D1351250

PRACTICAL PRINT MAKING

PRACTICAL PRINT MAKING

The complete guide to the latest techniques, tools and materials.

EDITED BY LOUISE WOODS

APPLE

A QUINTET BOOK

Published by the Apple Press
6 Blundell Street
London N7 9BH

ISBN 1-85076-709-2

This book was designed and produced by
Quintet Publishing Limited
6 Blundell Street
London N7 9BH

Art Director: Patrick Carpenter
Designer: Peter Laws
Project Editor: Clare Hubbard
Editor: Louise Woods

Typeset in Great Britain by
Central Southern Typesetters, Eastbourne
Manufactured in China by
Regent Publishing Services Ltd.
Printed in Singapore by
Star Standard Industries (Pte) Ltd.

Material in this book previously appeared in *The Complete Guide to Screenprinting* by Brad Faine; *The Encyclopedia of Printmaking Techniques* by Judy Martin and *Prints and Printmaking* edited by John Dawson.

Publisher's note

Working with printmaking chemicals demands care, as some you will be using are poisonous and/or corrosive. This means you must take precautions; always follow the manufacturer's instructions; always store chemicals securely in clearly marked non-food containers and keep them well out of the reach of children. As far as the techniques used to apply the chemicals, and the effects they produce are concerned, all statements, information and advice given here are believed to be true and accurate. However, neither the authors' copyright holder nor the publisher can accept any legal liability for errors or omissions.

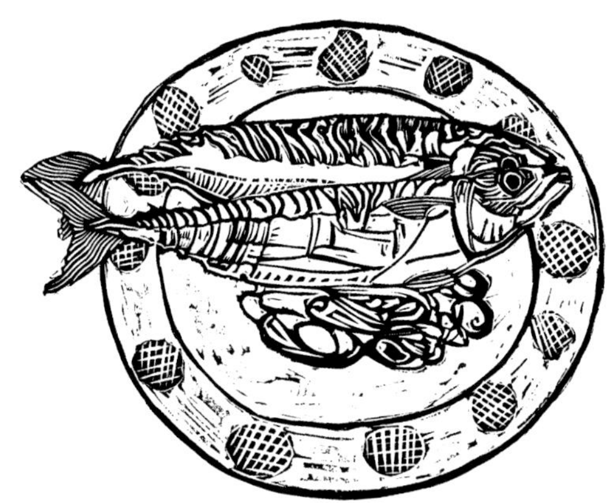

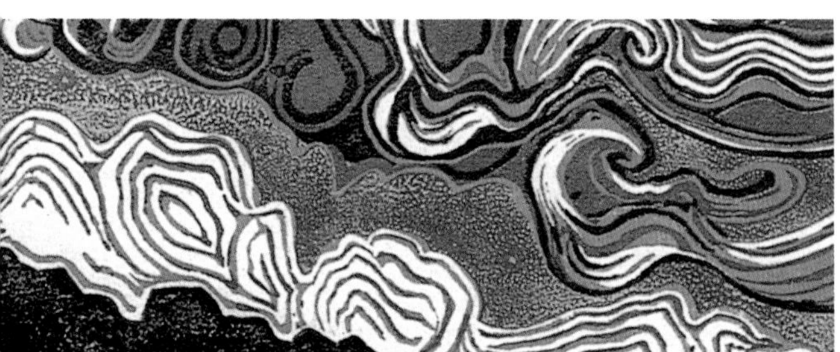

Contents

Introduction

Printmaking covers an impressively wide range of activities and pictorial matter – there is something for everyone here. But printmaking studios, with their strange, alchemical combinations of unfamiliar materials, purpose-made tools, and monumental machinery, can seem like alien territory, even to experienced artists quite comfortable with other kinds of studio practice.

However, there is no need to be daunted by the technicalities, because many of the printmaking processes are very straightforward and easy to grasp. Some, such as lithography and etching, are inherently more complex, but they can be learned in stages so that the newcomer can gradually build confidence and grow in ambition. In fact the necessity to follow specific technical procedures provides a framework for the creative side of image-making that many artists regard as a supportive element. As you become immersed in practicalities, the process itself suggests ways of interpreting your image.

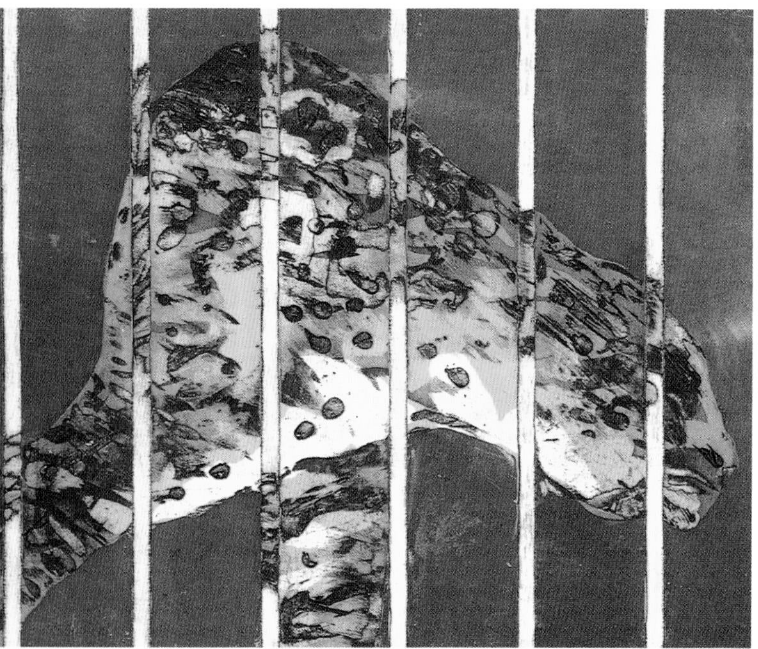

Jaguar Turning (etching) by Judy Martin
The "duotone" effect of this print comes from inking up the intaglio in black, then rolling over the surface with orange. As the black ink picks up on the roller, the color has to be laid in one pass with a roller large enough to cover the width of the plate.

This book is an invaluable introduction to printmaking methods, taking you step by step through the technical details as well as providing inspirational examples of prints in all media. Although some of the print processes have a long tradition and are carried out in much the same way as they always were, there can be no doubt that modern technology has made it easier to extend the potential of individual printmaking methods and to combine their effects in multi-media images.

Well-known professional artists who produce "edition" prints often have much of the processing carried out for them by equally professional print technicians, but in this book the priority is to relate the techniques and inspirational images to things you can easily achieve yourself with readily available equipment and facilities. Although it is necessary to have access to a properly equipped studio and presses in order to develop the full potential of most techniques, there are methods you can carry out from start to finish working on your kitchen or living-room table. Keep this in mind as you look through the book and choose the printmaking areas you might like to work with. Once you have understood the principles and mastered some basic techniques, you can bring your own inventiveness and creativity into play to adapt the chosen methods to suit your style of work and situation.

Setting up a print workshop

There is no doubt that the ideal situation for learning and practicing all the major printmaking processes is a properly equipped print studio. And for those who would like to devote some regular time to specific processes, it may be possible to hire time in a professional studio or join a co-operative of artists sharing printmaking facilities.

However, having no access, or very limited access, to a studio by no means disqualifies you from producing interesting prints. Monoprints, linocuts, woodcuts, wood engravings, and collage prints can all be prepared and printed at home.

At home, it is essential to match your equipment to the size and scope of the printed matter you intend to produce. This is an obvious point, perhaps, but one which is easily overlooked. Define the functions of the studio as closely as possible – are you going to prepare your drawings and working ideas prior to printmaking in the studio, or will you need additional working space there? The cost of setting up a studio need not be excessive – a modest but adequate space for one person can be established for relatively little.

The main advantage of using a print studio is access to a printing press, which enables you to produce reliable, good quality impressions quite quickly. But you can also produce finished prints from flat surfaces and blocks by a simple hand-printing method at home.

A flatbed press
The upright section of the press supports a heavy platen that moves downwards when the bar is pulled across. The flatbed is rolled out from underneath to position block and paper, then taken back underneath before pressure is applied.

PRINTING PRESSES

There are various printing presses, some dedicated to one printing method, others adaptable to more than one. A relief printing press typically relies on direct pressure. In flatbed presses such as the Albion and Columbian types, the block is placed on the bed of the press and an upper surface is brought down to exert heavy pressure on paper and block. An alternative is the old-style type-proofing press, formerly used by typesetters. This kind of press has a sunken bed in which a thick wood or wood-mounted linoleum block can be set. A cylinder with the paper attached is rolled across the block under pressure.

Intaglio printing is done on a roller press, a flat, heavy metal bed suspended between two rollers. The space between the rollers is adjusted to vary the pressure as required; the metal intaglio plate with paper laid on top is positioned on the bed, and the bed is passed between the rollers. This press can be adapted to relief printing provided that the original block is not too thick to be accommodated by the rollers. A relief printing press, however, cannot normally be used for intaglio because it does not exert sufficient pressure to force the paper down into the sunken areas of the plate.

For offset lithography, the use of a specialized press is required to carry out the printing process. This has a long bed on which the paper and plate are positioned side by side. A very large, heavy roller occupying the whole width of the bed trundles along its entire length, moved either by a handle or an electrically powered mechanism. The rubber "blanket" around the roller picks up ink from the plate as it passes forward, then puts it down on the paper as it moves back.

Large printing presses are cumbersome, heavy, and extremely expensive. Even if you could find an affordable secondhand one, you might need to have the floor of your workroom strengthened before the press could be installed. New roller-press models are more compact and lightweight. The capital outlay is considerable, but you will have a machine that will see service for years. On a smaller scale, table-top versions of the intaglio roller press are available at reasonable prices.

SCREENPRINTING FACILITIES

You can set up a screenprinting operation at home, since the basic equipment is self-contained, relatively lightweight, and can be constructed to a required size. You must have a flat surface for printing, so it is best to hinge the screen to a permanent printing bed or baseboard so it can be raised and lowered. Screens can be bought from some art and craft retailers, or you can make your own – there are specialist publications that explain this in full detail.

Operation of a flatbed press

1 The handle is turned the other way to take the bed right back underneath the platen, to position the block centrally, so that even pressure will be applied.

2 With the bed in position, the artist grasps the bar and pulls it towards him, which lowers the platen onto the bed. This takes some effort, as the downward pressure activated by the movement of the bar is powerful.

Proofing press

This kind of press was originally designed for printing type blocks to produce galley proofs of texts. The bed of the press accommodates the height of the type blocks, so is ideal for printing woodcut blocks and wood-mounted linoleum. The paper is fitted to the cylinder, which is then rolled over the inked block.

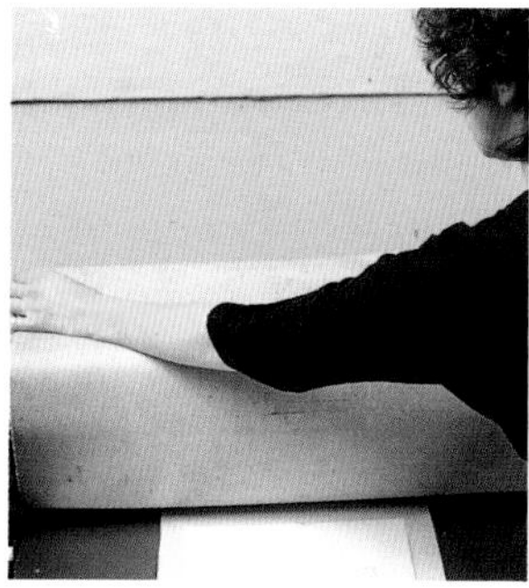

Etching press

A press for printing intaglio plates, which are only a few millimeters thick. When a geared handle is turned, a flat metal bed passes between two weighty metal rollers. To soften and spread the pressure, blankets are used to cushion the action of the rollers.

Basic equipment

A working surface is the first consideration. A solid heavy table with a flat working top is ideal, and the stronger it is, the better. Cover the working top with a good surface, either plastic self-adhesive sheeting, hardboard (masonite), zinc sheeting, or Formica™. These materials are all smooth and easy to keep clean. Newspaper is also adequate and is relatively easy to dispose of after use.

CLEANING CLOTHS

Materials such as old pieces of *clean* clothing, cotton dusters, cheesecloth, and paper towels can be used to clean the print table, ink palettes, inking rollers, squeegees, and brushes. Store them in a trunk or wooden packing case so they do not get dirty before they are needed.

CONTAINERS

All jars with screw lids, plastic seal-lid containers, yogurt pots, and clean, used, plastic food containers make suitable containers for storing liquids (not acids) or mixed printing inks.

STORAGE

Begin by storing all your material and tools in a workmanlike manner. Storage units such as wooden or cardboard boxes can be painted to give them a good appearance and improve their durability. Keep tools in boxes or drawers, or on wooden wall racks, so they do not become dirty or damaged when they are not being used. Store printing inks away from heat and direct sunlight, and keep all solvents in a fireproof metal cabinet or container. A secondhand metal filing cabinet is ideal for this purpose and is a worthwhile investment for safety.

As your ideas progress and become more ambitious, your paper requirements will become more complex. Storing papers properly in a flat plan chest will become a necessity. The influence of temperature, humidity, and light on paper is crucial.

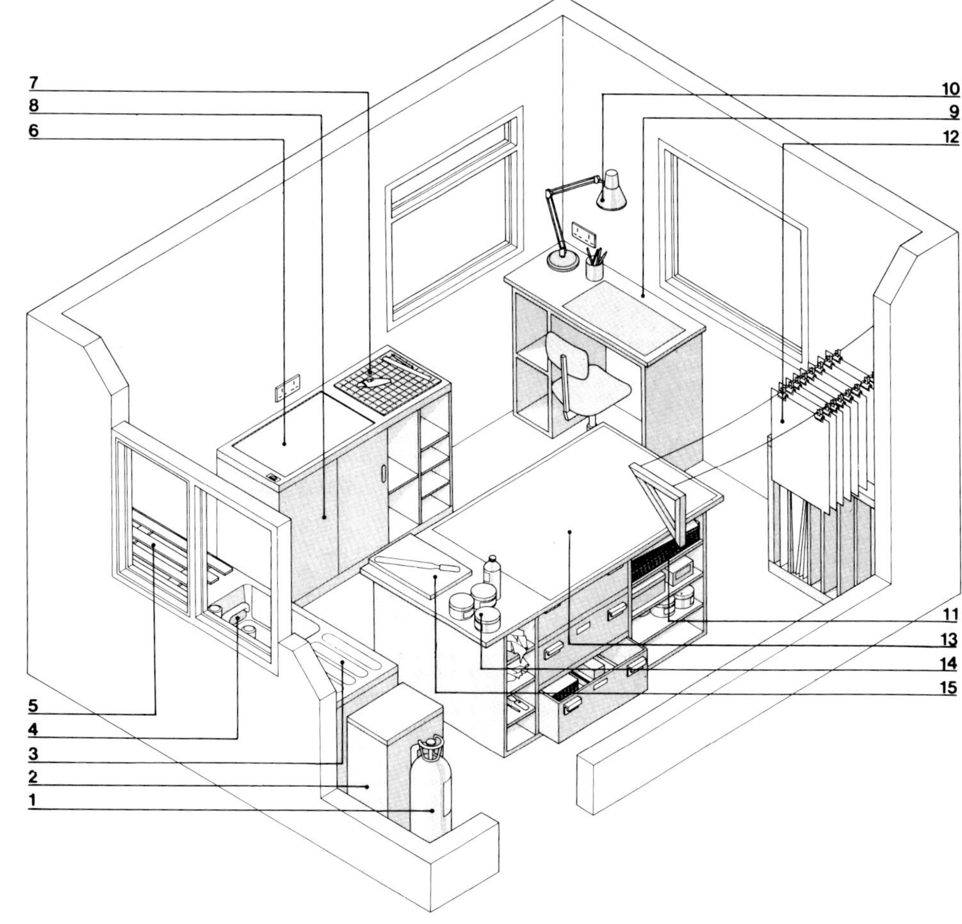

Basic studio layout for use without a mechanical press.

1. Fire extinguisher.
2. Metal cabinets for storing inks and solvents.
3. Draining area.
4. Sink.
5. Wooden drying racks.
6. Light box for viewing.
7. Cutting mat.
8. Storage for materials.
9. Drawing table in front of north-facing window.
10. Adjustable table lamp.
11. Paper storage.
12. Print-drying rack.
13. Printing and working surface with protective covering and storage underneath for tools. Strip lighting should run directly overhead, slightly in front of the working position.
14. Inks and solvents.
15. Ink palette.

Rubber rollers
Rollers are an essential piece of printmaking equipment. They are used to ink up the printing plate.

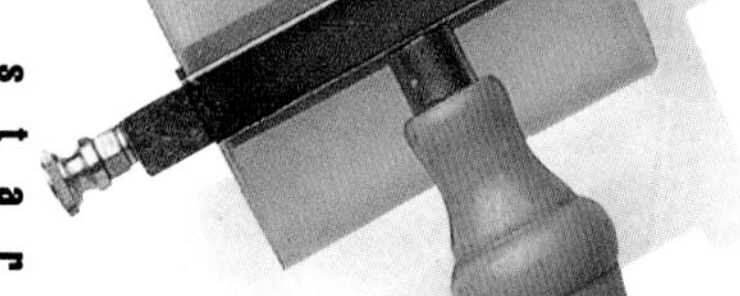

PALETTES

A palette is essential. The cheapest form of palette for mixing printing inks is a piece of strong white-coated, smooth cardboard. Alternatives are pieces of plain linoleum, non-ferrous metals such as zinc or copper, hardboard (masonite), plywood, laminated plastic, or thick glass with ground edges.

The best palette is a sheet of ground glass about 10 × 14 inches, approximately 1 inch thick. Its surface is extremely smooth, allowing you to mix inks quickly and cleanly with a palette knife.

PRINTING ROLLERS

A couple of rubber rollers to "ink up" your prepared printing surfaces are essential; for silkscreen printing you will also need to buy a good quality rubber squeegee. These tools can be bought at any good art shop. The various widths of rollers you choose will depend on your printmaking ambitions. Initially, for general use, buy both a hard and a soft roller about 4 inches in size. For more ambitious and meticulous printmaking you might consider buying a roller made out of gelatin which spreads an even layer of ink on almost any surface and is especially suitable for inking type. Rollers must be cleaned thoroughly after each working session and should not be laid face down for long periods of time, otherwise one side will begin to flatten and the roller will no longer lay ink evenly. Rollers and squeegees are best stored away from excessive heat, in a drawer or cupboard, or hung under cover in a tool rack.

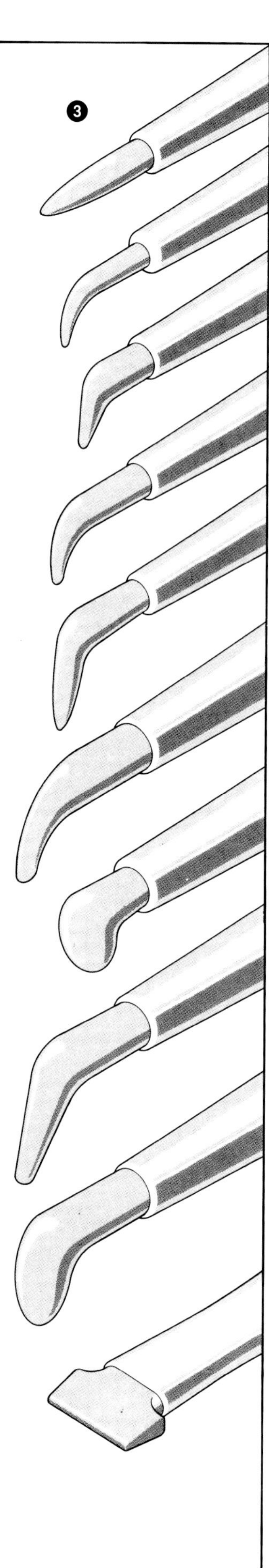

Different types of burnishers
1 A baren. This is a purpose-made tool for hand-printing. **2** A spoon used for hand-printing. **3** Burnishing tools used for intaglio work. The round-tipped tools are used for flattening and those with fine points are used for detailing.

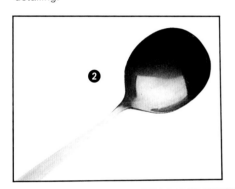

BURNISHERS

The simplest burnisher is the flat of your hand. Old smooth kitchen spoons, smooth rounded pebbles, or pieces of polished wood or metal are ideal for burnishing the reverse side of a sheet of paper as you apply an even pressure across the surface. Eventually you will need to buy steel or agate burnishers for such specialist functions as repolishing corrections or lightening surfaces in the plate, as in aquatint.

PRINT-DRYING EQUIPMENT

There are many ways to dry prints.

1. Lay the prints out on clean paper in cupboards or shelves.
2. Pin the prints, using mapping pins, onto wooden battens running across the wall of your studio.
3. Pin the prints onto a large sheet of soft board and stand it against a wall, or fasten it to the wall. (This is a good and very ueful way of viewing a progression of color prints.)
4. Pin the prints, using clothes pins or bulldog clips to a simple wooden clothes dryer, with smooth flat slats.
5. Stretch nylon lines across the studio, without interfering with your working areas, and pin out the prints like washing. Pins should be drilled with a small hole and threaded on the line so that they stay in place. If you have the space, two parallel nylon lines stretched from one side of the studio to the other, with threaded pins make an ideal print dryer.
6. Install a metal drying rack which has each frame hinged to lift easily.
7. A purpose-made ceiling rack enables each print to hang straight.

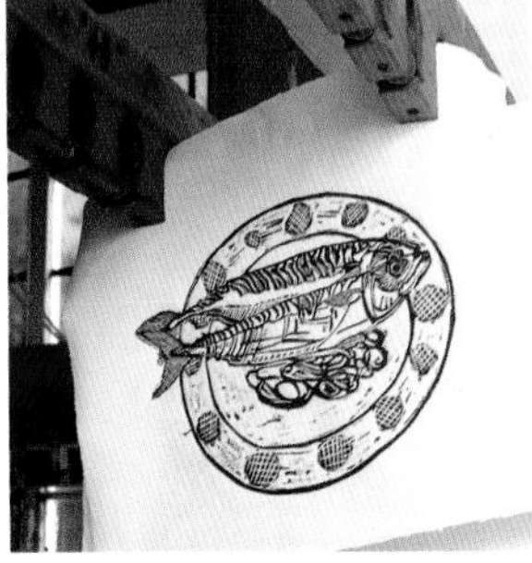

Metal drying racks
The metal frames form a stack, each frame hinged at the back so it can be lifted easily to slip in prints on lower layers. This kind of drying rack is highly suitable for relief prints, screenprints, and lithographs.

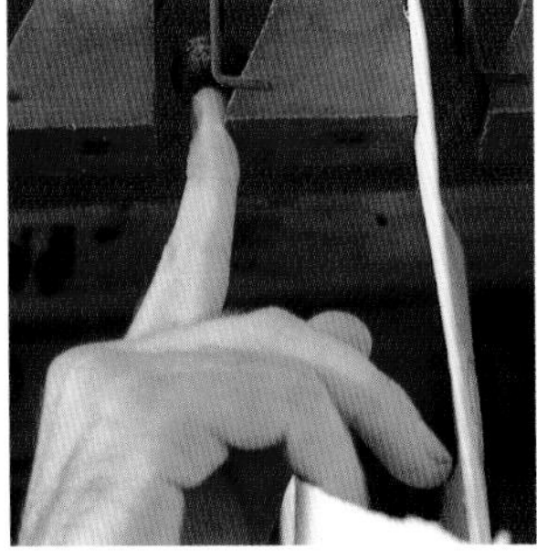

Ceiling racks
1 These purpose-made wooden racks have slots containing a ball-and-wire mechanism that grips the top edge of the print and allows the paper to hang straight.

2 To insert the print, the ball is pushed upwards and the paper slipped in against the wire. When the ball drops back, its own weight secures the paper. The same action releases the print.

Safety – chemicals and solvents

Safety factors are particularly important in both etching and lithography. Various stages of etching involve working on the metal plates with heat, acid, or flammable substances, while chemical preparations are used in lithography, and the flexible metal plates and mechanical press need careful management. However, under proper guidance, both processes are quite safe. Any chemical that gives off fumes must be used in an area with good ventilation, and goggles, a face mask, and rubber gloves are necessary precautions when you are dealing with acid or other caustic liquids.

Generally, however, your alertness to the safety angle should be much the same as when you are cooking or carrying out home repairs. Don't leave things to "cook" on a hotplate; don't let sharp tools lie about exposed or jumble up different types of equipment; immediately clean up liquids or inks that spill on the floor so that you don't slip.

Using Acid
When your fingers are likely to be in contact with acid, it is wise to wear rubber gloves.

CHEMICALS

When using chemicals, your working area should be free from any bulk supplies and should have on it only the materials required for the processing of the work in hand. The chemicals usually found in a printer's studio are acids to etch plates, chemicals to develop the image on a photo-sensitized plate, and solvents.

Nitric acid, either in dilute form or concentrated, will attack copper, zinc, and aluminum plates and is used as an etching solution. Hydrochloric acid, like nitric acid, also attacks copper, zinc, and aluminum. Ferric chloride solution is also used to etch printing plates. Sulfuric acid, especially in its concentrated form, is very dangerous and should be avoided, if at all possible, by purchasing and using a diluted form. All acids are dangerous and gloves and goggles should be worn when using them. Any spills should be neutralized with sodium carbonate and the contaminated areas washed well with water.

SOLVENTS

Organic solvents are used for cleaning plates and as diluents for certain printing inks. The common solvents used for cleaning and drying plates are acetone, propanol, and methyl alcohol. For degreasing, toluene and mineral spirit are much more efficient. All these solvents have low boiling points and they give off inflammable vapors. Sources of ignition such as naked flames and electrical sparks must be avoided at all costs. The lower the flash point, the more dangerous is the solvent.

STORAGE AND CARE

All chemicals and solutions should be labeled and any hazard symbols incorporated. Most chemical manufacturers now label their products with hazard symbols so that the user can see the potential hazard that the chemical poses.

As a general rule, chemicals should be stored in a dry, ventilated place away from the excesses of cold, heat, light, and dampness. Strong acids, normally supplied in glass bottles, should be stored in suitable non-corrodable trays at ground level. Solvents should be stored separately in a steel cupboard in the chemical store.

You should know about the properties of the various chemicals so that in the case of an emergency, such as a fire, you will know how to handle them. The fire authorities will help you to select the correct fire extinguisher.

Check with sanitary authorities before disposing of chemicals down the sink. Chemicals should be flushed down with a great deal of water; never pour inflammable solvents down sinks, basins, or lavatories.

1

2

3

4

5

6

Safety features

The acid bath in an etching studio is one of the most obviously hazardous work areas, which needs special facilities. This one sits below a ventilator hood, and can be completely enclosed by drawing down the plastic sides of the boxed-in area. The artist takes the precaution of using goggles and rubber gloves when working with the acid.

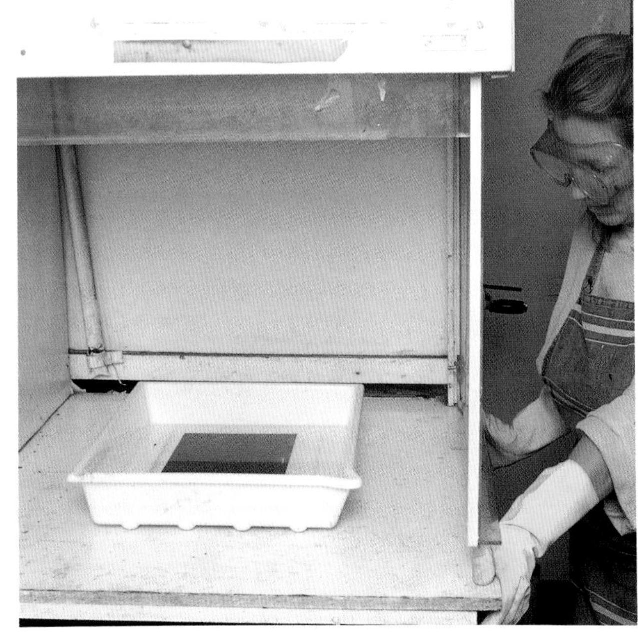

Acids

Acid	Use
Nitric	Etching
Acetic	Cleaning
Hydrochloric	Stencil removal
Phosphoric	Fountain solution – lithographic printing
Citric	Photographic processes, removing stencil gum
Sulfuric	Stencil removal

Toxic Chemicals

Chemical	Use
Ferric chloride	Etching
Potassium dichromate	Plate preparation
Ammonium dichromate	Plate preparation
Ammonium nitrate	Fountain solution
Potassium ferrocyanide	Etching positives
Mercuric chloride	Photographic intensification

Solvents

Solvent	Inflammable	Soluble	Boiling Point	Flash Point
Acetone	Yes	Water	132.8°F	64.4°F
Methyl alcohol	Yes	Water	149°F	43.8°F
Propanol	Yes	Water	179.6°F	73.4°F
Toluene	Yes	Insoluble	231.8°F	39.2°F
Xylene	Yes	Insoluble	276.8°F	73.4°F
Trichloroethene	No	Insoluble	165.2°F	

The tables list the acids and the chemicals that are used in printing.

Hazard Symbols

Used as warnings on containers and around areas where dangerous chemicals are stored.

1. Oxidizing
2. Harmful
3. Toxic
4. Explosive
5. Highly flammable
6. Corrosive

Paper

A wide selection of papers is useful for beginning to experiment with prints. One of the cheapest and most suitable forms of paper to begin with is photocopying paper. It comes packed in boxes, is easy to handle and store, and can be bought already trimmed in various sizes and colors of stock. Newsprint (newspapers), magazines, wrapping papers, tissue papers, pads of cartridge paper, typography paper, tracing paper, and layout paper all produce good prints. Pads of paper are relatively inexpensive, come in a range of sizes and thicknesses, and are very easy to keep clean and store. Inexpensive medium-weight rice paper takes a print beautifully. Usually made in Japan, it is available at most art suppliers.

More expensive papers, especially handmade printing papers, are also available at art suppliers, but until you become more experienced and skillful, the cheaper ranges will be more than adequate.

Most relief and screen prints can be made on almost any kind of paper – even on fabric – but the weight, thickness, and finish of the paper affects the appearance of the image.

For other printing surfaces, try using thin plywood, hardboard, canvas, burlap, white linen, cellophane, white card, laminated plastics, and even white-surfaced corrugated board. Experimenting with unusual surfaces will often produce surprising and pleasant results, but avoid using papers with a smooth, hard, shiny finish. This type of surface will repel both water-based and oil-based inks, and under pressure the inked block or plate may skid, giving a blurred image.

OTHER USES OF PAPER

Different kinds of papers have practical purposes in printmaking. In intaglio printing, blotting and tissue papers are needed to prepare and store the dampened printing paper; prints can be taken on a variety of surfaces, including fine handmade or good-quality moldmade drawing and watercolor papers. Textured and colored papers are useful for collage work and relief printing. To develop a printed image from an existing drawing, or working study, you will also need tracing and transfer papers.

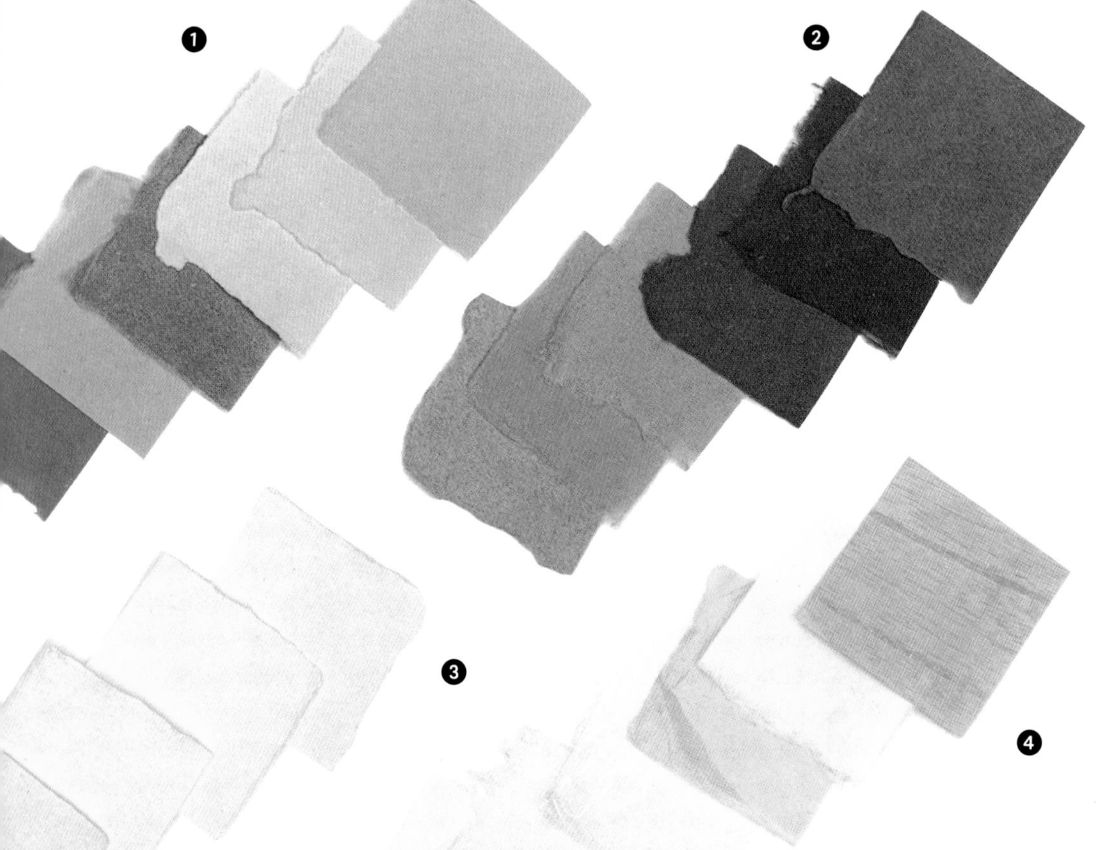

Papers
The range of papers which can be used for printing is enormous. A small sample is illustrated here. All of them are handmade and deckle-edged.
1, 2 A range of colored papers. **3** White papers variously textured. **4** Papers incorporating decorative grain. **5** Papers with shiny surfaces. They are usually coated with china clay.

Inks

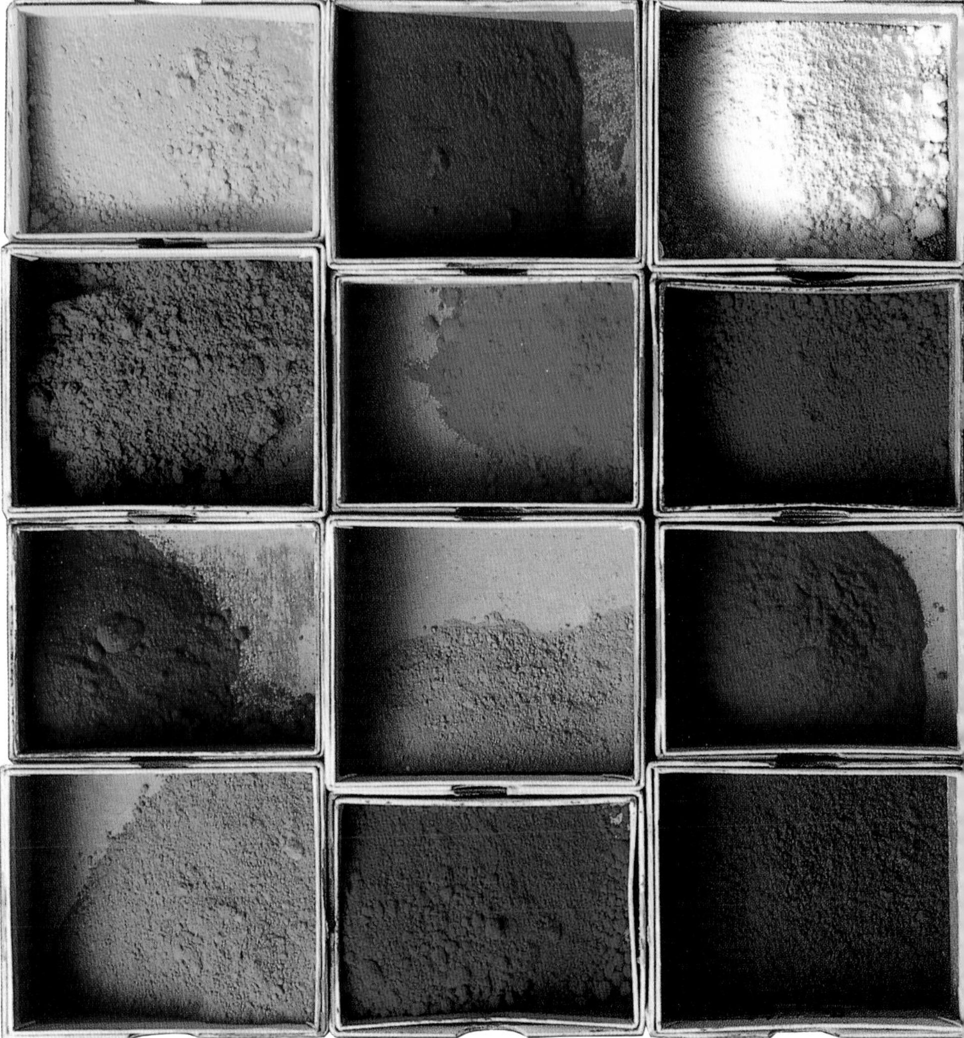

Ink in its simplest form is a colored pigment or dye mixed in a fluid which is known as the vehicle. Some pigments are found naturally, such as sepia which comes from the cuttle fish. Others are manufactured commercially.

The actual hue and brightness of a pigment depends upon the amount of light it absorbs and reflects. In addition, the color of the ink laid down on the paper is a function of its color strength, the shape and size of the pigment particle, and the degree of dispersion of the pigment in the vehicle. Pigments which are used for printing should be resistant to water, acids, alkalis, and organic solvents. Dyes are colored compounds which have solubility in the vehicle or the solvent which is used to make the ink. They have a high purity of color and give transparency to the ink. Sometimes they are used to tone inks, as in the case of the blacks. This toning results in blacks acquiring certain tones such as blue-black, green-black, or slate-black.

Different methods of printing require different properties from ink and paper, and proprietary-brand inks, available from specialist suppliers, are purpose-made for each one. Block-printing inks are more widely sold, and can be bought in most good art stores. In some cases – notably relief printing and screen-printing – you may find a choice between water-based or oil-based inks. Typically, oil-based types give the smoothest coverage and the most versatile effects, but the prints take longer to dry, and blocks or screens have to be cleaned up with the appropriate solvent. If in doubt, explain to the supplier what you intend to do and get advice on the right type and texture of ink and the color ranges available for your kind of work.

Pigments
Pigments come in a wide range of vivid hues. To convert them into ink they must be mixed with some type of vehicle. The vehicle is the liquid component of the ink and determines how the ink flows and its drying properties.

Types of ink

RELIEF INKS

The quality of relief inks varies widely. One type is newsprint ink, which uses a non-drying oil as the ink vehicle. It takes a long time to dry and even after a few days it can be smudged. Another type is jobbing ink which is used for printing such things as hand bills, programs, and invitations. A further type is a quick setting ink which produces a hard film on the paper surface and does not penetrate it. All these inks are viscous but nevertheless have the property of flowing and can be worked out by using a roller.

Lithographic ink
This ink has high color strength and is used very thinly.

Drawing inks
There are many drawing inks available. Some are suitable for technical pens and come in a variety of colors and other drawing inks can be used with brushes or mapping pens.

LITHOGRAPHIC INKS

The ink film deposited on the substrate from the lithographic printing plate is thin in comparison to inks used for, say, relief or screenprinting. This ink must have, therefore, a high color strength. It is very viscous but must be able to be rolled out.

GRAVURE (COMMERCIAL) INKS

Gravure ink is light and mobile compared with the viscous consistency of both relief and lithographic inks. The ink is a combination of a pigment and a solvent, frequently xylol, in which is dissolved a binder. The binder, after the solvent has evaporated, must retain the pigment and set into a hard, non-tacky material on the substrate. Binders vary from modified natural resins to synthetic binders based on vinyl polymers, or lacquers such as nitrocellulose. The choice of binder is influenced by the substrate so that these inks are designed individually for specific substrates. One characteristic of all of them is that they contain no hard particles which would damage the gravure ink cells.

ENGRAVING QUALITY INKS (INTAGLIO)

These are thick, greasy inks similar in composition to lithographic inks. In place of the mobile solvent xylol, however, they use a solvent with a high boiling point, so the drying time is somewhat slower. The ink appears on the paper as thick film and is raised up from the surface.

SCREEN INKS

Screen inks are soft and are pressed through a screen with a squeegee. The ink needs to be of such a consistency that it can flow easily.

INKS FOR BEGINNING PRINTING

Water-based printing inks are the best inks to buy when you start printing. Obtainable at any good art suppliers, they usually come in tubes and are easy to manage. They can be used straight from the tube, or can be diluted with a little clean cold water to obtain a better working consistency. Squeeze out just the amount you need, and make sure that your palette is clean. They are non-toxic, come in a range of good colors and wash off rollers, palette, palette knives, and working surfaces easily with cold water. Working clothes can also be cleaned with soap and water. Water-based inks should not be used on paper that is printed damp or used to print fabrics – they will run during the printing process.

Basic methods of printmaking

After Vincent (linocut)
by Paul Bartlett
In this linocut, the direct, graphic qualities are effectively employed to parallel the heavy, swirling brushwork of van Gogh's famous painting. It is printed from one block by the reduction method used for both linoleum and woodcut prints, re-cutting the design after printing each color. The ink has been rolled on thickly and overprinting produces some interesting areas of broken color.

The methods of producing a printed image can be divided into four main categories: relief printing, intaglio, planographic printing (from a flat surface, as in lithography), and stencil processes, as applied in screenprinting. In the relief printing techniques of linocut, woodcut, and wood engraving, the original flat surface of the wood or linoleum block represents the printing surface. Any parts of the design not to be printed are cut away, leaving the image raised in relief. This is inked and transferred to paper by direct pressure.

Intaglio processes – drypoint, mezzotint, and etching – are usually done on metal plates, and the design is incised or etched into the surface. It is the sunken lines and areas of the plate that are printed, by pushing ink into them and applying heavy pressure to press the paper into the inked marks; the original surface level of an intaglio plate represents the white in a black and white image.

Lithography is a planographic process. The image is drawn on a metal plate (or lithograph stone) and processed so that it "sets" into the grain of the surface. Lithographic prints can be taken by direct pressure or by offsetting. On an offset press, plate and paper are placed side by side; a roller travels over the plate and picks up the inked image; traveling back, it deposits the image on the paper.

Screenprinting is basically a stenciling process. The screen has a stretched, fine mesh which transmits an even layer of ink under pressure. To create the image, parts of the mesh must be blocked so they cannot allow the ink through. There are many different ways of preparing stencils, all of which produce different qualities in the imagery.

Animal Magic (etching)
by Mychael Barratt
Soft ground and aquatint contribute rich, deep tones to the characterful drawing in this image, which is also hand-colored to enhance the strong graphic effect and highlight the main subjects.

8 a.m. (lithograph)
by Elisabeth Harden
In preparing lithographic plates you have the same sensitivity of touch as in drawing or painting on paper. Crayon marks and washes can be gently faded out, to "lose" the edges of the image and disturb the effect of rectangular framing. It is possible to organize the balance of the composition so that printing on white paper makes the image appear as a free shape or, as here, loosely contained by a conventional format.

NEGATIVE AND POSITIVE

A printed image taken by direct pressure is always reversed on the paper because the original block or plate is in face to face contact with it. Relief and intaglio processes both produce reversed images, as does lithographic printing on a direct-pressure press. In offset lithography, the image is not reversed, because it is put down on the paper in the same position as it was picked up from the plate – an intermediary surface carries the inked image, and there is no direct contact between plate and paper. In screenprinting, too, the image is right-reading, because the ink passes through the screen mesh rather than being printed off from it.

This left-to-right reversal is not the only "opposite" element you have to keep in mind when preparing images for printing. Often you are required to work in negative – that is, the marks you make with your printmaking tools represent the non-printing areas of the design. In relief prints, the parts of the block that you actively cut away surround the parts that will read as the image. In screenprinting, where you are preparing a stencil to print, for example, blue areas of the image, the stencil itself will consist of all those areas that will not be blue. Conversely, in lithography and most intaglio processes, the marks you make are those that directly create the image.

These concepts can seem confusing when put into words; they start to make sense as you come to deal with them in practice.

Punta Sabbionẹ (screenprint)
by Moira Wills
Despite the solid color areas, this screenprint is very linear in character. The narrow loop of the sea creates a strong directional curve, defined by color changes rather than a visible outline. The colors contribute a well-chosen tonal balance to the image, creating a fresh, descriptive impression of the sunlit bay.

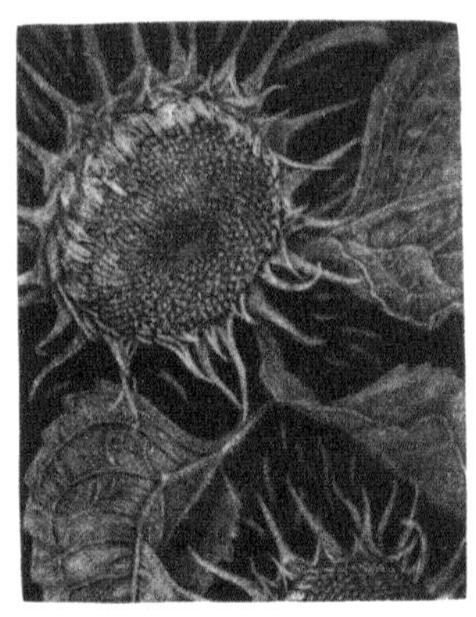

COLOR AND TEXTURE

Prints of the same subject carried out in the full range of media show some of the characteristic differences between printmaking processes and their effects. Monoprints and collage prints are technically quite simple to make, but can provide a wide range of painterly qualities. The intaglio methods of drypoint and mezzotint are primarily tonal, but differently approached – drypoint by drawing positively in black line and tone, mezzotint by burnishing whites out of dark texture. Similarly, wood engraving typically appears as white lines on black, while the other relief methods – woodcut and linocut – more often rely on black key-line images, although both are easily adapted to color printing. Etching, lithography, and screenprinting each incorporate a variety of techniques enabling equally varied, simple, or sophisticated surface effects.

An infinite variety of colors and textures can be achieved in printmaking from a simple subject.

Producing prints

Getting from the picture in your mind's eye to the finished print on paper is not just a matter of technical skill, but also of working with the medium appropriately at each stage of processing. This includes the way you initially conceive and prepare your image for print form. For the beginner, this is a chicken-and-egg situation – if you don't know what the process can do, how can you plan the final image? On the other hand, if you haven't begun with a definite visual idea, what are you to work on in order to learn how to print?

To find out what the particular marks and materials you apply will turn into when processed and printed, you can start off by working direct on a block, plate, or screen in a purely abstract manner. A test plate or block is not an unusual first step. You probably won't achieve a finished image with much form to it in this way, but you may find you have produced a useful reference chart for future use.

WORKING DRAWINGS

More commonly, you will start with some reference work – a sketch, drawing, painting, or photograph – as the basis for the print. The first thing to realize is that any form of printmaking is an interpretive, not a reproductive method. In other words, the print will not look exactly like the original. The working drawing is a guideline to composition, visual qualities such as the relationship of line work and solid color areas, and the overall scheme of color. These elements have to be translated into the new medium and cannot be copied exactly, although in all media you can trace and transfer an image as your starting point – it is not necessary to redraw the composition from scratch.

For the inexperienced printmaker interested in producing prints in two or more colors, the working drawing is an essential step. You have to make a separate block, screen, or plate for each main color, and work out whether you can overprint colors to produce mixed hues. Sometimes, once you have isolated the areas for

The working drawing
The composition of this still life is worked out in a detailed pencil and watercolor sketch. The artist needs to establish the overall shapes clearly and plot the color and tonal variations within them. These are to be translated into a three-color print.

1st printing
1 Yellow is the dominant color, contributing to each aspect of the still life, so it covers a broad area of the first printing plate. However, it will not have this full-strength effect in the final print. Being light-toned, it will recede against the other colors.

2nd printing
2 The red obviously has to be strongest in the tomatoes, and will print lightly over the yellow on the bowl in order to produce a warm orange. In the peppers, it is used tonally rather than as a distinct color, to create the subtle shadows that model the forms.

printing one color, you will find that an originally realistic image is reduced to a series of more or less abstract shapes, and you cannot relate this to the other colors without some initial guideline. It may be best to make a fairly detailed working drawing and trace off each color element with some accuracy. As you learn more of your craft, you can cut down the detail of this preliminary stage and simplify your plan to the bare essentials. Experienced printmakers may start straight in without doing this at all because they feel confident of working direct with the print medium and can anticipate how the stages of the process will gradually pull together.

PROOFING AND PRINTING

In order to understand how the image is translating into print, proofs are taken at various stages. These working proofs also act as guidelines for further stages, such as the continued cutting of a block or processing of a plate; until you have seen the image as it prints, you will not know where to develop it further or where to make necessary corrections and adjustments.

On a relief block, you can take a rubbing rather than a printed proof, which is less laborious and gives you a fair idea of the image quality. An etching can be proofed at any stage, but on a mezzotint or drypoint plate the printing areas are relatively fragile – too many proofs cause the surface to deteriorate – so what you gain from proofing you may lose in the final printing.

When you are ready to take the final prints you can run a whole edition. An edition is a numbered set of identical prints. In commercial terms, the numbering is a safeguard of their value, and professional artists' plates or blocks are cancelled after an edition has been completed. The artist chooses the number of prints in an edition; sometimes it may depend on how the printing surface stands up to wear, as with drypoint and mezzotint. An artist's proof is a finished print that does not form part of the edition set – the first few trials of the final printing may become artist's proofs if the quality is good.

Peppers and Tomatoes (relief print) by Elisabeth Harden
The print is less heavily modeled than the original, since it contains no black that would correspond to the pencil drawing. The bright colors have a lush, fresh feeling appropriate to the subject. Dark shadows emerge from the overprinting of all three colors.

3rd printing
3 The green printing has a more linear character, defining the contours of the forms. As with the red, the color has two functions, providing local color in the green pepper and enhancing the detail and modeling of the red and yellow fruits.

CHAPTER TWO

RELIEF PRINTING

Monoprints

Beach People (monoprint) by June Ann Sullivan
The image is prepared for printing using etching inks, with solvent to vary the textures. Where the ink is thickest, the colors are vivid and rich. Together with broad white highlights where the paper is left bare, this creates the sunny mood of the picture. The foreground was added using transparent ink base with a touch of color.

A monoprint, as its name implies, is a one-off impression made by applying printing ink to a flat surface and transferring it to paper. The method excludes one of the usual main purposes of printmaking, which is to obtain multiple copies of a single image, but the marks and textures obtained are characteristically different from those drawn or painted directly on paper. Monoprint is of particular interest to beginners in printmaking because no presses or special studio equipment are needed.

Embroidered Hat (monoprint) by Carole Katchen
The printed impression reflects the spontaneity of vigorous brush-drawn lines in this rendering. Their boldness is enhanced by the transition through subtle color variations that describe different parts of the figure. Open, irregular shapes created by the outline drawing are nicely offset by the repetitive detail of the pattern areas.

TOOLS AND MATERIALS

The printing surface can be anything which is flat, smooth, and non-absorbent. Suitable materials are a sheet of glass, plastic, or metal; a slab of polished stone; or a section of plastic-faced wood or composition

Monoprint equipment
1 Brushes; **2** papers; **3** glass mixing slab; **4** block-printing inks; **5** palette knife; **6** roller.

board. To create your image, you can apply block-printing inks (or oil paints) using any suitable implements – brushes, rollers, sticks, rags, sponges, or palette knives – to build up the design, just as though you were drawing or painting on paper. Then you simply lay a sheet of paper over it and rub firmly but evenly across the back of the paper.

It is not necessary to have access to a relief press, or any other press for that matter, in order to take a print from your plate or block. Indeed, printmakers, particularly the Japanese printmakers, often prefer to use a hand system of printing since it gives a more individual result which looks less mechanical than a print taken from a press. The most popular hand method is to use some form of burnisher, specially shaped for the job. However, a simple wooden spoon or a large smooth pebble can be used to rub over the back of the paper.

It is most important to avoid movement of the paper while rubbing it down to the inked block, as it will cause doubling or smudging and this can be a real problem if you are printing more than a single color. The paper used for direct rubbing should be strong enough to stand up to this treatment, although if you really do want to use thin paper, some kind of protection can be used, such as a thin card placed over it. When you lift the paper, the final image is printed in reverse, as with relief printing methods.

OVERPRINTING

Monoprints can be graphic monochrome studies or vigorous multi-colored images. You can also overprint; for example, to build up thin color "glazes", develop dark tones, or lay in line work over solid color areas. You do this by taking your first print, then cleaning off the working surface and reworking with ink to take a second impression.

To overprint accurately, you need to use a simple form of registration. You can simply align the paper to the edges of the surface you are printing from, or if this is not large enough to give a good margin of paper around the printed image, you can lay a larger registration sheet beneath, visible on at least two sides, and align the printing paper to that.

In the demonstration sequence shown here, the artist places a working sketch beneath the sheet of glass as a guide for each painting stage and for registration of overprintings.

Although you cannot produce a series of prints by re-inking, as you can with a etched plate or incised block, you can sometimes obtain two or three impressions from one inking, they will become gradually fainter, coarser-textured, and less colorful. There are various ways you can experiment with this medium, apart from the way you prepare the initial design. Variations in thickness of the ink and the pressure you apply to the back of the paper will affect both the tone and texture of the print.

Overprinting

1 For the first stage of a three-stage print, the artist rolls out a layer of ink on glass. A sketch guide is positioned underneath the glass.

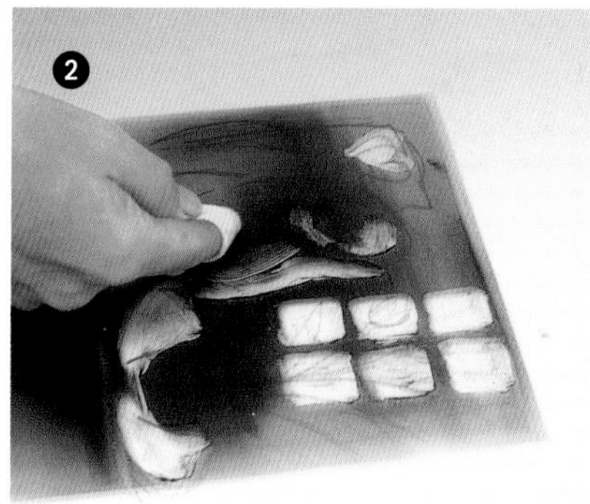

2 By dragging and lifting the ink with a rag dampened with mineral spirit, she draws broad shapes in the color area.

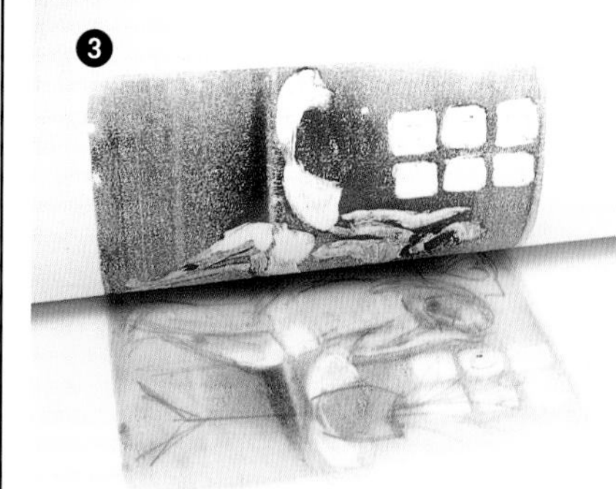

3 The paper is placed over the glass sheet, aligned to the left-hand edge of the working drawing below the glass sheet, and the print is taken by hand-rubbing. This gives a soft, moody monochrome image.

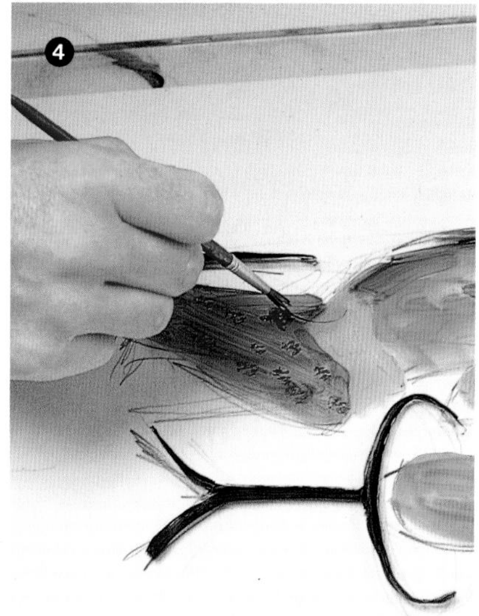

4 The second stage is prepared by painting on the glass with several colors. The underlying sketch is the guide for positioning the colors so they will overprint accurately on the monochrome image.

5 The monochrome print is aligned to the left-hand edge of the paper beneath the glass and laid down over the painting, which is again printed off by hand-rubbing on the back of the paper.

6 The artist partially removes the painting by cleaning it off with mineral spirit on a rag. She then reworks the dark-toned areas with fresh ink and takes a third impression.

7 In the finished print, the overprinting has produced a variety of tones and textures that create a simply stated, but atmospheric, image.

LINEAR DRAWING

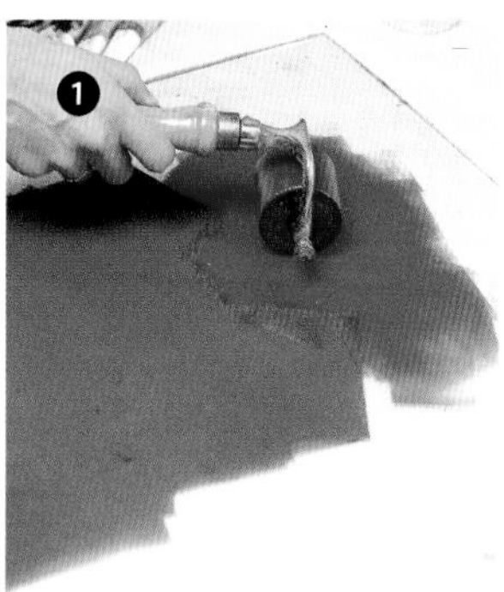

1 Block-printing ink is rolled out thinly on the glass slab. The color areas are roughly estimated in relation to the subject to be drawn.

2 A sheet of paper is laid down over the ink, and the wooden end of a paintbrush is used to draw on the back of the paper. Alternatively, you can use a pencil, knitting needle, or other suitable implement.

3 The impression shows a soft but strong line quality that gives an expressive character to the drawing. The background is lightly textured through contact with the rolled-out colors.

DEVELOPING TEXTURES

1 This experimental sequence investigates patterns and textures relating to water and wave patterns. Colored inks are squeezed onto the glass directly from the tube.

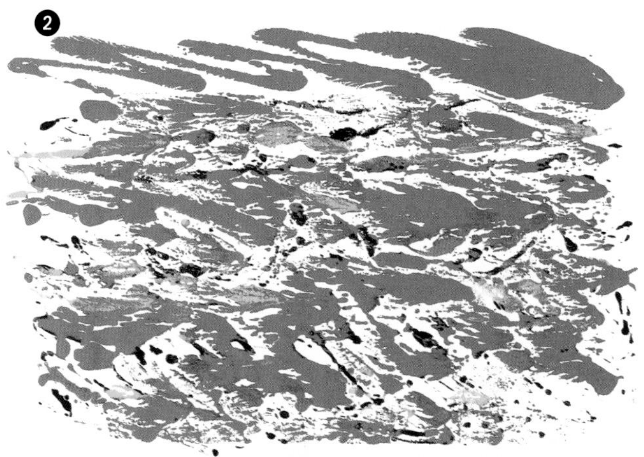

2 A simple blotting off onto paper spreads the ink marks and produces a vigorously textured surface. There is always a random element to these very basic printing techniques.

3 The artist works into the painting on glass by blotting the colors again and adding fresh ink. The top band of the color layers is rolled out to create a feeling of the division between sea and sky.

4 Paper is placed over the ink, and using a pencil the artist begins to draw roughly scribbled wave patterns, working the hatched textures in different directions.

5 Progress can be checked at any stage by peeling back the paper; keep one edge in place so that the paper goes back in exactly the same position. If the image is not strong enough, the pressure of the pencil marks can be varied or reworked.

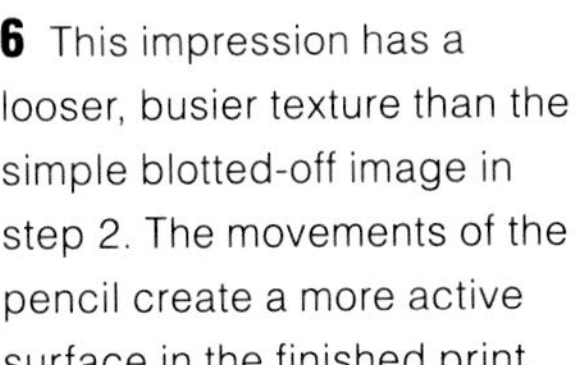

6 This impression has a looser, busier texture than the simple blotted-off image in step 2. The movements of the pencil create a more active surface in the finished print.

Collage

This area of printmaking provides the opportunity to produce interesting and varied printed images without the use of specialist materials and tools. The basic principle of collage is relief printing, in which the design is formed by the contrast between positive (raised) areas of the printing block and negative (cut-away) sections, and can be adapted to handmade blocks constructed from a wide range of materials. These are assembled on a flat base to form a relief block with different surface levels. Suitable materials include paper, cardboard, fabric, and string; found objects such as bottle tops and buttons; or acrylic mediums, which are applied in fluid form but dry to form hard, rubbery textures. This flexibility enables you to combine different substances and textures. You ink with a roller as if it were a wood or linoleum block. To print, you can use the hand-burnishing method of rubbing the paper down onto the inked block with a spoon or similar tool, though a relief printing press gives you a stronger, denser image.

TOOLS AND MATERIALS

The only tools you need are a craft knife and scissors for cutting your materials and a roller for inking up the block. Choosing materials for the collage is a matter of judgement and experience. It is not possible to predict absolutely the effect a particular material will make. Sometimes the roller picks up much more or less of the surface texture than you anticipate, though you can adjust the effects a little in the pressures you apply to inking up and printing. It is useful to experiment with small samples before selecting

River Scene (collage print) by John Elliot
An interesting combination of techniques has been used to produce this unusual, textured effect. The line work was printed from a zinc plate made by a commercial printer, from the artist's original drawing. The broader impressions of tone and color were overlaid from relief "blocks" of varying levels cut out of illustration board. Inking with soft oil pastel rather than printing inks provided the gentle, textural color gradations.

1

your materials for a particular kind of image.

Among the simplest and most readily available materials are different kinds of card and papers – you can save offcuts and packaging materials, looking for varied weights and textures. String, wool, ribbon, and braid are all effective. Adhesive tapes are useful for forming linear and geometric motifs.

An all-purpose acrylic adhesive such as PVA works as both the means of gluing materials to the support and as an independent printing element. The viscous white medium can be thickly applied with a pen, brush, or knife; it dries into a clear, rubbery surface that retains its original texture and prints well. It also makes an excellent binder for loose-textured materials such as sand or rice.

Equipment for collage blocks

1 Buttons; **2** paper and card; **3** craft knives; **4** scissors; **5** yarn; **6** PVA adhesive; **7** pasta; **8** pulses; **9** wood shavings.

Braid and yarn ▶

Scraps of fancy braids and yarns from a knitting or sewing basket contribute unusual pattern qualities. Because the materials are absorbent, you may need to ink and print a few times before the full impression comes through.

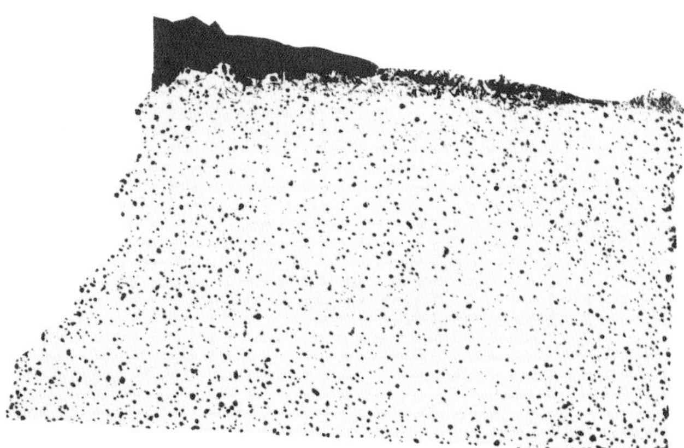

◀ Cardboard

In addition to selecting different textures and thicknesses of cardboard to create variations in your print, you can cut into the surface and peel back the top layer to make hard edges and rough, broken textures.

Sandpaper ▲

The gritty surface of sandpaper prints a fine pattern of irregular dots. The solid color at the top of this section comes from tearing the material so that the abrasive layer is pulled away, leaving only the base paper.

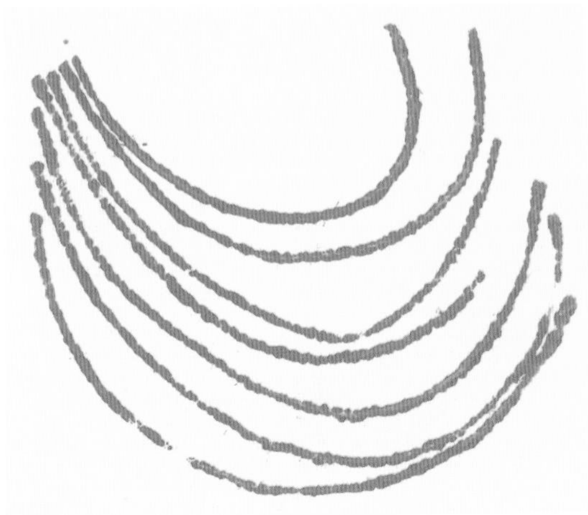

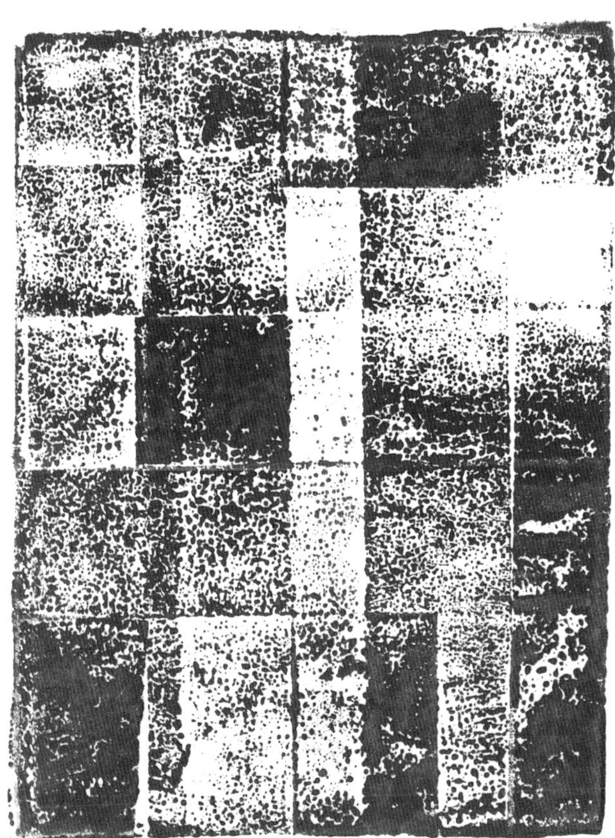

String ▲
Pieces of string create distinct, fine lines, but with a pleasing burred texture. Different effects will be obtained according to the weight and thickness of the string, and the fibers from which it is made.

Adhesive tapes ▶
Masking tape has a rough finish that prints as a mottled or striated texture. Smooth, finer tapes allow the ink to print off more evenly. The edges print as dark or light lines, depending on the thickness of the tape.

▲ Split peas
Loose materials such as beans, sand, or wood chippings can be glued to the collage base by pressing them into a layer of acrylic medium and allowing it to dry. The patterns that print are more random than you might expect, in this case because the hard peas have irregular surfaces.

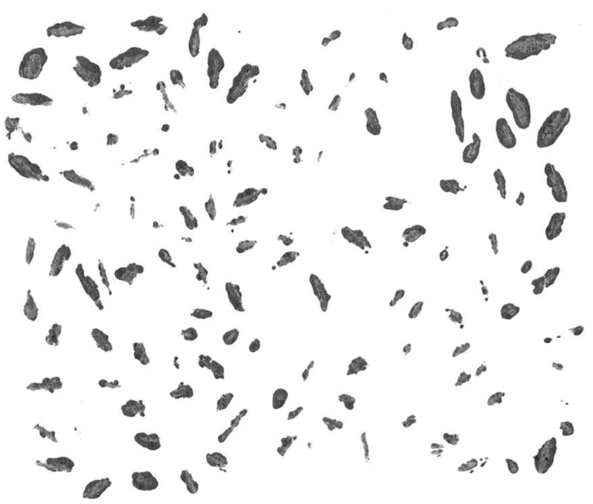

Rice
A hand-proofed print from a layer of rice stuck in acrylic medium, produces a coarse stipple effect. With all such materials you will obtain a slightly stronger texture if you print on a press, because of the more intense, even contact between printing surface and paper.

MAKING THE COLLAGE

1 The materials are glued to a cardboard base. Let the adhesive dry completely before printing. This example is a hilly landscape constructed from various thicknesses and finishes of cardboard, sandpaper, string, and crumpled tissue for the sky.

2 In the first proof the softer cardboard layers reveal a "honeycomb" texture under the pressure of printing. This appears too evenly distributed and mechanical, so additional materials are added to the block.

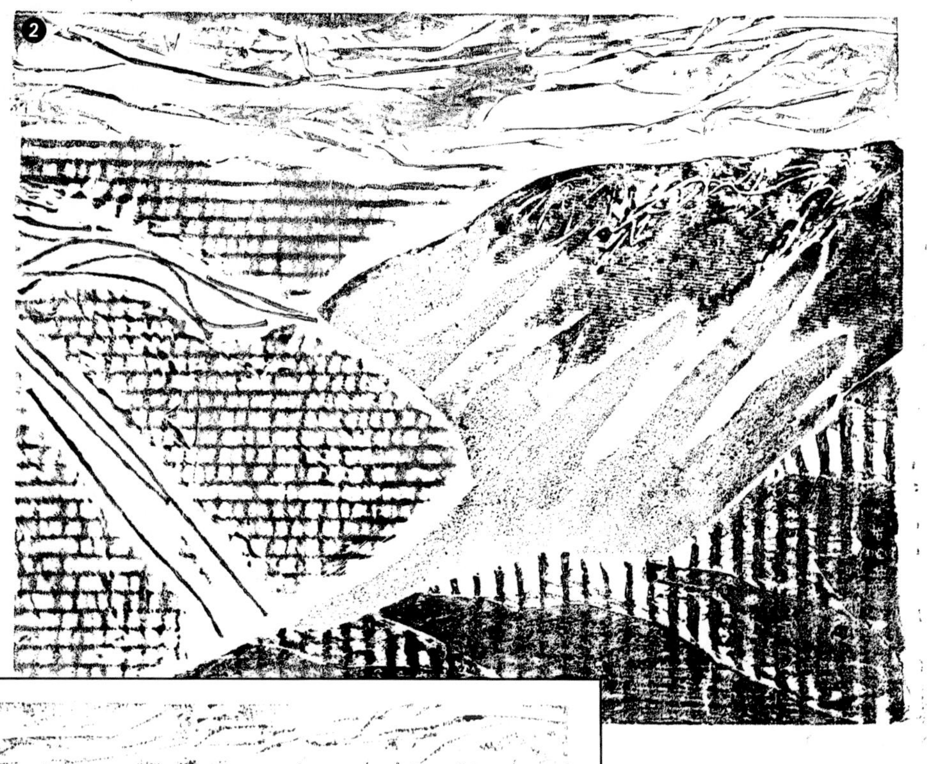

3 This proof has a more satisfactory contrast of textured and solid color areas. In the foreground, thin card pieces create strong black shapes. The upper slopes of the hills are more densely textured where a thick layer of acrylic medium has been loosely brushed on.

Linocuts

This is also an excellent printmaking technique for the complete beginner. The process of preparing the block is relatively simple, you can quickly produce a strikingly original image. A printing press is not essential, so you can satisfactorily complete the whole process without access to specialized studio facilities.

Linoleum is a sympathetic medium in that it is relatively soft and easy to cut, but because of its pliability, it is not suitable for very fine line work. Monochrome linocuts make use of the material's graphic potential, exploiting bold shapes, and patterns. Printing in two or three colors allows many possibilities for texturing and shading the image.

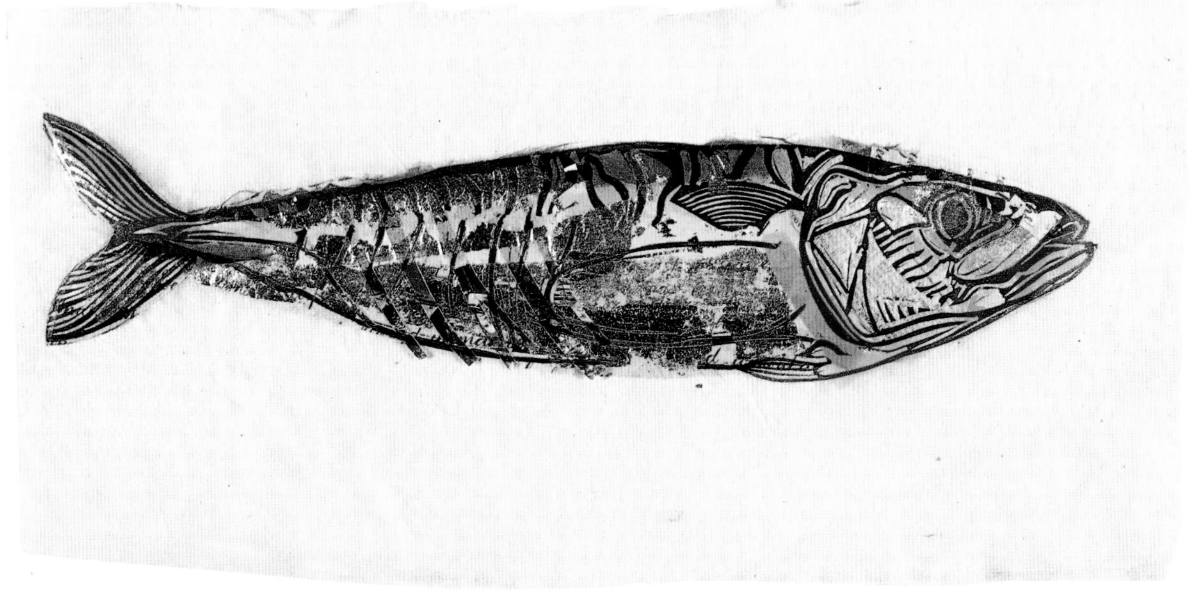

Mackerel (linocut)
by Ian Mowforth
The simple, graphic shape and patterning of the fish is provided by the linoleum block. The glittering colors of the fish skin come from a collage of various materials – silver leaf, colored tissues, and printed papers. These were assembled on thin textured paper, which was then laid over the inked block to print the linocut. Because the paper is translucent, it was possible to see through it clearly to register the collage correctly over the black line work on the block.

▲ *Audley End* (linocut)
▲ by Edward Bawden.
This linocut print was made using five blocks and five colors, one for each block.

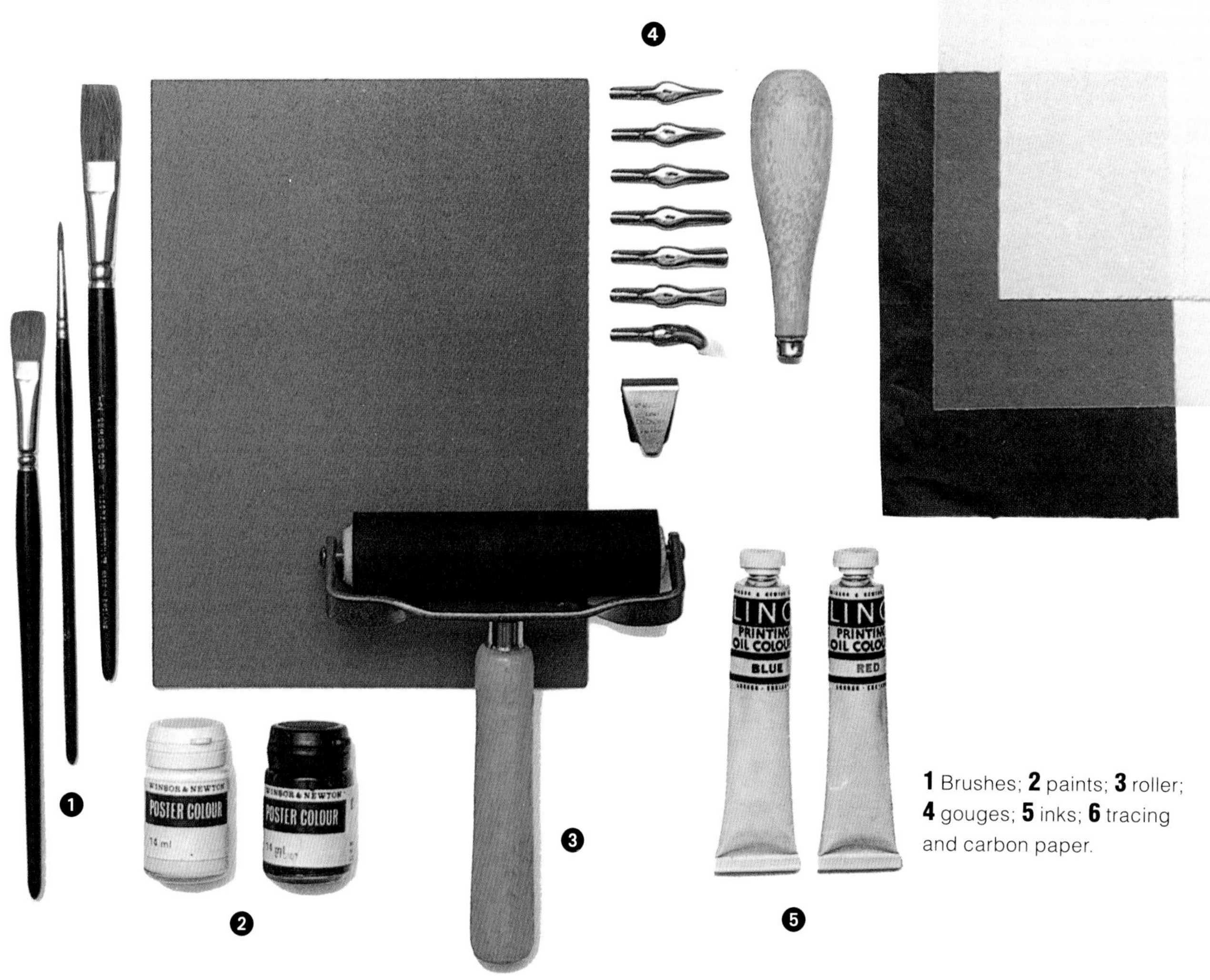

1 Brushes; **2** paints; **3** roller; **4** gouges; **5** inks; **6** tracing and carbon paper.

TOOLS AND MATERIALS

Linoleum is a corky, composite sheet material with a burlap backing. You can obtain small pre-cut linoleum blocks from most art material stores, and large pieces or rolls up to 3 feet wide from specialist suppliers of printmaking materials.

The quality of linoleum varies; sometimes the block is very smooth and compact, but the texture can also be grainy and liable to crumble when cut. It deteriorates with age, becoming hard and brittle. Warming the block before you start cutting helps to soften a "difficult" texture, easing the passage of the tools. Linoleum has a naturally oily feel, but the surface can be degreased before you start work by wiping it with denatured alcohol or rubbing it gently with a fine-grade sandpaper.

The principal linoleum-cutting tools are gouges and V-tools of different sizes. You can also use an ordinary craft knife to cut grooves in the block or to outline areas to be cleared with the gouges. Blunt tools can easily tear soft linoleum, so they should be kept sharp.

The block is inked with a roller. Different sizes and types are available, made of rubber, gelatin, or plastic. Inexpensive rollers are often too hard to give even coverage; a softer roller is more sensitive to any variations in the linoleum surface.

Gouge marks

The gouge makes a bold stroke that can be clean-edged or lightly toothed. This sample shows long and short cuts with (from left to right) medium-sized, fine, and broad gouges. The rough-edged mark is made by easing the tool from side to side, as well as forward.

Developing texture

A more complex textured effect can be obtained by quite simple means when you are overprinting colors. This shows where the same marks of the V-tool have been recut more broadly for the black printing.

V-tool marks

A comparable range of marks made with medium-sized, fine, and broad V-tools. The beginning of the cut is tapered where the "V" bites into the linoleum. You can end the cut with a taper by easing the tool up gradually, or form a squared end by stopping the stroke abruptly.

Line and tone

The tools can be used to cut the main shape in outline or to cut away the surrounding areas, leaving the outline in relief. You may even wish to combine the two approaches in one design, and should plan how you will make the transition between solid shapes and line work.

SHARPENING A GOUGE

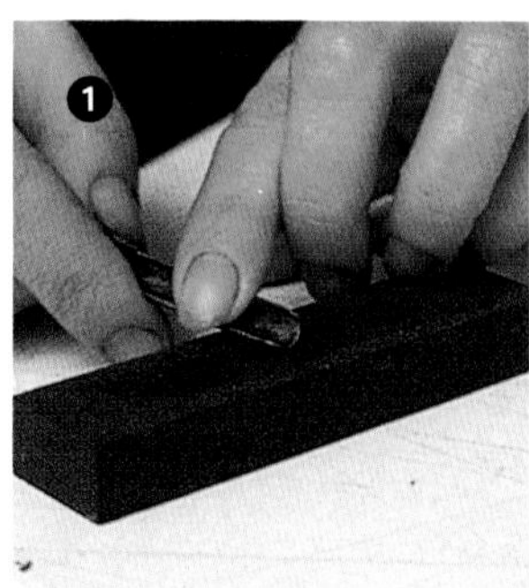

1 Place the curved blade of the gouge on an oilstone and rock it from side to side so the whole edge makes contact with the stone.

2 Sharpen the inner edge of the blade with a broad slipstone. Support the tool firmly while rubbing the stone back and forth.

SHARPENING A V-TOOL

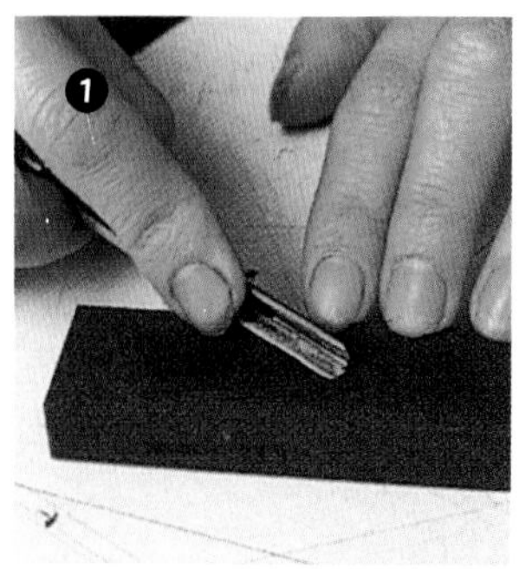

1 Put one side of the blade flat on the oilstone and rub it back and forth. Repeat with the other side to sharpen both outer facets and the point between them.

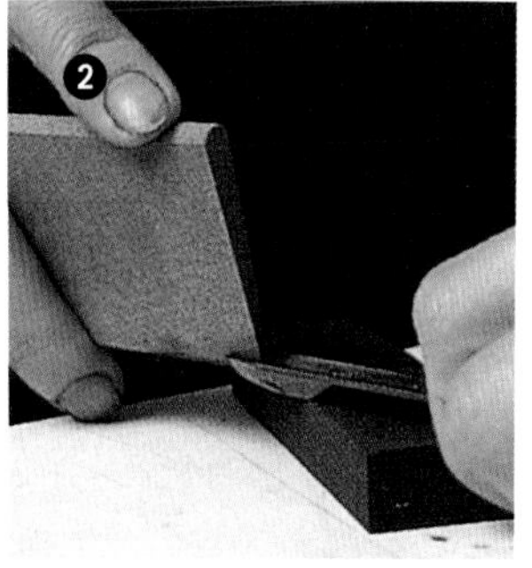

2 To sharpen the inner edges, you need a fine slipstone that fits into the "V." Support the shaft of the tool as for the gouge, while moving the stone inside the blade.

PLANNING THE IMAGE

Begin by sketching out the design onto tracing paper, which can then be turned over and the design transferred onto the surface of the linoleum. It is important that this guideline image should not be too elaborate, otherwise the design may appear too fussy when it is printed. With brush or pen, paint in white the areas which you are going to cut away, and paint in black those areas which are to be kept. This will give you a good idea of what the final print will look like. Alternatively, you can sketch directly onto the block. If you make errors, you can either draw over them, or wipe out the error with a suitable solvent and rework the area completely.

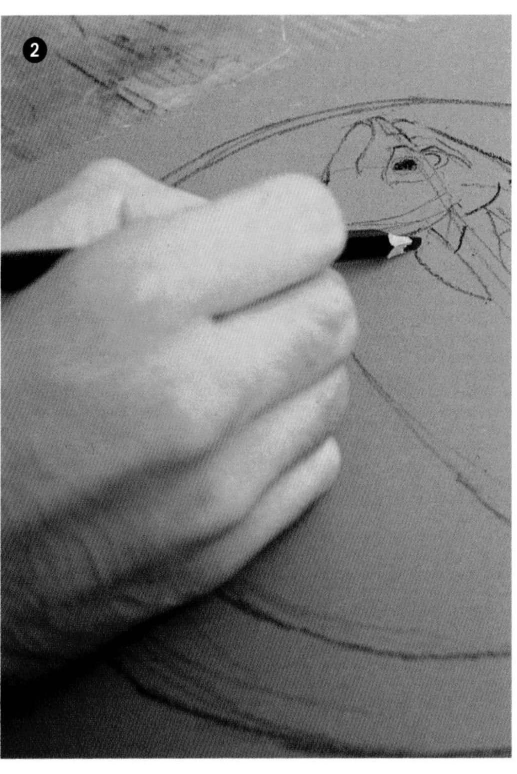

2 The markings on the fish form the most intricate part of the design and they are drawn in some detail. The shape of the plate has been drawn to position the whole design on the center of the block.

3 The pattern on the plate is indicated very loosely, leaving the artist an open choice as to how to treat those areas as the cutting of the design develops.

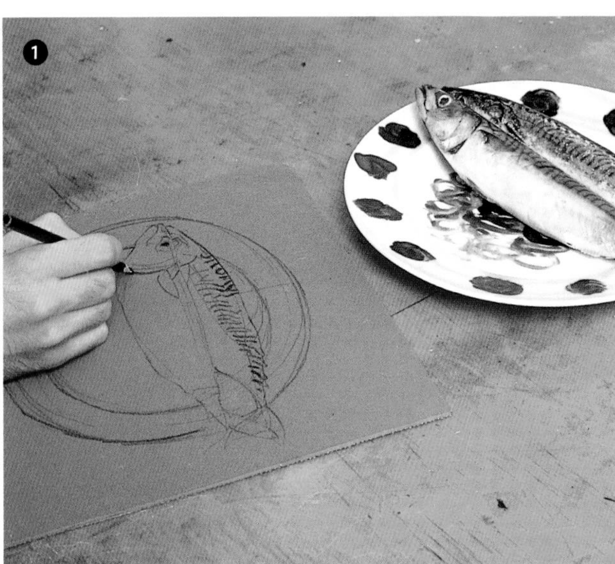

1 For this demonstration of cutting a monochrome image, the artist works directly from the subject, drawing on the block with a black waxy pencil.

CUTTING THE BLOCK

When you are cutting the linoleum you need to be able to control the tools properly and this is made easier if the bench or tabletop is set at a comfortable height and preferably at a slight angle to the body. During cutting you should rotate and move the block to facilitate the movement of the cutting tool as it is pushed through the material.

There is no particular order or sequence to cutting into the design. For example, you can begin with narrow cuts outlining the overall shapes, then work into detail and clear any large "white" areas; or you can work from one side to another, completing each section as you go. You will soon learn to judge which tools provide the right width of cut and how much pressure you need to apply. Providing that the linoleum has a good thickness (something in the order of ¼ inch), it is quite easy to gouge out without damaging the canvas backing.

Avoid working too heavily, as it is easy to slip and cut into a section that should be left uncut. Move the tool easily and evenly; if you angle a knife or V-tool blade too sharply, you may undercut the linoleum, which makes lines and edges unstable.

If you have a large area to clear (which is "non-reading" in the print), or you are shaping the outer edges of the block, you need not do all the work with the gouges. You can cut away the surplus linoleum with a craft knife or scissors.

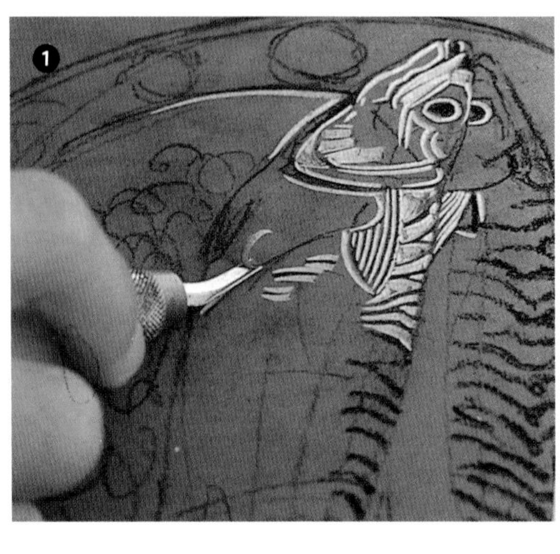

1 Initially a V-tool is used to establish fine outlines and work into the detail of the fish head and body.

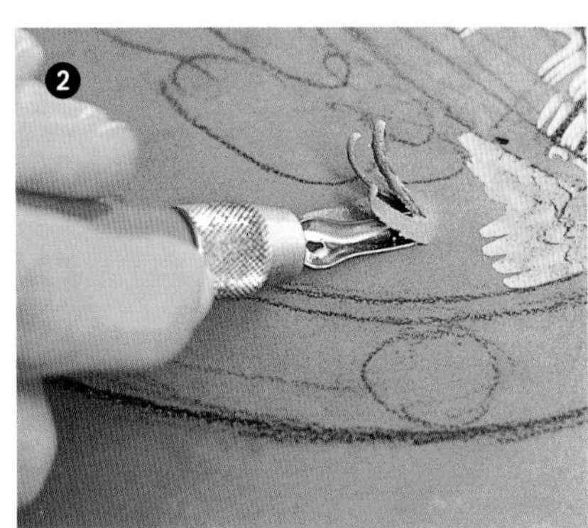

2 Once the markings of both fishes have been described with careful line work, the artist begins to clear the "white" areas, working rapidly with a broad gouge.

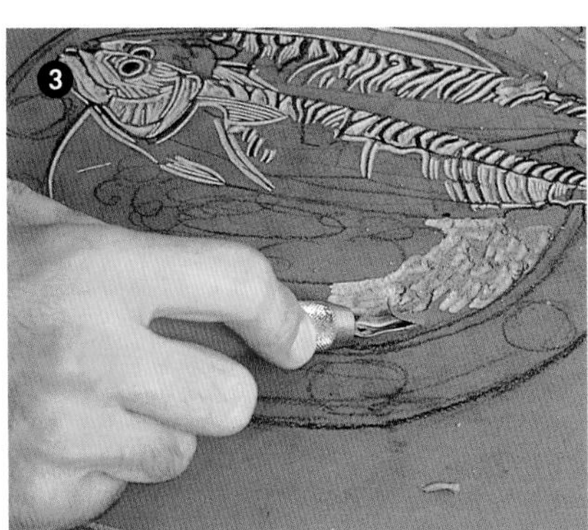

3 The gouge is used roughly so that the lowered surface of the block retains some relief texture that will print.

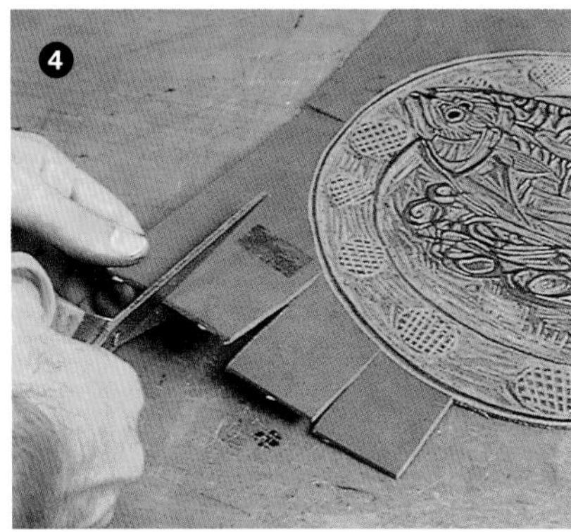

4 The outer border does not print . The artist cuts the linoleum away. The shape of the plate is outlined with a V-tool, then cuts are made from the edge towards the outline.

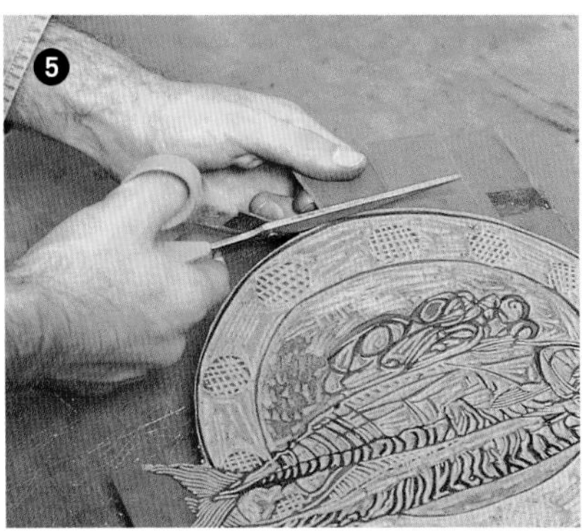

5 The edge-cuts make the linoleum more flexible, and easier to cut. If the border area were cut with a gouge, some residual marks might appear on the print, but removing the surplus ensures a clean outline.

PROOFING AND PRINTING

For a monochrome print like the example shown here, you can check the progress of the cutting without actually rolling up and printing the block. Simply place a piece of paper over the surface and take a rubbing with a pencil. This will be accurate enough to show you where further cutting is required, and whether there is a good balance of negative and positive areas.

When the block is ready to print, roll out the ink thinly on the inking slab, then roll it over the raised areas of the linoleum firmly and evenly. You can work back and forth in all directions, and if you put down too much ink you can take up some of the excess by running the roller in one direction only.

You can take a print either by placing paper over the block and rubbing with a baren, a spoon, or any other suitable smooth, curved tool; or you can print on a flatbed, cylinder, or proofing press.

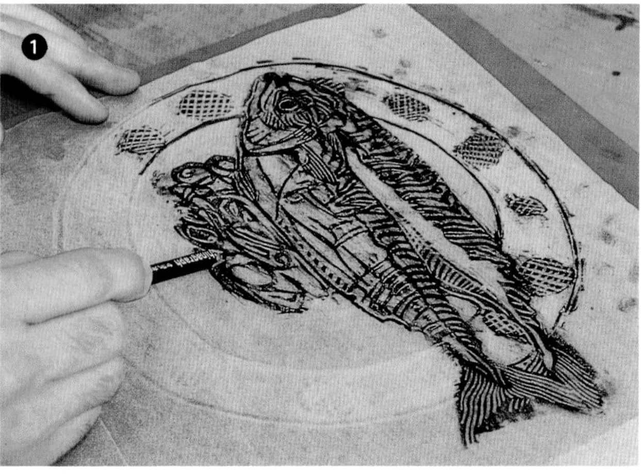

1 Rather than ink the block to pull a proof, the artist takes a rubbing on thin paper with a graphite pencil. Any refinements needed can be cleanly cut before printing.

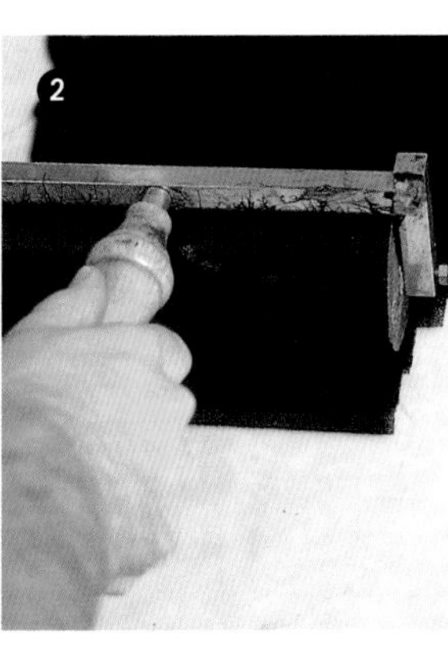

2 When the design is complete, it can be inked and printed. To roll ink out, spread it across the glass slab with a palette knife, then work outwards with the roller until the ink forms a thin coating.

3 You can work in all directions when rolling up the block. Go over it as many times as you need to coat it evenly with color, picking up more ink on the roller as necessary.

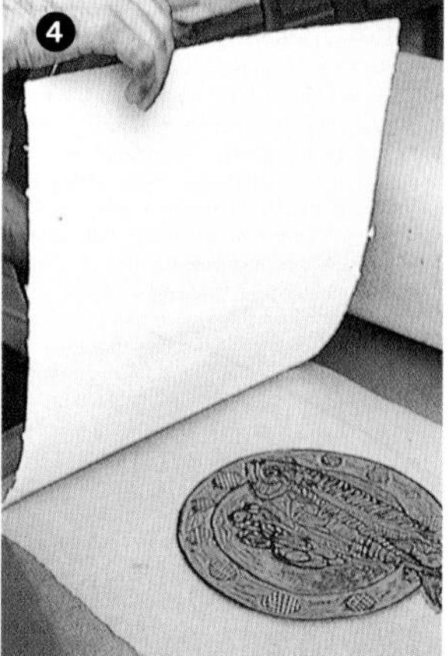

4 Position the inked block on a clean sheet of paper on the bed of the press. Align the printing paper to the base sheet, so the printed image will be centrally placed, and lower the paper onto the block.

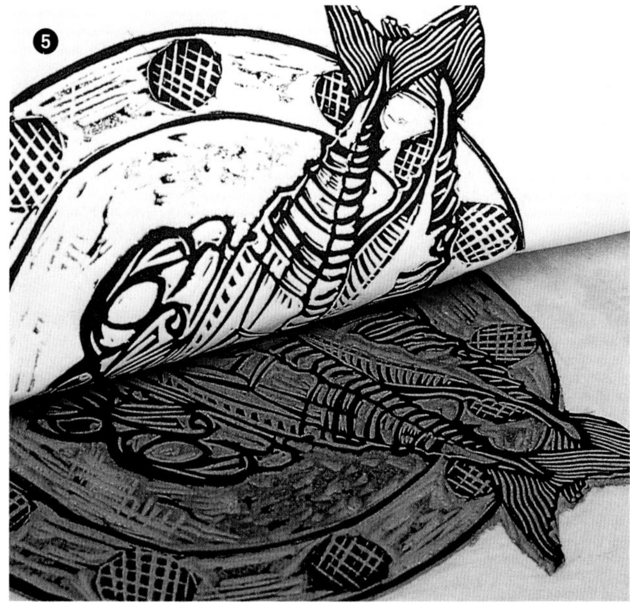

5 Activate the press to exert even pressure on the block and paper. Take hold of one corner of the printing paper and peel it back gently from the block.

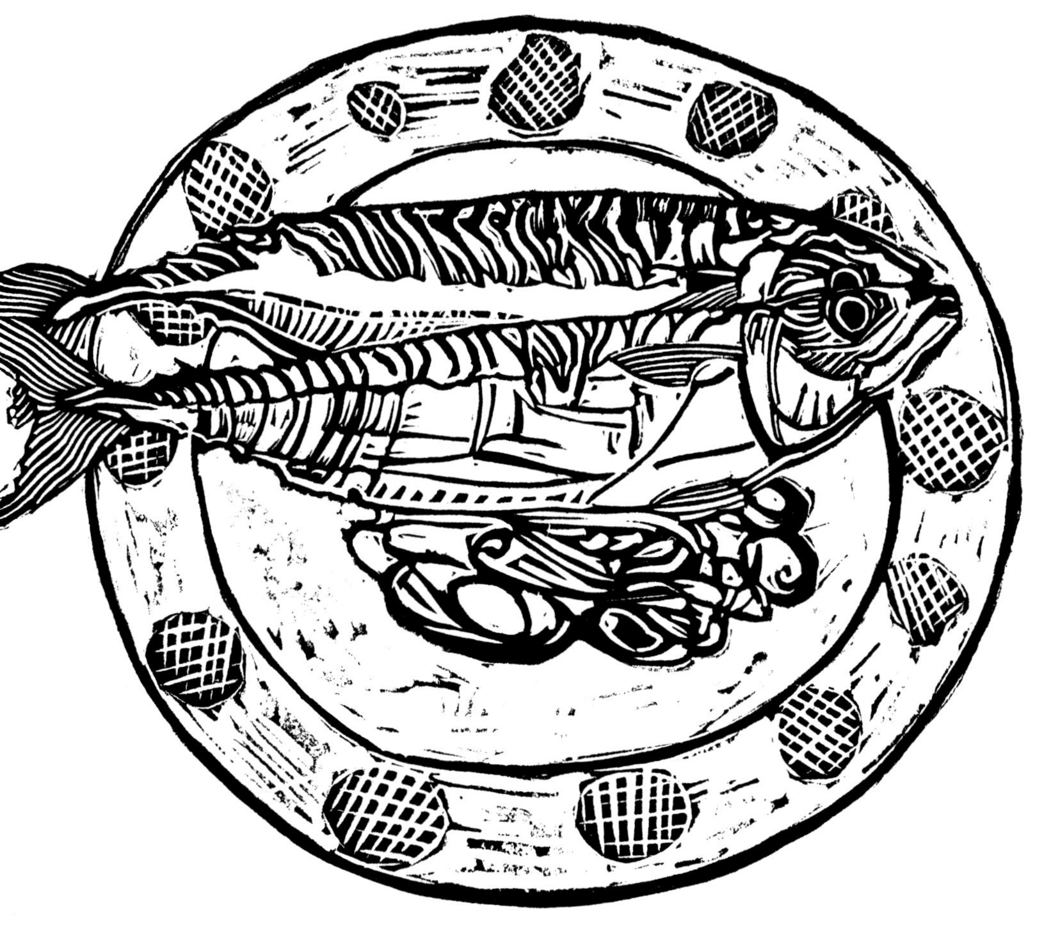

This print has a bold, graphic style, with crisp black line work nicely offset by the incidental patches of rough texture in the whites. Variations in the line widths give a pleasing "hand-done" quality without detracting from the clarity of the image.

PRINTING WITHOUT A PRESS

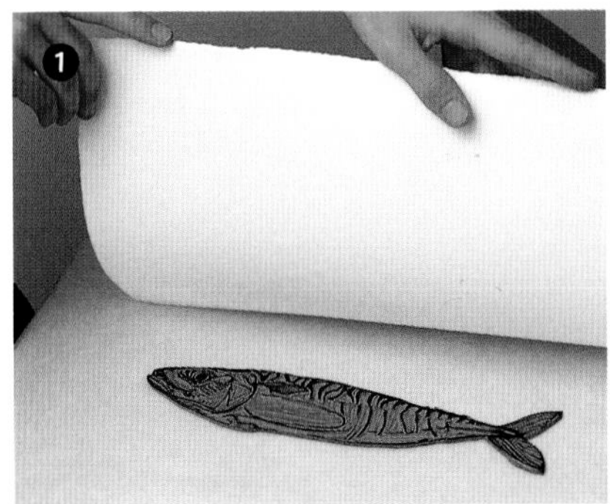

1 If you have no access to a press, you can use this hand-printing method, also known as burnishing. Ink the block and position it on a clean base sheet. Lay the printing paper over it.

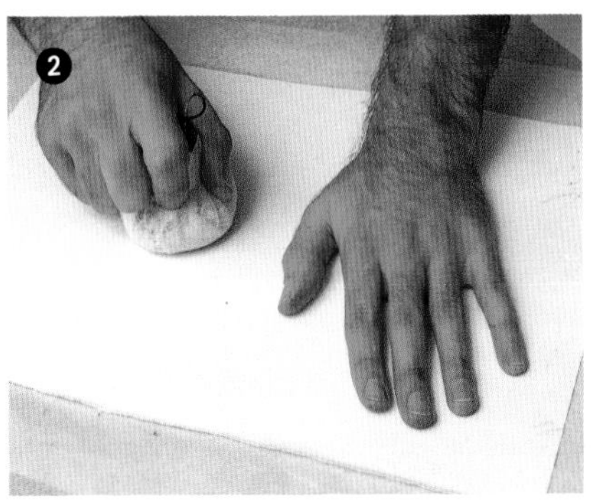

2 Use a rounded implement such as a purpose-made baren, the back of a spoon, or, as here, an etching dabber wrapped in cheesecloth, to rub firmly and evenly all over the back of the printing sheet.

3 A print taken by this method is naturally lighter colored than one taken on a press, because the pressure is less intense. As you continue to take prints and the ink layer on the block builds up, the image will become increasingly dark and more even.

COLOR PRINTING

Multi-colored linocuts can be prepared by one of two methods. In the reduction process, successive cuts are made in the same block, and a new color is printed at various stages. The other method is to register the design on separate blocks, one for each color. The reduction method (demonstrated on p46), may be easier to register for printing, as it is the same block you are using at each stage; but the block is gradually destroyed by the continuing work, so you have to be confident about how much of the surface is to be removed for each printing.

Using two or more blocks gives you more time to think through the cutting stages, and you can proof all the colors to compare and amend the different areas. However, any slight variations in the dimensions or shape of the blocks' outer edges can make it difficult to align each printing.

To cut two or more blocks, you can use a master tracing to place the image on each, but a more accurate method is to cut the first block and use it as the key block for offsetting the image onto the uncut linoleum pieces. As shown here, the method used to register block and paper for the offsetting is then also used to register the overprintings.

SEPARATE BLOCK METHOD

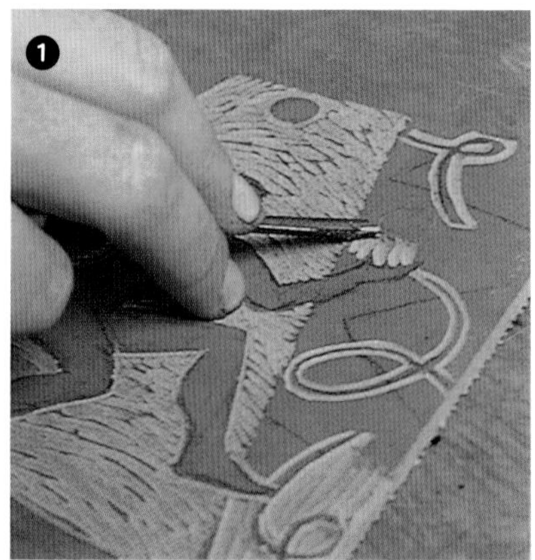

1 Cut your block for the first color, using the appropriate marks and textures for the effect you wish to achieve.

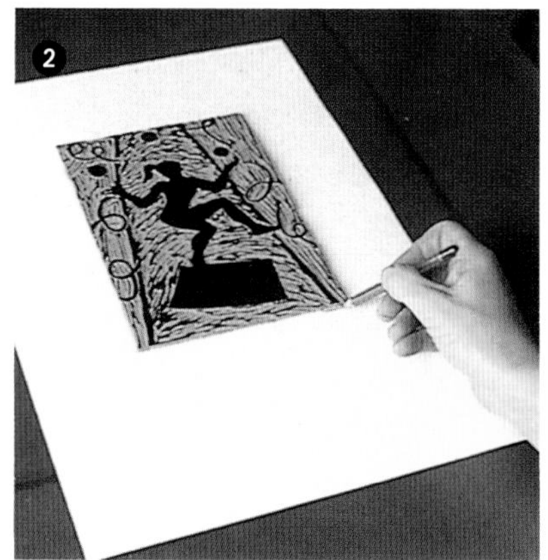

2 Ink up the first block in black and lay it centered on a clean sheet of paper on the bed of the press. With a pencil, mark the edges and corners of the block on the base sheet. This sheet will form your guide for registering subsequent printings. Take a print from the block on smooth paper.

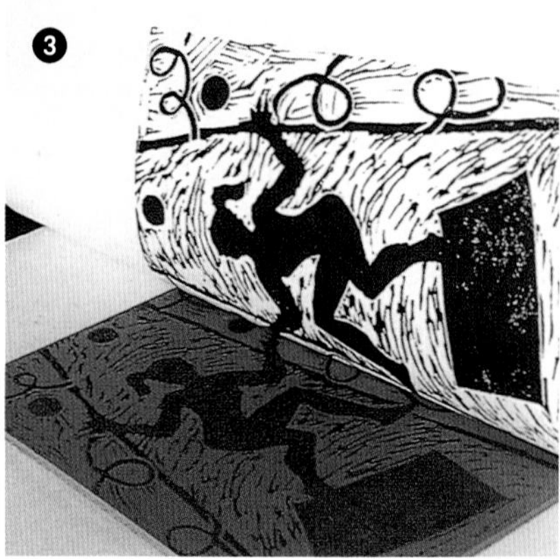

3 Lay the uncut second block in the marked area on the base sheet and place the black print over it, aligned to the edges of the base sheet. Run this through the press so that the print transfers color onto the clean linoleum block.

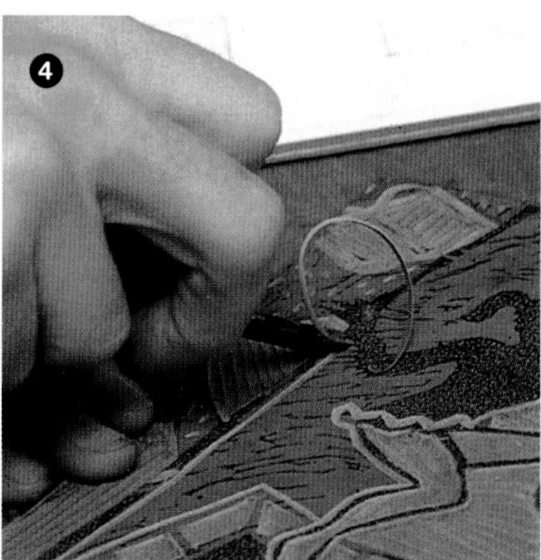

4 Use the shapes offset from the first block as a guide to cutting your design for the second color. Pay special attention to areas where the two colors will overprint, and also any shapes that must register exactly.

5 Roll up and print the first block in the required color. Here it is printed in red. This is the same block that was printed black in steps 2 and 3 to offset the image.

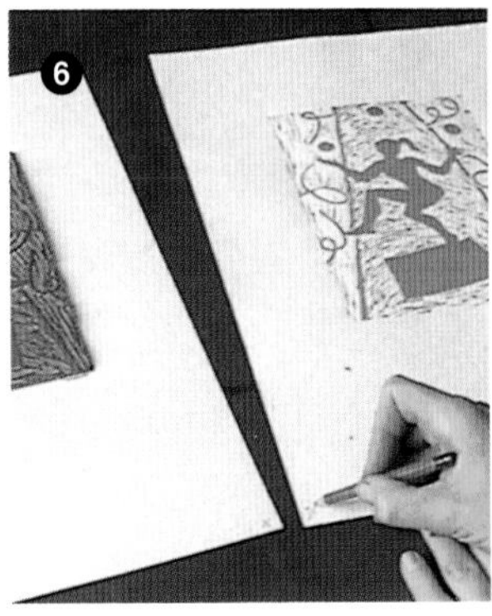

6 You may find it helpful to mark one corner of the base sheet and the corresponding corner of the print with a small cross. Each time you come to print from a second or subsequent block, match the crosses and then align from that corner. This is particularly valuable when you are printing several colors, as the prints can appear quite abstract in the early stages and it is easy to make an error in overprinting.

7 Roll up the second block in the required color – in this example it is to print black over red. Position the block on the base sheet, register the printed image over it and run them through the press.

8 This extremely lively image combines solid blocks of color with roughly worked, gouged textures and bold patterns made with the V-tool. The registration of colors on the figure is deliberately inexact to add to the sense of movement, but where required, background shapes have overprinted cleanly along the same outlines.

Registering on the press

This method of registration is a simple alternative to the use of a base sheet. Mark the positions for the block and printing paper directly onto the bed of the press, using small strips of card attached with masking tape. Butt the corner of the block to the inner cards. Next slip the corner of the paper in to align with the outer registration stops, before lowering the full sheet over the block.

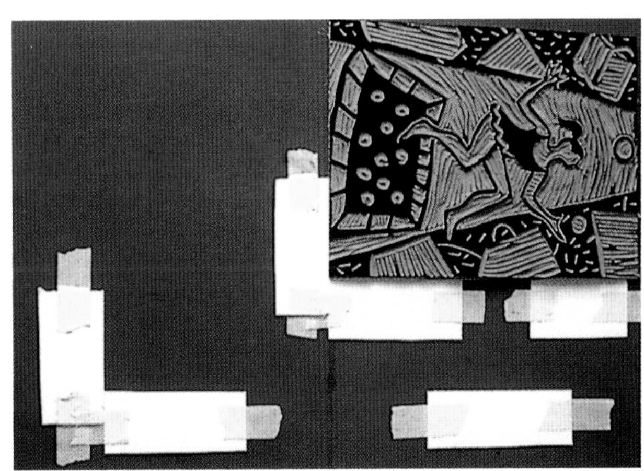

Woodcuts

Catnaps Edition (woodcut) by Jonathan Heale
A simple, everyday subject becomes an unusual, witty composition, when seen from an unexpected angle. By treating the human subject almost as a background element, the artist finds a strong combination of large and small shapes and makes the most of the bright patterning that frames the simple, elegant form of the cat. The print is a black-and-white woodcut, hand-colored with watercolor paint.

Woodcut printing is very similar in technique and process to linocut, but different in style and surface quality due to the properties of the base material. Woodcuts are made on the side grain of the wood, in other words on pieces of wood which have been cut from a tree so that the grain runs along the surface. These cuts are also referred to as plankwoods.

The natural pattern and direction of the grain are therefore integrated with the textures and patterns made by the cutting process.

Almost any wood can be adapted for this purpose, though sycamore, lime, pear, cherry, and boxwood are the most popular. The last, which is very tough, is usually reserved for wood engraving. Secondhand furniture and demolition timber are also sources of material. Really any wood which has dried out and which is not warped is suitable for the beginner. Indeed, cheap offcuts are ideal for they allow him or her to experiment and take risks with the knowledge that expensive materials are not being wasted. It is not easy to produce a finished composition the first time that you tackle a woodcut, so some time spent acquiring the basic skills involved in cutting a relief image will not be spent in vain.

In linocutting the tools cut easily in all directions, but for woodcuts it is easier to cut along or with the grain than across or against it. The type of wood used – how heavily grained and hard or soft it is – will also affect the print. You can obtain interesting variations between clean and ragged edges, sharp knife cuts, or broadly gouged channels. Woodcuts are associated with the aggressive, jagged graphics of European Expressionists, but also with the clarity and formality of Japanese color prints, so a wide range of variations is possible.

TOOLS AND MATERIALS

A useful aspect of the woodcut process for beginners is that you can use almost any type of wood. Instead of buying specially prepared blocks you can pick up offcuts of plywood or timber from a lumberyard. Pine boards and plywood sheets, inexpensive and readily available, are highly suitable for trying out the cutting techniques and gaining confidence with the medium. They are relatively coarse and liable to

Two Geisha Girls (woodcut)
by Utamaro II
Illustrated here are five stages in the printing of a color wood block. In all, 16 printings were necessary to produce the final print. Four blocks combined more than one color while the other 12 blocks were used for one color only. A large number of blocks were needed because the Japanese inks failed to mix satisfactorily. Each area in the design which needed a different color required a separate block. The first block was the key block which printed the black outline. Each subsequent block introduced a new color into the composition. The detail shows the printing of the gray which constituted the ninth stage in the development of the print. Careful registration was vital to ensure that the color blocks related accurately to the key block.

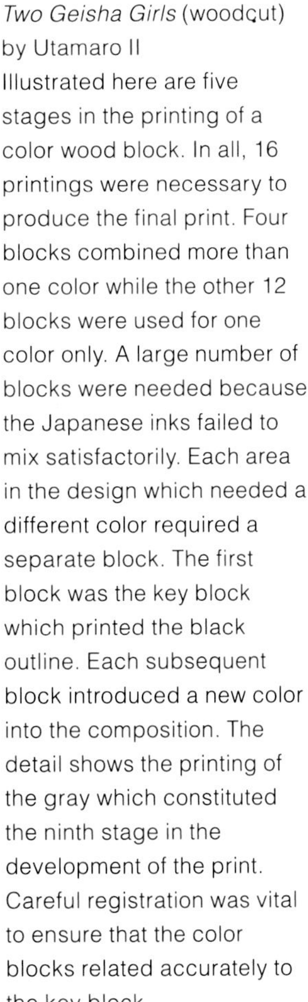

Woodcut equipment
1 Side-grain wood blocks; **2** gouges and V-tools; **3** craft knife; **4** cutting knife, for fine-line work on block; **5**, **6** push knife and palette knife; **7** block-printing ink.

splinter, but are also soft to cut and have pleasing, pronounced grain patterns. As you become interested in the process of woodcut and practiced in the techniques, you can investigate finer, denser woods that allow more delicate control. The only way to discover and exploit the characteristics of different types is to try them.

Tools for woodcut include the V-tools and gouges also used for linocut. The interchangeable gouge sets, however, are unsuitable as they are not strong enough; use the metal-shafted individual gouges. Cutting knives are extensively used in woodcut; specialist tools are available from printmaking suppliers or you can use a sturdy craft knife. Chisels are also useful tools for abrading the surface and clearing large areas.

Prints are made from wood blocks in exactly the same way as from linoleum: the surface is inked and the print can be taken by hand or on a press. Thin plywood can be printed on a cylinder or flatbed press. A thick wood block must be printed by the direct pressure of a flatbed press, or on a type-proofing press where the block can be packed into a sunken bed and the paper rolled over it.

CUTTING THE BLOCK

Some artists cut directly into the block without preparation. Others may prepare the surface by sandpapering or brushing with a wire brush to remove any loose fibers and bring up the grain pattern. As with linoleum, you can draw onto the surface with pencils, markers, or brush and ink, or trace down a design using transfer paper. You can, if you wish, stain the surface all over by rubbing it with diluted printing ink; this enables you to see the cut marks very clearly as you progress.

Wood is quite a responsive surface, and you can obtain good effects from a variety of different marks. Try to get the feel of the tool as you cut, particularly as you change its angle to the grain. Pushing a gouge easily along the grain produces even, clean-edged cuts, but cutting too boldly across it can cause major splintering that strips too much of the surface.

The width of the gouge you choose has to be matched to the elements of your design, but otherwise the choice of tool is a matter of common sense – there is obviously more labor involved in trying to clear a large area with a narrow gouge than with a wide one. In an open area, you may leave small ridges that will print as a broken texture; this can be effective, but if after proofing you find it is not suitable you can clean up the shape and remove any cutting marks.

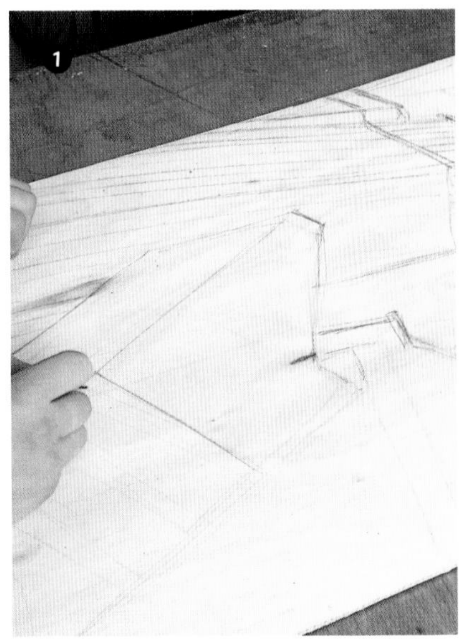

1 Unless your design is small-scale, or you are very confident in cutting, it is best to draw a fairly detailed outline of the image on the wood block.

2 In this example, the image depends upon some intricate pattern-making in the structures of the buildings. The artist draws this in detail, filling in lines and shapes that feature strongly.

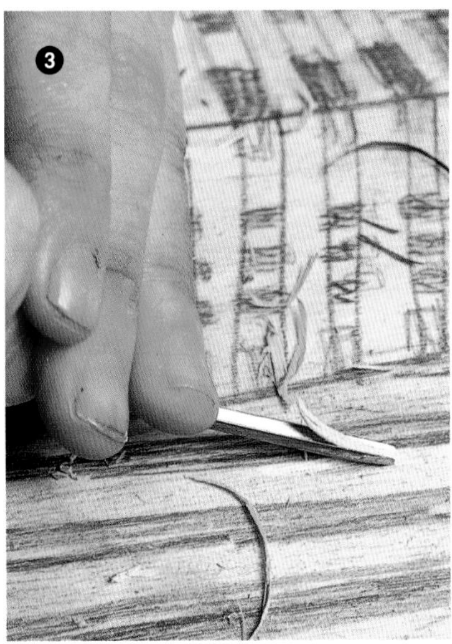

3 She begins cutting the broadest lines, stripping the wood rapidly with a gouge. As with linoleum, there is no particular rule as to where you should start.

4 Because the print will consist of a four-color sequence, the cutting at this stage is relatively limited, consisting only of those elements that will appear white in the final print. Fine detail is worked in using a narrow gouge.

COLOR PRINTING

This demonstration shows a four-color wood block cut and printed by the reduction method. In the first cutting, only the areas to remain white are taken out, and the block is printed with the first color rolled all over the surface. In the second stage, the areas to remain as the first color are removed, and the whole block is printed in yellow. In the third stage, areas to remain yellow are cut out and the block is printed in blue. Finally the blue areas are cut away and the remaining relief surface is overprinted in black.

With the reduction method it is not necessary to follow the process of offsetting demonstrated for linocut, but you can use the same registration process to ensure that the colors overprint accurately. In this case, however, having printed the first color, the artist registers the block for each subsequent printing by laying it face down on the print.

PRINTING AND OVERPRINTING

1 When the first stage of cutting is complete, you can immediately print the first color. You may wish to take one proof first to check the balance of the image and the effectiveness of individual shapes. Roll up the whole block with an even, smooth layer of ink.

USING GOUGES

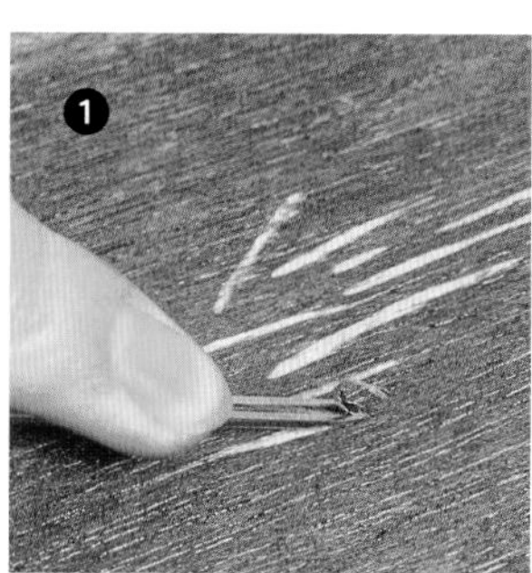

1 All woodcut tools cut most easily along the grain of the wood. A small gouge makes clean-edged fine lines suitable for outlining or hatched textures.

2 The print shows how the grain of the wood contributes a specific background texture, where the relief surface is allowed to print as large areas of dark tone.

3 Broad gouges are used for line work. In addition, by keeping the cuts very close together or overlapping them, broad gouges can be used to clear areas of the block.

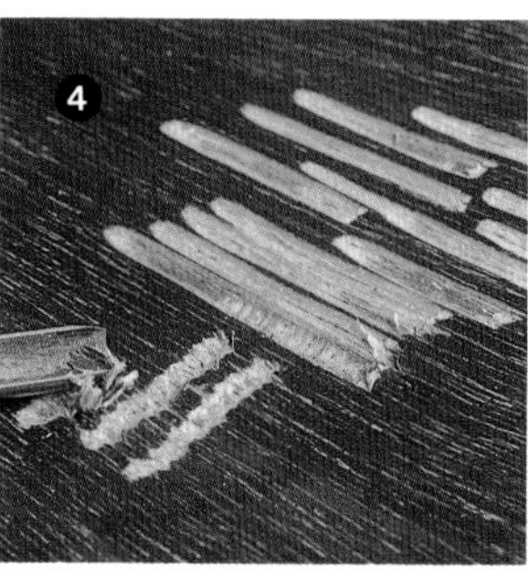

4 Pushing the gouge across rather than along the grain, you encounter more resistance and may need to ease the gouge from side to side as it moves forward.

2 Run the print through the press and peel back the paper carefully. Once you have begun to lift the paper, it is advisable not to lay it back down, as any slight shift can create a double image.

3 At the second cutting stage, remove all areas of the block that will appear as the first color – in this case, beige – in the final print.

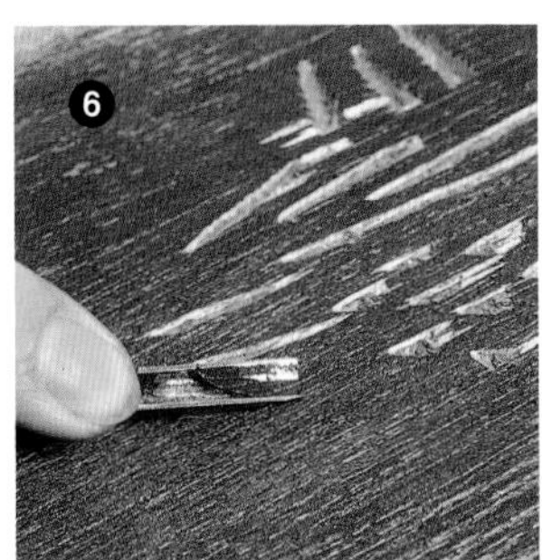

5 Although the width of the tool mark does not vary very much, you can see how working along or across the grain produces different edge qualities.

6 The V-tool reacts similarly to the gouge in terms of the direction it takes; but if the angled blade is sharp, the cross-grain resistance may be less influential because the cutting edge is less broad.

7 A V-tool cut begins sharply and broadens as the full width of the blade bites into the wood. Short, angular cuts produce interesting, irregular coarse textures.

8 The actual character of each mark may be less important than the way the tools are used to cut particular elements in the design, but this sample block demonstrates a wide range of textures obtained with only three tools.

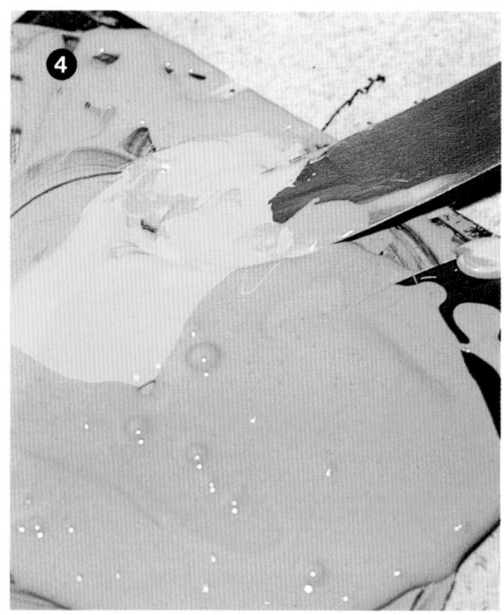

4 If you have to mix a special color when printing, make sure you have a quantity that will cover the number of prints you wish to make; it can be difficult to match a mixed hue.

5 Roll up the block in the second color, working the ink in all directions to produce an even, smooth coating. It is advisable to have a roller that relates well to the size of the block. A large brayer is being used here.

6 To register the second color over the first, the artist lays the block face down on the original print, judging the alignment of edges and corners by eye.

7 The cutting in the third stage consists of removing all the areas of the image that should appear yellow in the final print. An experienced artist may work directly on the block; for a beginner, it is advisable to use a previously prepared color study as a helpful guide.

8 There may be a lot of detailed cutting at the final stage, because in order to allow the previous three colors to show through, much of the remaining relief surface becomes linear in character.

9 Large areas of the block have now been cleared, particularly the sky, which is very open. The cutting is deliberately rough, so that a lightly textured impression will show up between the more emphatic lines.

▲ **Stage proof: one**
In a print made by the reduction method, the first color printing may include a lot of broad, flat color areas where the detail will be created by the cutting for subsequent colors. When printing is completed, clean the ink from the block immediately with solvent and a rag.

▲ **Stage proof: two**
The second color printing begins to suggest the three-dimensional depth in the image, but because the two colors are close in tone, the change is not dramatic.

◄ **Stage proof: three**
The overprinting in blue, using the same registration technique as for the yellow, produces a more appreciable variation in the image, both because the color is lighter than those underneath and because the textures are becoming more complex.

▲ **Stage proof: four**
The black printing sharpens the image and gives it a much bolder, more graphic feeling, pulling together all the shapes. This is the effect that the artist has been carrying in her mind throughout the cutting processes. The radical changes that occur with each successive stage are a very exciting feature of color printing. Although with experience you can anticipate many aspects of the color interactions, the overall result can still contain surprising and unexpectedly pleasing details.

Wood engravings

The wood engraving is a variation of the woodcut. The main difference is that in wood engraving the wood is cut across the grain rather than plankwise, along the grain. For the artist it means that he or she can work freely with the tools in any direction. Furthermore, because the wood is harder when cut in this way, he or she can use the more intricate tools of the engraver and is not merely reliant on the knife and the gouge.

Wood engraving is typically a monochrome method (although the relief surface can be inked in any color), since the engraved work is too

◀ *Room 61* (wood engraving) by Roland Stringer
The delicate touch of the engraving tools gives a distinct charm to printed textures in a small-scale wood engraving.

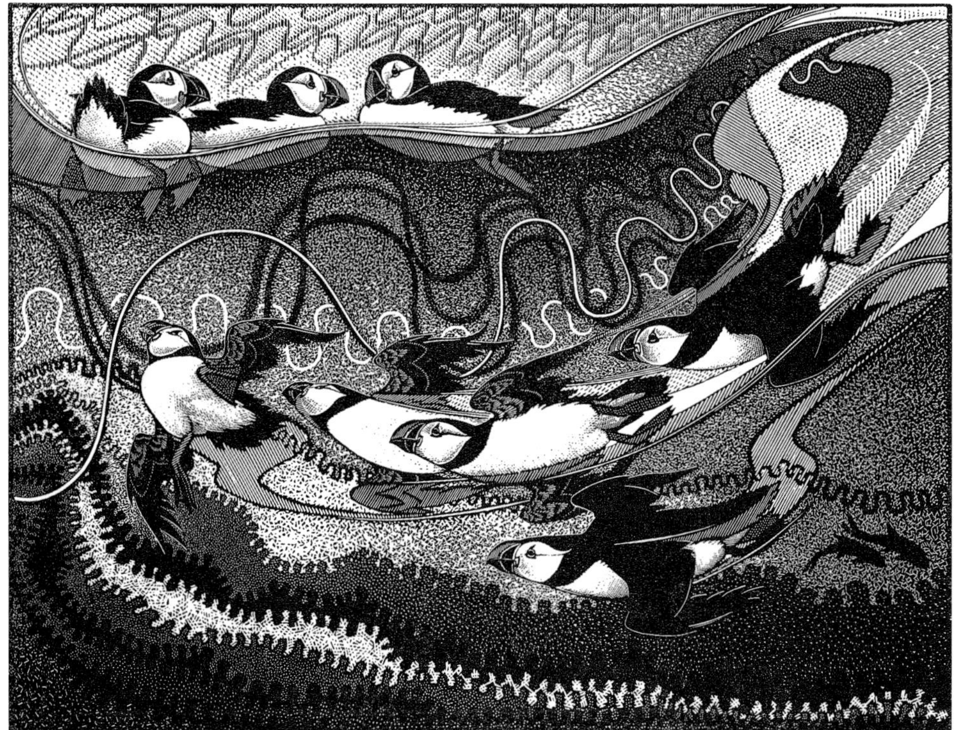

▲ *British Birds* (wood engraving) by Thomas Bewick
The delicacy of the detailing in this print made in 1797 reflects Bewick's training as a metal engraver. That a wood engraving should have been used in a natural history book is testimony to its ability to print fine detail.

◀ *Puffins* (wood engraving) by Colin Paynton
The hard end-grain blocks used in wood engraving enable the artist to control fine cutting techniques that create intricate texture. The halftone effect of stippling and hatching is beautifully balanced with solid areas of black and white.

detailed and tight to allow the processes of re-cutting and overprinting that can be exploited with sidegrain wood and linoleum. Printing in black, or a very dark-toned color, best conveys the subtle graphic effects of the engraving.

TOOLS AND MATERIALS

The preferred wood for end-grain blocks is box, which has a tight grain but is relatively soft and easy to engrave. This is a slow-growing, small tree, so wood-engraving blocks are usually only 2 to 3 inches across – larger blocks are made by jointing small pieces together. They are expensive as the wood must be properly seasoned and prepared, and you do need to obtain the blocks from a specialist supplier. Holly, pear, or maple – cheaper substitutes – may also be available. In addition, compact blocks of plywood or manufactured board can be used. (When you begin engraving you might use man-made substitutes which are of a similar density but much cheaper. Good examples of such materials are Lucite™ and Perspex™.)

To prepare the wood for engraving, one surface is planed smooth before it is brought up to a highly polished state by the application of glass paper. It is worth pointing out that the beginner will probably find this is a very time-consuming task and that in the end the finished article will in no way match the quality of the ones supplied by professional block makers.

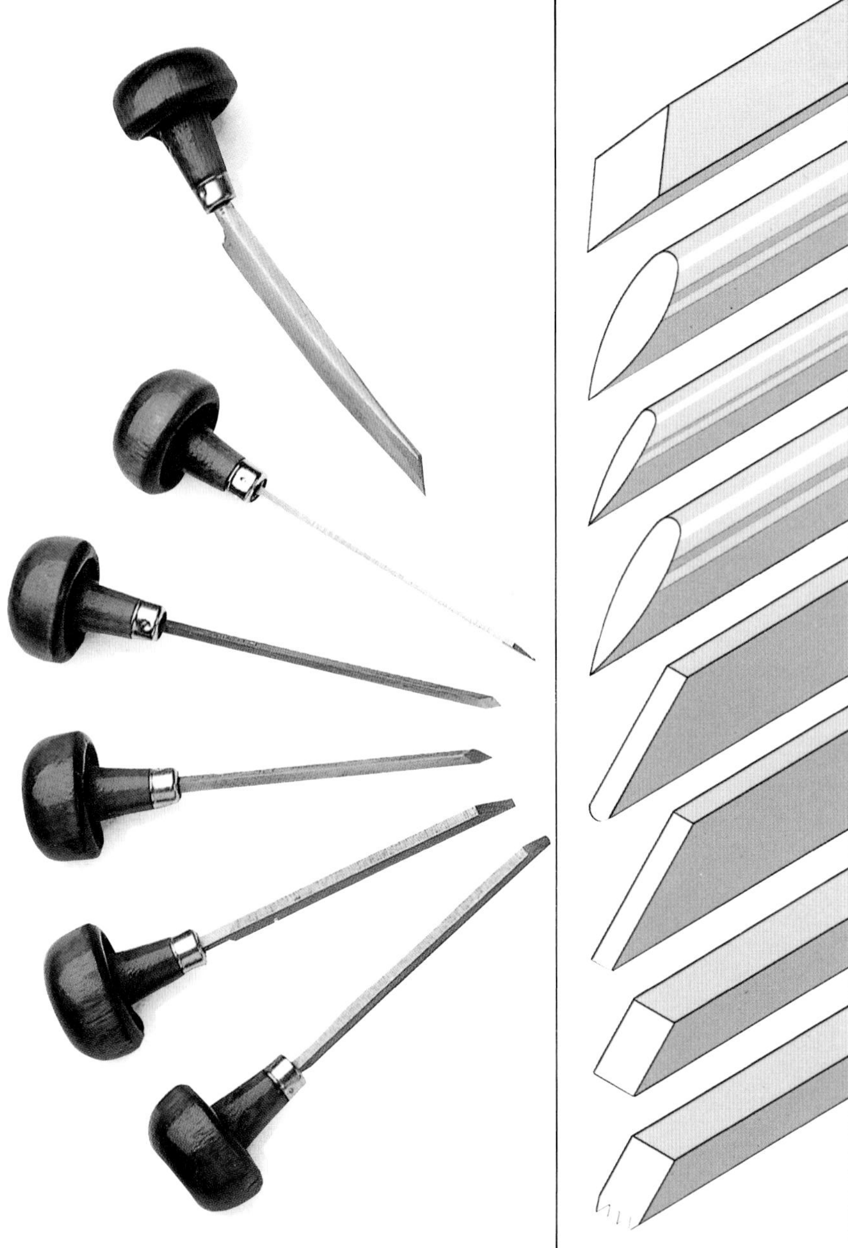

▲ Blade sections of wood engraving tools. From top to bottom: a gravure or lozenge, a spitstick, two tint tools, a round scauper, a square scauper, a chisel, and a multi-tint tool. (Above left) Tools used in engraving.

The engraving tools are fine shafts of metal, faceted and sharpened to form various shapes of cutting tip. The main types are the lozenge-shaped graver for general line work; the elliptical spitsticker, designed for cutting curves; the squared or rounded scauper, used for broad marks, and clearing areas of the block; and the fine tint tool, which maintains a line of uniform width. It is important to keep the tools sharp, as blunt tools slip and slide on the close-grained surface. Tools can be

Wood engraving equipment
1 End-grain wood blocks; **2** glass mixing slab; **3** block-printing ink; **4** palette knife; **5** roller.

sharpened by a professional for a small charge, although during the course of engraving, a little gentle rubbing of the straight back edges of the gravers will keep them in good condition while a whetstone can be used to remove the slight burr which will collect on the tools.

To cut curves and angles you turn the block rather than the tool. To facilitate the movement, it can be mounted on the traditional engraver's sandbag, but you can work just as effectively by resting the block on a book wrapped in a cloth. Raising the block also helps you to grip it and hold it steady.

The block-printing ink for wood engraving should be quite stiff, or it may flood the delicate marks. A small gelatin or rubber roller is adequate for inking the little wood blocks.

A traditional sandbag. An equally effective item can be made by wrapping a large book in a cloth.

DRAWING ON THE BLOCK

A drawing can be made directly on the block or a prepared design can be traced down. If you are working in a way that produces a white-line image, you may find it easiest to darken the surface of the block with ink. You can then make your tracing with white transfer paper, so that the initial drawing corresponds to what you expect to see in the print.

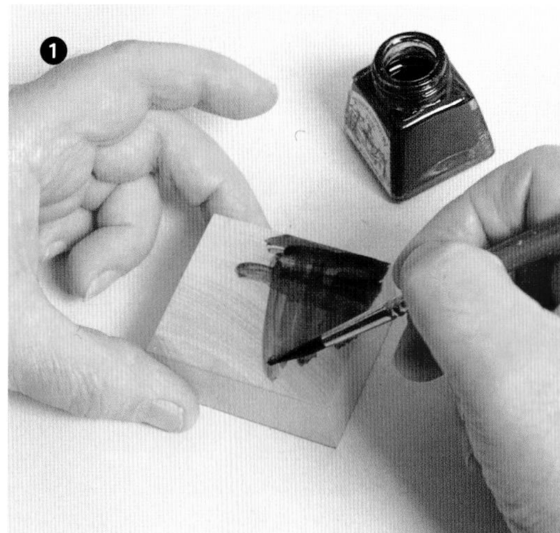

1 Paint the upper surface of the block with a thin coat of black drawing ink and allow it to dry completely.

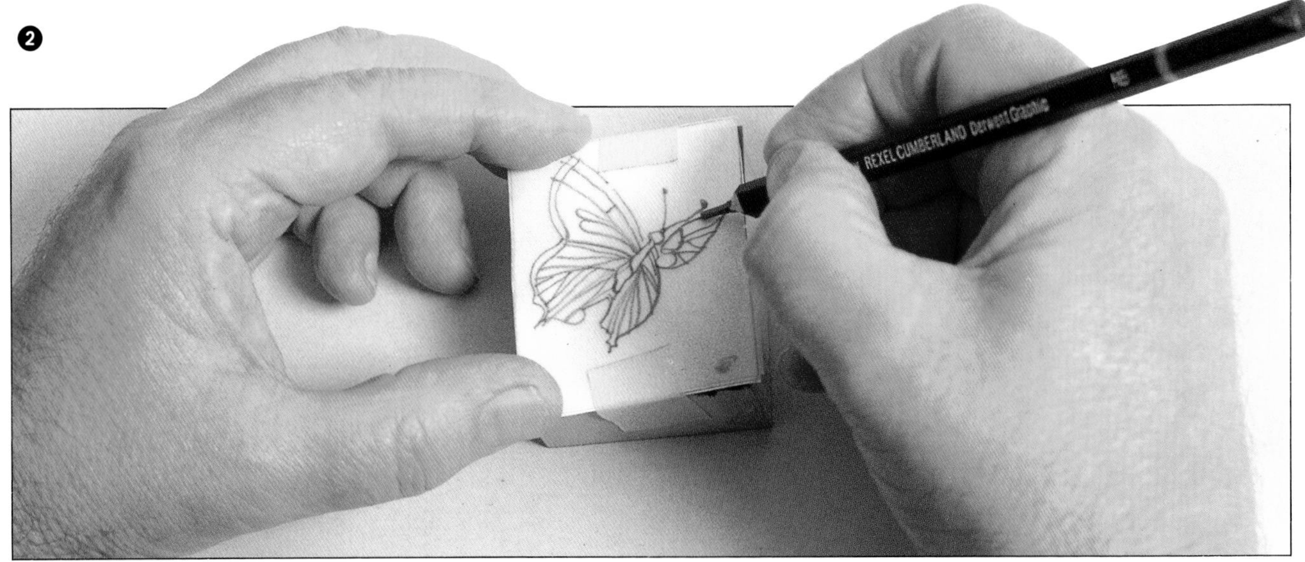

2 Place a piece of white, or light-colored, transfer paper on the block and put your drawing over it. Tape it to the edge of the block and go over the design in pencil to trace it down.

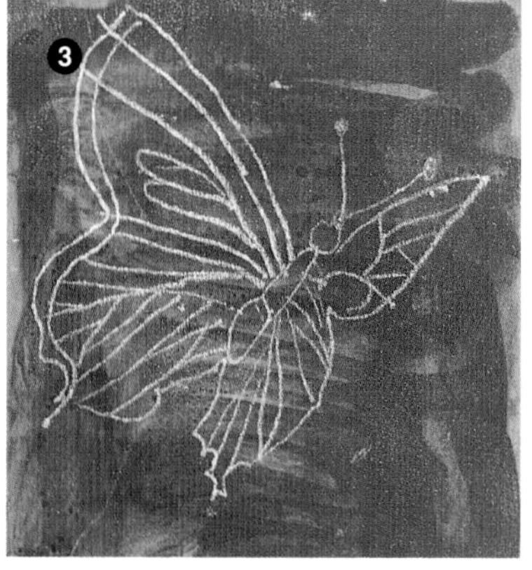

3 The transferred drawing in white on black gives an idea of the way the print will appear, but you do not need to fill in all the detail at this stage – this can be developed as you cut.

CUTTING THE BLOCK

A common fault with beginners is to overcut. It is not easy to replace wood after it has been cut away so it is sensible to work slowly, so that you can see how your image is progressing. There are a number of approaches to wood engraving which you will discover as you develop more skill and expertise.

The technique of engraving requires the development of quite controlled cutting, certainly more than is needed for the woodcut, so to begin with you would be well advised to confine yourself to unambitious designs. When using one of the tools previously mentioned, hold the handle in the palm of the hand and use the thumb to keep control of the point. When you are pushing the tool forward into the material, make sure that the angle of entry is not too steep or the point will jam and stop cutting. Equally, if the angle is too shallow, the point will tend to slip across the surface of the wood. Do not attempt to cut a long straight line with one cut; it is better to do a series of short cuts which then connect up to make the total length of the line required.

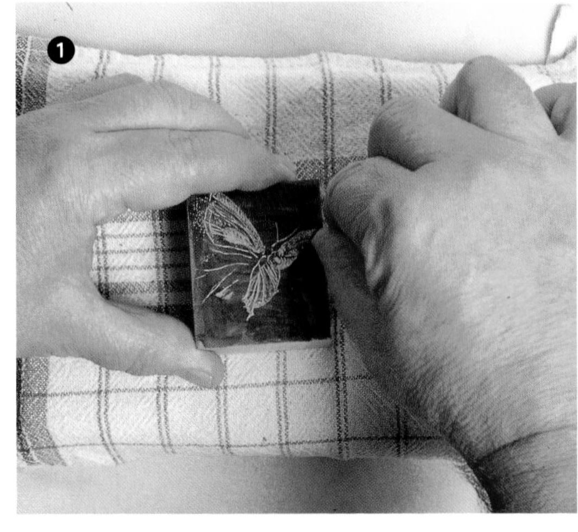

1 Support the block on a raised surface while you cut and hold it firmly by its edges. A book wrapped in cloth is the support used here.

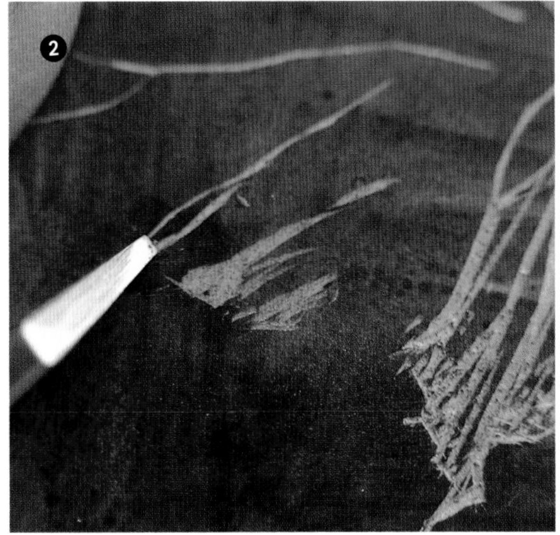

2 Work into different areas of the design with the appropriate tool. This picture shows a graver being used for stippled detail.

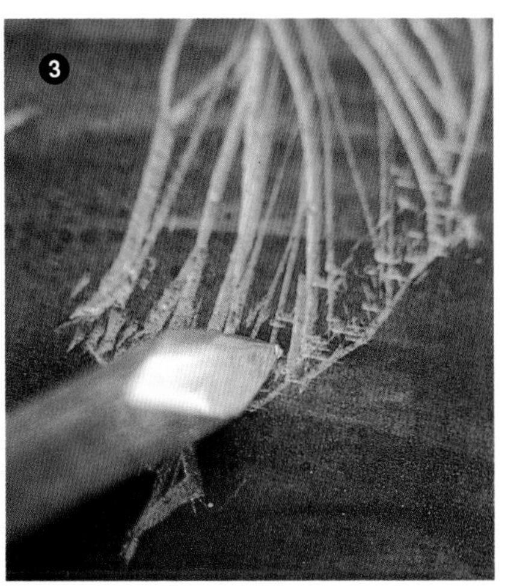

3 The scauper is used to draw strong, lines and to clear small areas of the block; note the shallow angle of the tip on the surface of the work.

4 Work the cutting to a more or less finished stage before taking a proof. Most of the detail should be in place, with only minor refinements to do after proofing.

PROOFING AND PRINTING

Once you have inked the block to take a proof, it is less easy to see the design clearly as the ink will have stained some of the finer lines. Proofing is thus best left until the work is quite advanced. You can then make any refinements needed in the cutting before you take final prints. Do not clean off the ink with a solvent after proofing – just wipe it with a rag to remove the excess.

In keeping with the overall character of the process, the method of inking should be particularly careful and controlled. You need only make one pass of the roller over the block in each direction. It is important not to over-ink the relief surface or the color will spread into and fill the engraved lines.

1 Roll out the ink on a glass mixing slab. Use quite a stiff block-printing ink so it will not flood the delicate lines cut into the wood block.

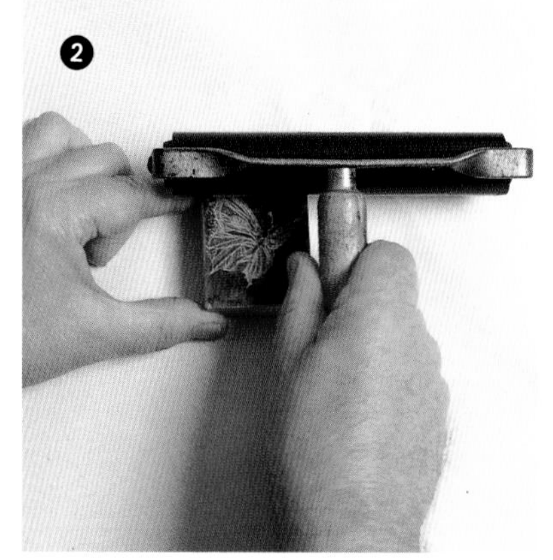

2 Roll up the surface of the block, being careful not to over-ink. You need only make one pass of the roller in each direction across the surface.

4 When you see the result of the proof, you can decide what further work is necessary before final prints are taken. Here, the artist decides some extra highlighting is needed.

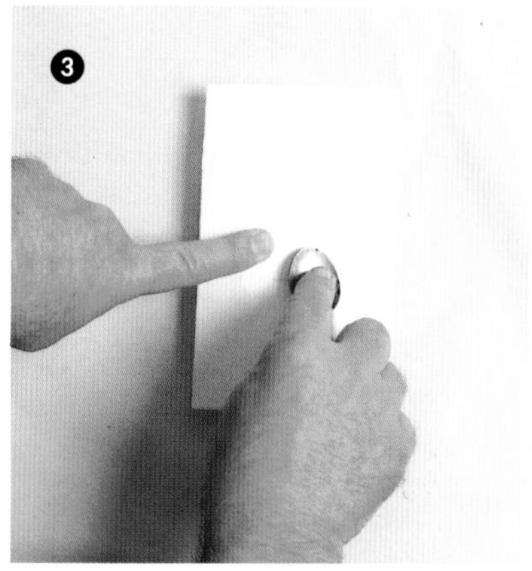

3 Use a lightweight printing paper that will pick up all the detail. Because the block is small, it is easy to take the proof by burnishing with the back of a small spoon. Place the paper on the block and rub it down firmly.

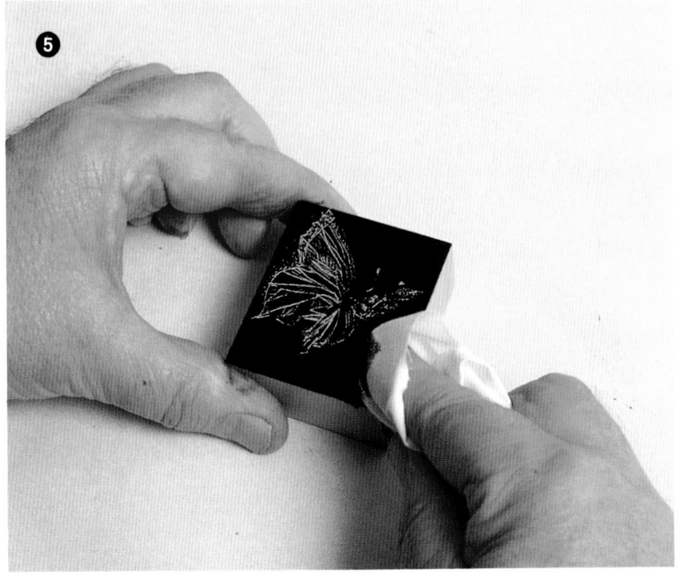

5 Before continuing to cut, wipe the excess ink off the block with a clean rag. Do not use a solvent, as this will flood the cuts and stain them, making it difficult for you to see the design.

7 This attractive image demonstrates the small-scale character of wood engraving, and the way it is necessary to balance the tones and textures by controlling the weight and direction of the various marks.

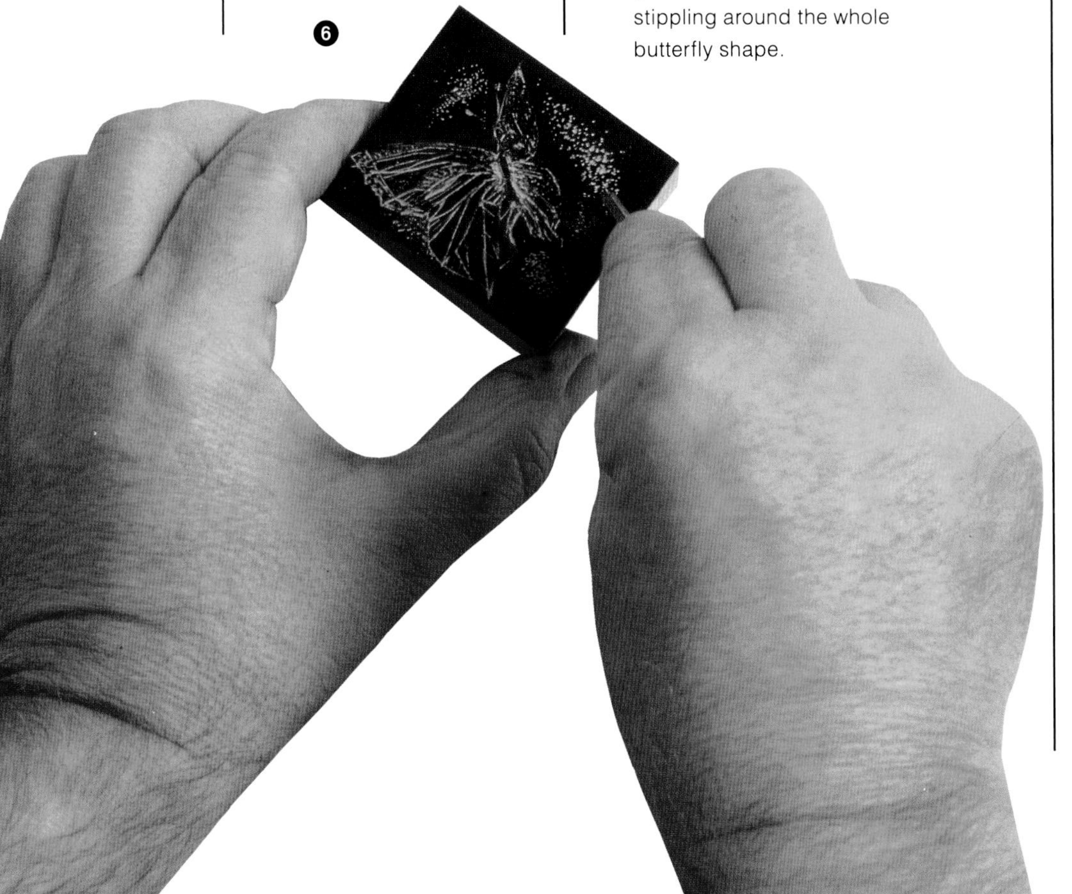

6 As the final stage on this engraving, the artist uses a graver to cut a halo of fine stippling around the whole butterfly shape.

Relief etching

Etching is an intaglio process which can be adapted to relief printing. Etching involves the erosion of unprotected areas of a metal plate by immersion in acid. Those areas which are left intact after the etch will later come out in the print while those areas which were corroded by the acid appear as the non-printing areas. The process is usually used to define areas rather than lines.

TOOLS AND MATERIALS

The list of equipment is not as extensive as that needed for engraving. No tools are needed for cutting the metal as that laborious task is done by the acid. You will need your plate (usually zinc), stop-out varnish, a sable brush, nitric acid, and a tray for immersing the plate in acid.

The First Book of Urizen (relief etching) by William Blake
This etching was made in 1794 for the title page of a book which was one of Blake's *Prophetic Books*.

Orpheus Taming the Animals (relief etching) Anon
A plate made by etching in about 1630. It was never intended for printing as the edges are unbevelled and the signature is not reversed. It was probably intended as a panel for a box.

PREPARING THE PLATE

The first priority is to clean the zinc plate thoroughly, removing grease and fingerprints. If this is not done properly, the stop-out varnish will not adhere to the plate and the acid may corrode areas of the plate that you wanted left intact. Next, polish the plate with a mixture of chalk and water made up into a paste. After washing the plate with water, it should be passed through a weak solution of nitric acid (five parts nitric acid to 95 parts water). Finally, wipe the surface with a piece of clean rag or cotton wool and then dry with some blotting paper and a hot air blower.

The plate will now be ready to design. Using a fine sable brush and stop-out varnish, paint the design directly onto the prepared metal plate. Bear in mind that the image must be reversed right to left if any lettering is to appear in the print. It is also important that the back of the plate is protected by painting out with the varnish, although you can buy plates which have a resist backing.

There is one important point which you must take into account when preparing your design. If you want to print a line, you should prepare the surface of the plate so that the acid eats away two parallel grooves leaving a thin shoulder of metal which will print as a line. There is, inevitably, a tendency for the acid to attack the sides of these shoulders and if the action goes too far the image support will be eaten away and the shoulder will collapse.

One way of avoiding this is to immerse the plate into the acid for only a very short time thereby limiting the depth of the etch. However, if you do this, be careful when you are inking up because the areas which have been etched will only be shallow and liable to pick up ink which will then appear in the final print.

1 Paint the design directly on the plate with stop-out varnish and a fine paintbrush.

2 Pour a 10% solution of acid into a suitable flat-bottomed dish from a stainless steel measure. Immerse the plate in the acid and brush away bubbles as they form during the biting.

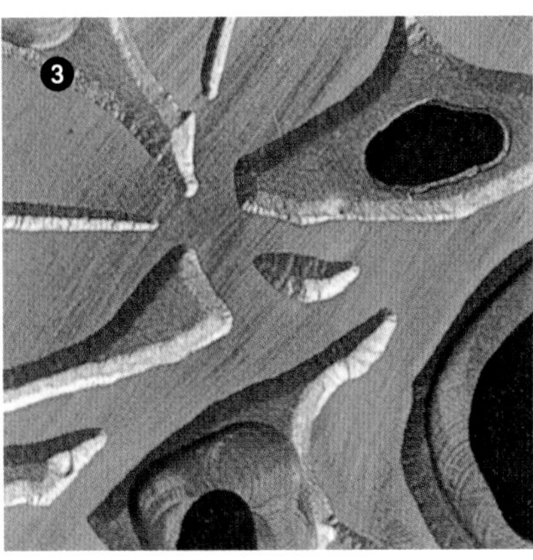

3 Rinse the plate in running water and clean off the stop-out varnish with turpentine. The plate is deeply etched, leaving the design as clean areas of raised metal.

ETCHING THE PLATE

Once you have drawn your design with the stop-out varnish, only the etching remains to be done. This can be carried out in a stainless steel or plastic polyethylene tray of a size large enough to accommodate the largest plate which you intend to etch. Place it near a window or, even better, out of doors, where the toxic fumes of nitric oxide can escape. Ideally, some form of fume extraction hood should enclose the dish while etching is carried out. The etching solution can now be made up ready for use in the tray from one part nitric acid and ten parts water. The water should be poured into the tray first and the acid added gently to it from a stainless steel measure.

The etching action of the nitric acid solution produces bubbles of hydrogen gas over the surface of the zinc plate. The plate must be lifted up by one edge so that all the acid drains off the surface and back into the dish. A hook for lifting the edge can be made out of a piece of bent metal which has been heavily lacquered with bitumen paint or polyurethane varnish. If attention is not given to this, uneven etching will take place.

Midsummer Night (relief etching) by William Giles
This print, a relief etching, was made using six plates. The most striking quality of the print is the subtle, mottled effect, created over the whole surface. This was achieved by inking up the metal plates with watercolors instead of the usual oil-based inks.

Photo etching (relief)

Photo etching, like relief etching, has the advantage of requiring no cutting skill. The acid does all the hard work. In simple terms, a photo etching is done by exposing a metal plate, prepared with photo resist coating, to a light source which is passed through a transparent sheet on which an image has been created in negative, the part of the image which is not going to print being opaque. The photo resist hardens where it is exposed to the light but where it has not been exposed it can be washed away. The plate is then ready to be etched in the normal way.

There are a number of ways of preparing an image, although the easiest one is to draw your design with photo-opaque ink on to a transparent plastic sheet. Paint out those areas which you do not wish to print so that they are not exposed to the light source and can be easily removed from the plate, so that when it is etched those areas will be corroded.

Any image can be created in negative, in order to produce a photo etching.

EXPOSING THE PLATE

The next stage of the process is to expose the plate to light which has passed through your film. The photo resist, which is crucial to the whole process, can either be applied to the plate yourself, or you can use a plate which has had the resist applied by the manufacturer. You now place the negative on the plate. It must be in close contact in order to stop the light from spreading where it is not wanted and this is best achieved by placing a piece of heavy glass over the film. The next step is to expose the plate to light for the length of time needed for the resist to harden. The exposure time will vary according to the type of light which is used. A domestic suntan lamp, for instance, is relatively weak so that the exposure time would have to be quite lengthy. After the exposure, the plate has to be washed to remove the unhardened resist. An area of hardened resist representing the positive image will be left on the surface of the plate. After this only the etching remains to be done. This part of the process is exactly the same as for relief etching, described in the previous section.

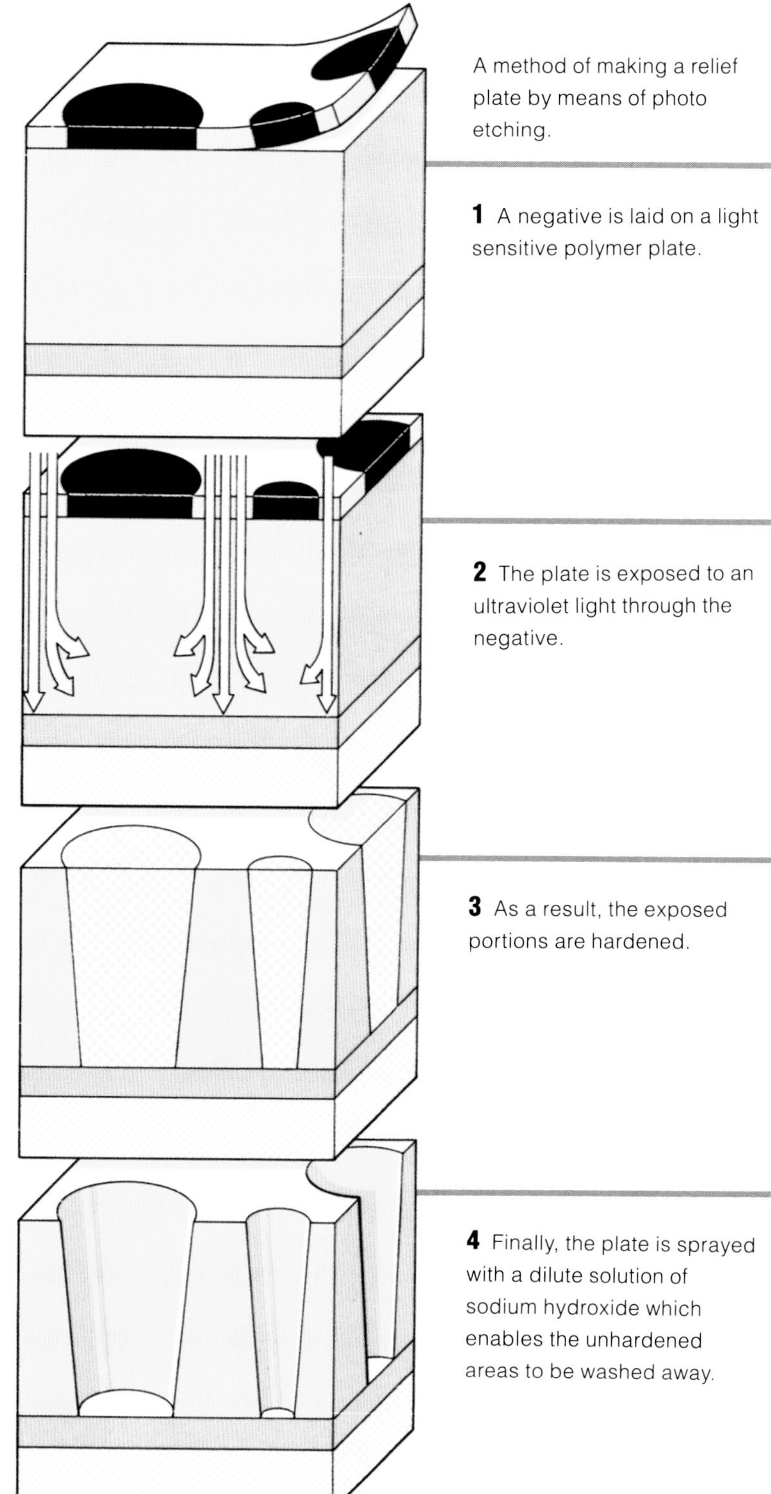

A method of making a relief plate by means of photo etching.

1 A negative is laid on a light sensitive polymer plate.

2 The plate is exposed to an ultraviolet light through the negative.

3 As a result, the exposed portions are hardened.

4 Finally, the plate is sprayed with a dilute solution of sodium hydroxide which enables the unhardened areas to be washed away.

CHAPTER THREE

INTAGLIO PRINTING

Intaglio printing, which derives its name from the Italian word *intaglione*, meaning to engrave or cut, covers a number of techniques, all of which involve the incision of designs into metal plates. Ink is later rubbed in so that an image can be transferred onto paper.

The principles of intaglio printing are the same whether applied to industrial printing or printmaking. After the ink is applied to the plate and rubbed into the grooves, all the surfaces in relief are cleaned of all traces of ink. In the industrial process this is done by means of a scraper while printmakers clean off the ink with a piece of tarlatan or scrim. Printing paper is then placed on the plate before both are run through a press. A powerful press is essential because the paper has to be forced into the grooves on the plate so that the ink is picked up. Finally, the print is peeled off the press.

Window (mezzotint) ▶
by Philip Coombs
This mezzotint image was printed from two plates in separate colors. The first plate was light-toned, printed in alizarin crimson; the second, with the image scraped but not burnished into the plate's rocked texture, was inked in Prussian blue and superimposed. The result is a mergence of the two colors, enhancing the atmospheric character of the print and contributing warm lights.

▲ *Daily News* (etching)
by Carole Katchen
The everyday occurrence makes a memorable image when the artist is alert to both the narrative and pictorial qualities. The tonal contrast is emphasized, but both dark and light areas contain much subtle, active texture.

PREPARING THE PLATE

Crucial to all intaglio printing is the plate. Several metals can be used for this although copper and zinc are the most popular. Copper is suitable for all intaglio techniques. It is economical to buy and is available in sheet form from most metal suppliers. It is usable on both sides. Unfortunately, it has not usually had the care lavished on it that is needed for printing, so that burnishing and polishing is often necessary before it can be used.

Zinc is cheaper than copper but it is not a good material to use for fine line engraving and fewer prints can be taken from it compared to copper. For the beginner, however, it is the ideal plate. It is easily polished and burnished and can be reworked quite easily.

Most suppliers will sell metal plates to size, but if they do not, the plate can be cut using a simple tool called a drawtool. This is a hard, sharp, steel point which is drawn towards you along a steel straight edge. If the tool is sharp, just a few incisions are needed and the plate can be broken along the cut line.

After cutting the plate to size, it is most important to bevel the edges as these may be very sharp and dangerous. The plate is put along the edge of a table and a file or scraper run along it at an angle of 45°. This will create the beveled edge.

The working surface has to be scrupulously clean and smooth as the tiniest scratch in the metal will come out in the print. These can sometimes be removed by using a burnisher. This pushes the burr down and can smooth out the metal along the edge of a scratch. If the burr is too pronounced, a scraper should be used to remove it, followed by burnishing and and polishing. For fine polishing use a household metal cleaner.

A badly damaged plate can be ground down with the use of a block of charcoal, using turpentine substitute as a lubricant, again to be followed by burnishing and repolishing. If the damage is too deep to be removed by any of these methods, a snakestone can be used to grind and rub the metal down. This produces a dent in the plate, which can then be hammered out carefully from the reverse side.

The tools and equipment needed to prepare the plate are: drawtool, scraper, burnisher, snakestone, file, emery papers, steel wool, household metal cleaner, charcoal block, cotton wool, cotton rags, turpentine, benzine, ammonia, and whiting.

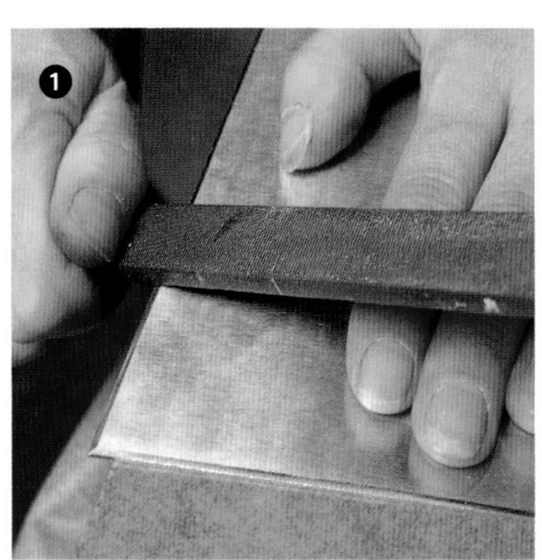

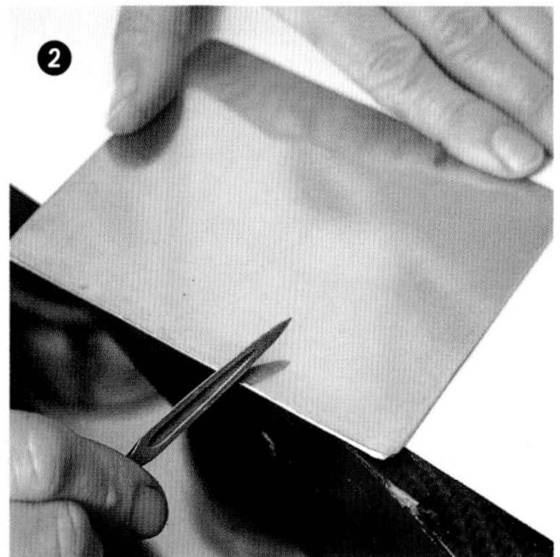

BEVELING THE PLATE

1 Position the plate so that it is firmly supported but one edge just protrudes from the edge of the work surface. File all along the edge of the plate, keeping the file at an angle of 45°. Repeat on all sides of the plate.

2 To smooth any marks that the file has left, you can work along the beveled edges with a scraper held at the same angle. Shave the metal lightly with the scraper blade.

3 You can leave mitered corners or, if you prefer, round them off completely. Because intaglio prints have a slightly embossed effect, the edges of the plate do leave a clear impression on the paper, so they should be even and clean.

DEGREASING THE PLATE

Before laying the acid-resistant ground, the surface of the plate must be clean and completely free of grease, otherwise the ground may adhere imperfectly and cause the effect known as "foul-biting." This is when blemishes allow non-printing areas of the plate to become mildly and irregularly corroded, affecting the quality of the plate.

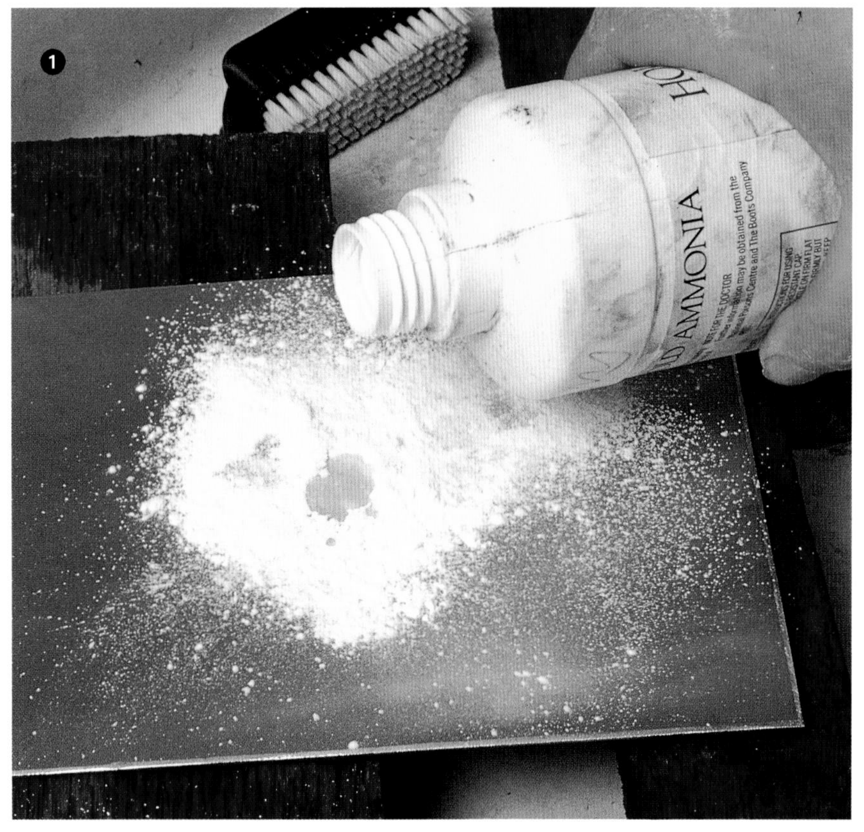

1 Put a small heap of French chalk or whiting on the plate and pour in a few drops of household ammonia.

2 Work the ammonia and chalk into a paste and rub it across the whole plate surface, using a lightweight scrubbing brush, cotton wool, or a soft rag.

3 Rinse off the plate with clean water. If it is completely degreased, the water will flow evenly across the surface. If the water runs around remaining grease spots, repeat the process. Then dry off the plate.

Engraving

Engraving is the oldest of the intaglio techniques of printmaking. Metal is removed from the plate in narrow grooves by the burin or graver.

TOOLS AND MATERIALS

The burin consists usually of a square steel rod fitted into a wooden handle at one end so that it can fit snugly into the palm of the hand. At the other end it is cut at an angle of 45° from one corner of the square to the other. This produces a sharp point and three cutting planes. Square burins are the most common, though other shapes are introduced for special effects. When engraving, the burin is often held at a very shallow angle to the plate and is pushed forward as an extension of the hand, with the forefinger and thumb steering it in the desired direction.

For good results, it is essential that your burins are sharp and properly prepared. To achieve this, the two

The print of the two wrestlers with its few strong lines which appear on the paper like gashes, is starkly contrasted with the more traditional portrait illustrated left in which the lines have been organized so that the figure is defined by carefully modulated tonalities. Both the viewpoint of the subject as well as technique of the top print give some idea of the extent to which the art of engraving can be modified and experimented with.

Engraving ►
Once the plate has been prepared you can begin to engrave your design. The equipment required is simple. You should acquire a sandbag or some kind of support on which to rest the plate when you are engraving it, and burins with which to engrave. Two should be enough to begin with; one with one sharp edge which can be used for jabbing, and another specifically sharpened for line cutting. As well as burins you will also need carbon paper; a pen or hard pencil; nitric acid; and an etching needle.

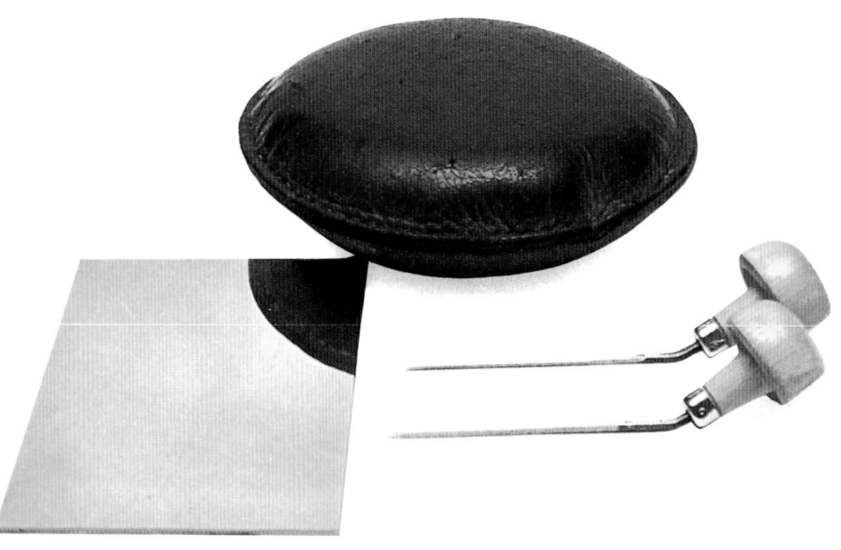

bottom planes are sharpened on a fine oilstone with a light oil used as a lubricant. When both planes are true, the angled facet of the cutting edge is put flat on the stone and moved back and forth at the correct angle without rocking. Repeated sharpening of the two bottom planes during engraving is necessary. Only sharp tools work efficiently.

It is generally advisable, when inexperienced, to practice cutting on scrap plates. You must learn to control the burin and you will be able to discover the varied types of lines which can be cut.

ENGRAVING THE PLATE

An engraving produces a mirror image of what has been created on the plate, so the design must be considered carefully. The simplest way is to prepare the drawing on transfer or transparent paper and then, with the help of carbon paper, transfer it through the back onto the plate. The weak, greasy lines act as a very mild resistant, if the metal is immersed in a weak nitric acid solution for a few seconds. After cleaning with denatured alcohol or benzine, the image will come up shiny against the dull background.

An incomplete line can now be made by pushing the burin gently forward into the metal and slightly downward. A fine spiral of metal will come away from the plate. You can then relieve the pressure, bit by bit, so that the burin reaches the surface of the plate. The line will be pointed and fade out at both ends.

Hard lines can be made by cutting into the metal in the manner described above but then stopping when the burin reaches its deepest point. You can then turn the plate and retrace the line in the opposite direction, so deepening the point of entry of the first cut. When cutting all these lines you will be left with fine spirals of metal which can be removed with a scraper.

The deeper the lines are cut, the darker they will come out in print. If lines are not dark enough, they can be re-cut. To produce a curved line you should turn the plate and not the burin. To do this the plate is held in one hand and rested on a sandbag or support while turning. Dots can be made by jabbing the burin into the metal and turning the plate.

Shadow and tonal effects are obtained by engraving lines quite close and parallel to each other, gradually increasing the distance. Cross-hatching is another way of creating tonal variations. Lines are drawn parallel to each other in one direction, then more parallel lines are drawn at right angles to these. If the area needs to be darker still, further lines can be drawn at 45° to the earlier ones.

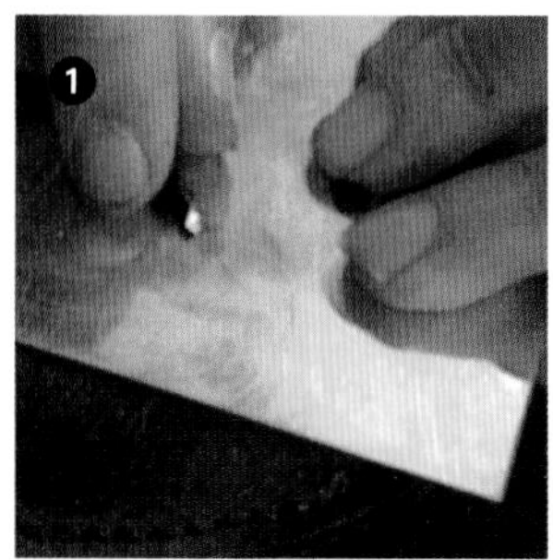

1 To cut a straight line, push the burin smoothly through the metal, keeping the tool at a shallow angle to the plate and guiding it with the forefinger. It should not be necessary to force the blade.

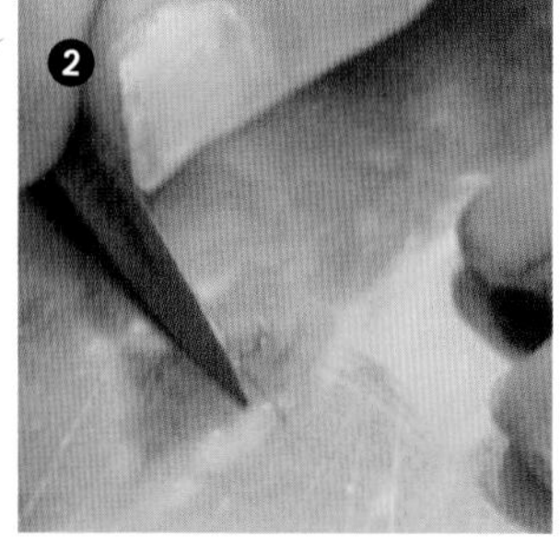

2 A small burr of waste metal is thrown up as the line is cut. Remove the burr carefully with a scraper, without marking the clean metal on either side of the cut.

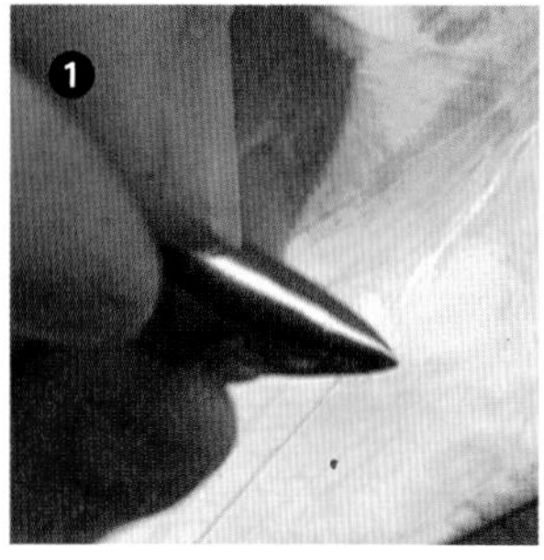

Removing scratches

1 Even a tiny scratch or incorrect cut in the metal will print. To remove unwanted marks rub over the scratched area with a burnisher.

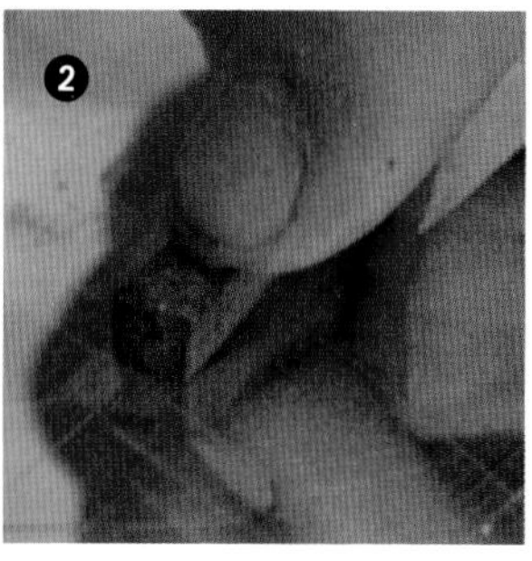

2 As an alternative method of removing scratches, gently rub the surface of the plate with a small snakestone.

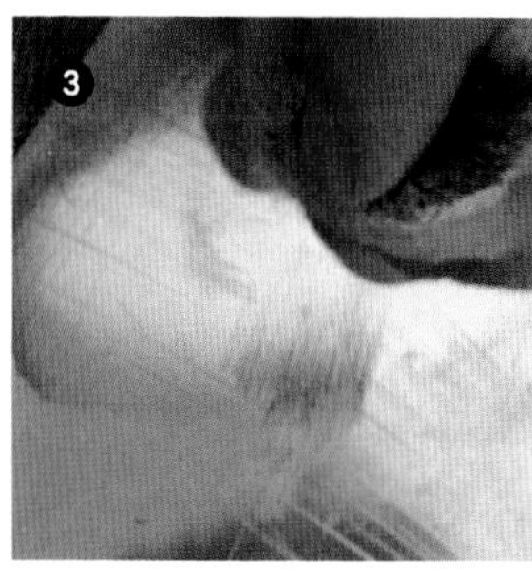

3 Bring up the surface of the plate with metal polish on a piece of cotton wool. This cleans and polishes the plate enabling you to see whether the plate is smooth and free of scratches.

Drypoint

▲ *Young Girl* (drypoint) by Paul Cesar Helen
This print was worked entirely in drypoint. The extraordinary quality of the lines was achieved by scraping off the burr.

◀ This drypoint engraving shows how tone has been created by hatched lines and stippling.

Because it is the simplest and most direct of the intaglio processes, drypoint is an interesting introduction to working on metal, especially if you have limited access to printmaking facilities. The technique consists of scratching into the surface of a metal plate using a strong, sharp point. The point is used to score the surface, which causes a ridge of metal – called the burr – to be thrown up on one or both sides of the line. This burr holds more ink than the relatively shallow scratches and contributes a velvety, rich quality to the impression.

Its main disadvantage in comparison with other intaglio printmaking methods is that the burrs wear down quickly under the normal actions of inking the plate and passing it through the press, so the number of good-quality prints that can be taken is limited.

Drypoint equipment
1 zinc and copper plates; **2** combined scraper and burnisher; **3** drypoint needle; **4** combined drypoint needle and burnisher.

TOOLS AND MATERIALS

The only materials needed are a plate and a point. Copper or zinc plates are commonly used. Zinc, being a softer metal, is easier to work but produces fewer good impressions. In theory, only one drawing tool is necessary – a hardened steel needle. More sophisticated needles with diamond or sapphire points are available: they never need sharpening but are expensive. The point of the needle should be round, without flat sides or facets, so that metal is not removed from the plate. There are other tools which can be used for special effects, such as roulettes – tiny spiked wheels which can be rolled over the plate, making small dots.

DRAWING ON THE PLATE

Any of the effects associated with line drawing can be expressed through drypoint. You can vary line qualities by altering the pressure and angle of the tool, using the point to score or pick at the metal. The burr is raised most consistently by holding the tool upright or at a steep angle.

If you incline the needle to one side, the burr is thrown up on one side of the line only, creating a rough furry effect on that side. As in engraving, close lines or crosshatching will give dark results, and deeper lines will print blacker than lightly scratched ones.

The character of the drawing can rely mainly on outline or contour, but if you want to introduce tonal areas to

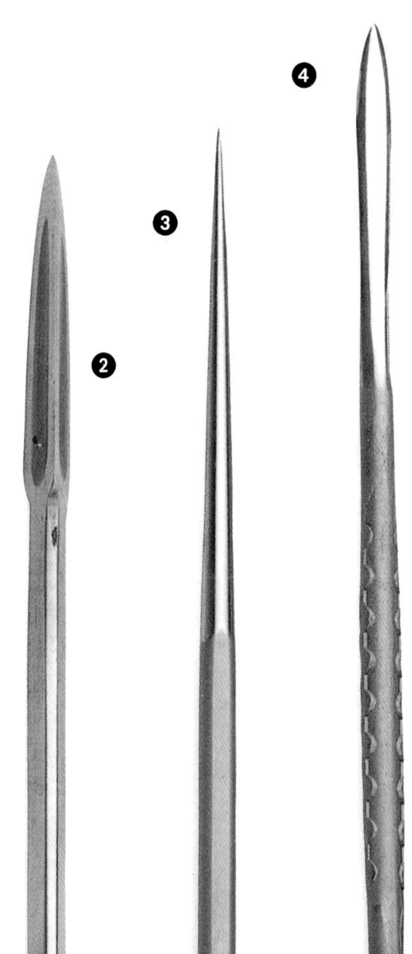

your print you can do so by means of conventional drawing techniques such as hatching and crosshatching with close-set parallel lines, or a form of stippling achieved with short, stabbing marks. However, the final state of the print need not depend solely on the positive marks made by the point; you can also use a scraper or burnisher to remove the burr, thus lightening up an area that has been overworked.

Because of the relative fragility of the drypoint image, working proofs that allow you to check the progress of the drawing must be kept to a minimum.

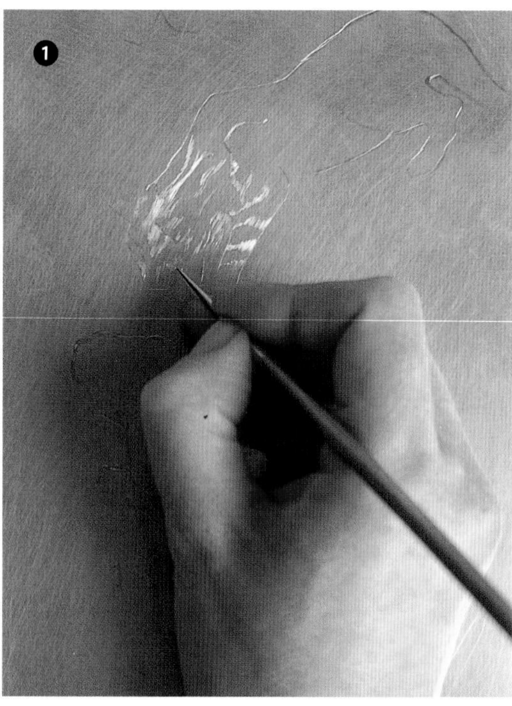

1 Start to draw on the plate with the needle as you would with a pencil on paper. It is easiest to sketch out a few faint guidelines first, then gradually strengthen the lines and develop the textures.

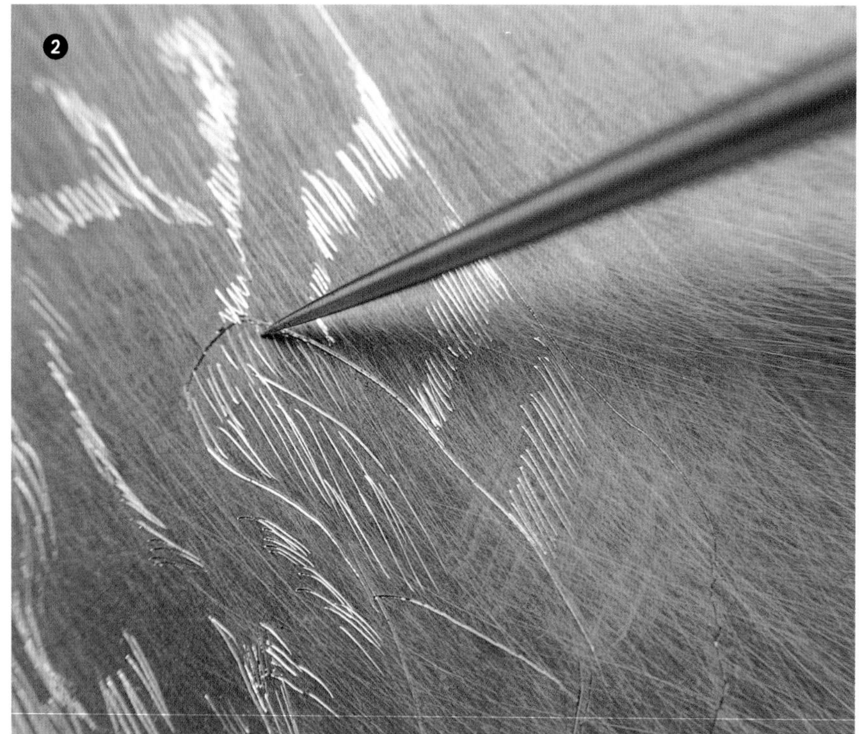

2 Changing the angle of the tool enables you to create more or less burr on the line, while more pressure gives you increased thickness. Try to vary the line qualities expressively, according to the details of your subject.

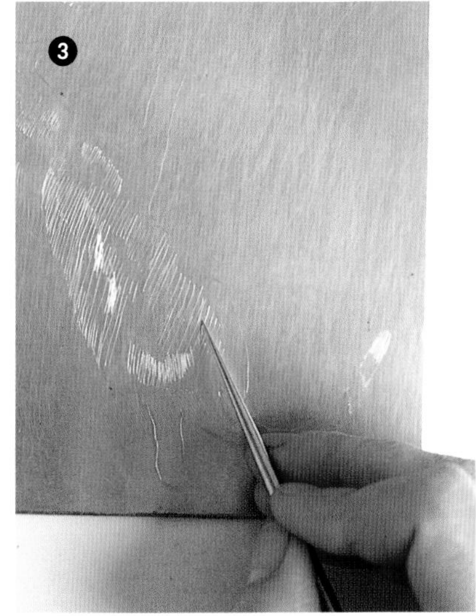

3 You can create grayed areas by hatching blocks of fine parallel lines. The closer the lines and the more burred the marks, the heavier the tonal emphasis will be.

4 Once the design is fully drawn out, take a proof to check the image. In this example the shapes are judged to be satisfactory, however it is felt that the tones are not yet rich enough

5 The drawing is worked much more heavily on the plate with hatched and stippled textures. A second proof is taken as work on the plate nears completion and, using this as a guide, some unwanted lines are smoothed out with the burnisher.

Finished print
The first print from the finished plate has a very rich tone, with dense blacks on the darker cat. This is due to the heavy burr created by the stippled marks. Compare this with the later print, shown on p68, where the dark tones have faded as the burr wears down in printing. Altogether ten acceptable prints were taken from this plate.

Etching

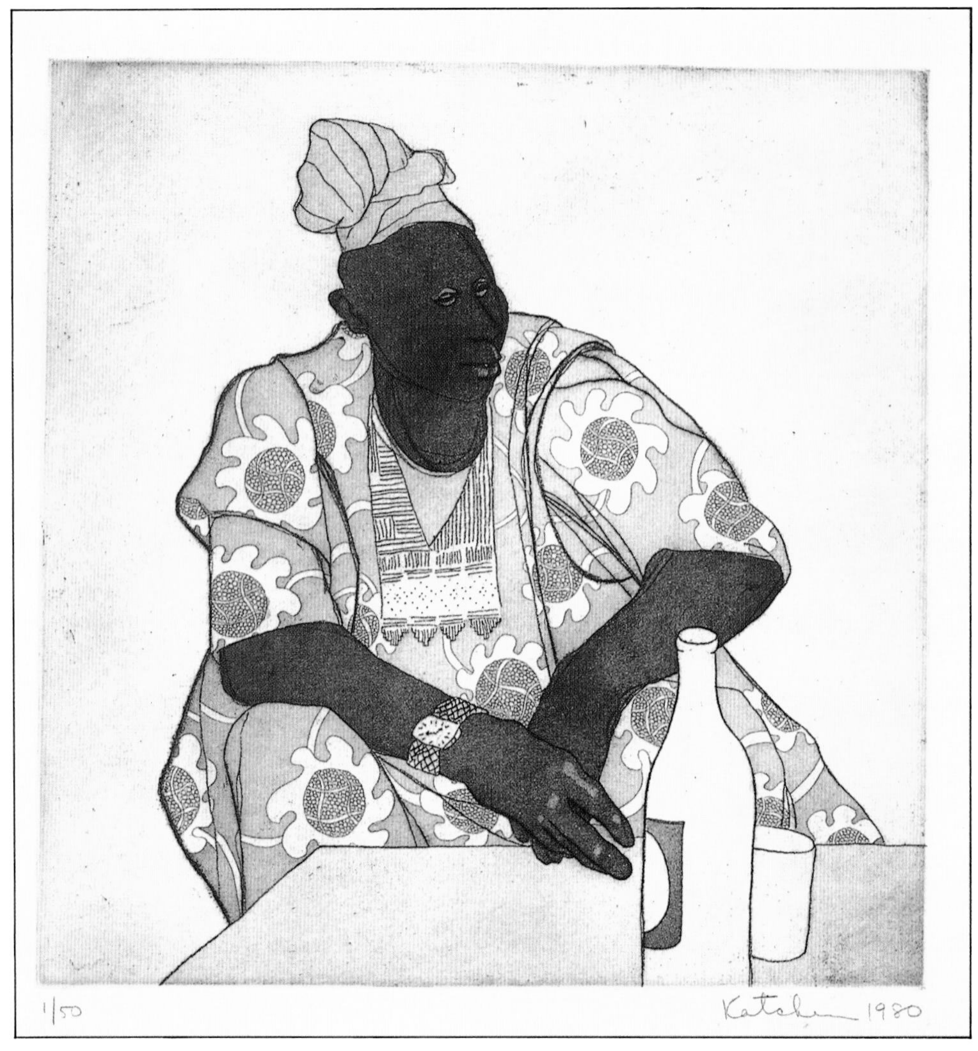

Yoruba Man (etching)
by Carole Katchen
The figure makes a beautiful, fluid shape placed boldly at the center of the image. An overly symmetrical sense of balance is avoided by the slant of his relaxed posture and the off-center shape of the table leading out of the frame in the foreground, which together make a diagonal pull through the image. The contrast of tonal shading and plain against patterned areas is perfectly judged.

The essential difference between etching techniques and the other intaglio methods is that the marks are not achieved by incising or scraping the metal. The image is developed by corroding the metal plate with acid, using acid-resistant grounds to protect the areas not to be etched.

The variety of materials and techniques that can be applied to etching makes it a remarkably versatile and expressive area of printmaking. Different ways of manipulating the grounds, the mark-making processes, the action, and extent of the corrosion, and the printing process give the artist an infinite range of creative opportunities.

TOOLS AND MATERIALS

To produce even the most basic etched impression you will need quite a wide range of materials and equipment, and it is essential to learn the techniques under supervision in a safe and properly equipped studio. Safety factors are particularly important. At various stages the plate has to be heated on a hotplate or burner, and the process of etching involves using an acid bath which should be sited well away from other work areas, which must be well ventilated to remove fumes.

The simplest range of etching equipment consists of a metal plate, acid-resistant ground and varnish, an etching needle, and an acid bath. Copper or zinc plates are usually chosen, although steel and other metals are also suitable. Copper

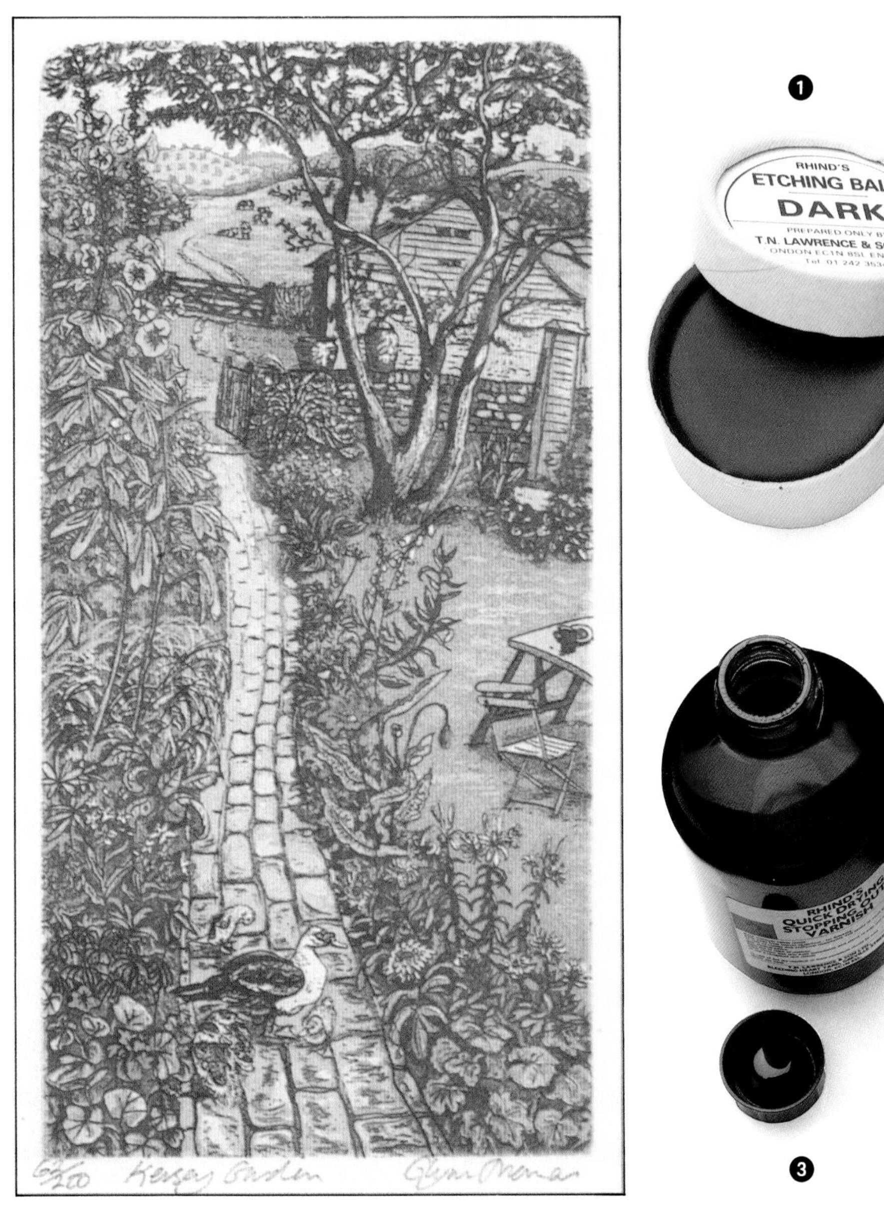

Kersey Garden (etching)
by Glynn Thomas
The yellow-green predominant in this charming composition gives a sunny, bright tone to the image, with the contrast of brown and dark green contributing space and depth. These colors were inked all together on the plate and printed in one. The brilliant red and yellow touches in the flowers were painted on the cleaned plate and overprinted.

Etching equipment
1 Hard ground; **2** soft ground; **3** stopping-out varnish; **4** liquid hard ground.

provides more refined effects of line and tone and, being harder, stands up better to the wear and tear of inking and printing. But zinc (or a zinc-like alloy offered by some suppliers) is a perfectly adequate and less expensive material on which to learn the craft.

Etching grounds are either hard or soft. The hard ground is the standard one for line etching, while the soft ground creates different, particular, surface effects. Both are available in sold cake form, and are melted onto the plate and spread with a dabber or roller. Alternatively, a liquid hard ground can be used. Stopping-out varnish is an acid-resistant liquid applied to reinforce the ground in areas not to be etched, or to cover up exposed metal.

The etching needle is a smooth, lightweight metal point. It should not be too sharp, as it is important that it does not scratch the metal as you draw into the ground. It is advisable to obtain a purpose-made tool, but you can improvise with a darning needle attached firmly to a pen or brush handle. The type and strength of acid solution, or mordant, depends on the metal being used and the intensity of the corrosive effect that is required.

Further materials and equipment are needed for the aquatint process (see p82) and for printing the plate, but the basic method of printing for all intaglio images is the same. If you use a professionally equipped etching studio, either for commercial hire or as part of an educational institution, it will have all the facilities you need for any of the techniques and processes described here.

PREPARING THE PLATE

The plate is prepared in the manner described on p65, which should leave it clean, smooth, scratch-free, and grease-free. Remember that "foul-biting" may occur if the surface of the plate is not well prepared.

Etching equipment
1 zinc and copper plates; **2** Leather-covered dabber; **3** burnisher; **4** etching needle; **5** scraper; **6** feathers for clearing acid bubbles from plate; **7** clamp for holding plate during smoking.

APPLYING HARD GROUND

In an etching the grooves on the plate are made chemically by acid which corrodes and eats into the metal. It is done by coating the plate with an acid-resisting film which is called the ground. Into this ground an image is drawn with a needle so that the metal is exposed underneath. The plate is then immersed in a bath of acid that erodes the exposed metal. When the desired depth has been obtained, the ground is cleaned off so that prints can be taken from the plate.

The ground must be applied evenly to form an effective acid-resistant coating that is durable, but can be lifted easily and cleanly as you draw into it with the etching needle. The solid ball of hard ground, as you buy it from the supplier, is shiny and brown-black. The basic ingredients are bitumen, wax, and rosin (colophony), but there are various recipes and some etchers prefer to make their own. It is applied to a warmed plate, which has been heated gently on a hotplate. Dabs of ground melt onto the surface of the metal and are rolled out in all directions to form a smooth, thin coating. The completed ground is a warm, golden brown color.

It is important not to "overcook" the ground, as too much heat causes it first to slide on the surface, then to coagulate and stick to the applicator so that the coating becomes lumpy and uneven. If this happens, cool the plate, clean it off, and start again. Getting the right touch in grounding a plate is a matter of practice; you may find a forward pass of the roller lays down the coating, and a quick backward roll will lift any excess.

Applying hard ground

1 Put the degreased plate on the hotplate and let it warm through. Dab the ball of hard ground onto the surface, allowing it to melt into random smears.

2 Use a hard-wearing roller to spread the ground evenly across the plate, working in all directions.

3 Continue to work with the roller, traveling from side to side both ways on the plate until the ground is thin and even, and a uniform golden-brown color.

Smoking the ground

Secure the plate at one edge in a pair of pliers or hand-held clamp. Put a small fold of paper at the edge to prevent the tool marking the plate surface. Light three or four tapers twisted together to make a long flame. Move the flame under the plate in a circling motion, so that only the smoke trail from the tapers touches the ground. Continue until the ground darkens all over.

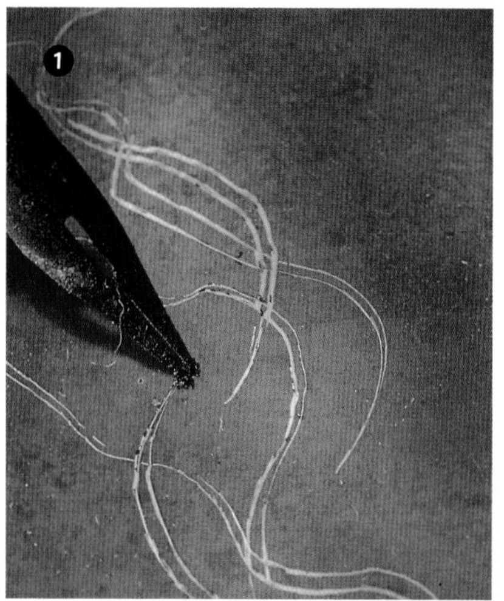

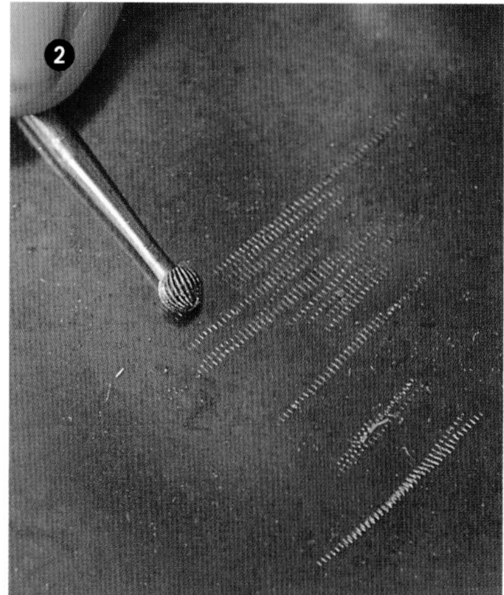

Alternative tools

1 You can use other implements to work into the ground. An ordinary dip pen makes calligraphic, double lines because of the split in the nib.

2 A small roulette – this is a dentist's drill bit – rolled over the ground makes a lightly toothed linear pattern.

SMOKING THE GROUND

Smoking the ground with tapers, which hardens it slightly and turns it a darker color, is not essential, but it does make it easier to see the marks of your drawing with the needle. Wax tapers are used, which give off a dark smoke that deposits carbon on the ground. Only the smoky trail from the tapers, not the naked flame, should touch the ground, which turns black and shiny as it carbonizes. Using the center of the flame can scorch the ground, and it will begin to flake.

DRAWING ON THE PLATE

Once the ground has been smoked and allowed to cool, you are ready to start drawing. If you wish to put down guidelines, you can draw on the

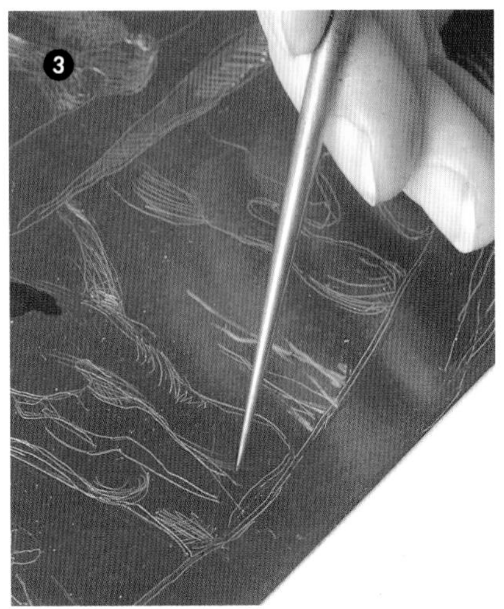

Drawing on the plate

1 If you are transferring an existing design to the plate, cover it with transfer or carbon paper and lay a trace of your drawing on top.

2 Tape down one edge of the trace so that it is anchored in position. Go over the drawing with a pencil so the transfer paper lays down the lines on the ground beneath.

3 Draw directly into the ground with an etching needle as freely as you would draw on paper with a pencil. Avoid scratching into the surface of the metal. The lines you make should just lift the ground cleanly.

ground with a soft, blunted pencil or trace down your design using transfer paper. However, the point of any print process is to exploit the characteristics of the materials and methods, so don't try to copy a preparatory drawing too slavishly – let the composition evolve freely on the plate.

You can manipulate the etching needle in just the same ways as you would a pencil or pen. The important thing to remember is that it need only lift the ground – it is actually a disadvantage if it scratches into the metal – so do not apply too much pressure. The work of cutting into the metal is all done by the acid, and if your lines are unevenly scored into the plate, this will affect the quality of the acid bite. You do need to expose the plate cleanly, however; if you can still see a thin brown film across the line the ground is not fully removed.

STOPPING OUT

Before etching, every part of the plate surface that is not deliberately exposed as part of the image to be etched must be completely protected

Stopping out

When the drawing on the ground is complete, paint stopping-out varnish over any non-printing areas where the ground is imperfect. Finally, stop out the edges and back of the plate as necessary, so no bare metal will be exposed to the acid except in the drawing.

by an acid-resistant covering. This involves painting the back and the beveled edges of the plate with stopping-out varnish – the plate may have been supplied with a prepared acid-resist backing, but the edges must still be stopped out.

On the front of the plate, any part of the ground where there is no drawing can be covered with varnish to prevent foul-biting. You can also use stopping-out varnish to refine lines scratched too coarsely in the ground or to cover errors.

BITING THE PLATE

The action of acid on metal is called the "bite." One of the difficulties for the beginner is that there are no simple rules for estimating how long the plate needs to be in the acid bath. The speed and strength of the bite varies according to a number of factors – the types of metal and strength of acid used, the extent of plate surface exposed to acid, the temperature of the acid bath, and that of the studio environment. You also have to consider the effect you wish to achieve – whether the lines should be fine and shallow-bitten, or deep and strong. This is all learned by experience, but even so it remains a relatively unpredictable technique. However, it is true to say that the longer the plate is immersed in the acid (etched), the deeper the lines will become and the blacker they will print. Given this, the design can be made accordingly by immersing the complete image for a short time and then painting out all the lines that you want to print lightly with an acid-resisting varnish. The plate can then be immersed again in the acid, so deepening the remaining lines. By repeating this process, a wide range of tonal values can be created.

In between the etches, the plate must be examined carefully, and any areas where the ground is lifting should be painted out with the stop-out varnish.

A plate can be bitten in stages to produce different line qualities. All the lines are bitten for a certain length of time, then the plate is removed from the acid, rinsed and dried, the fine lines covered with stopping-out varnish, and the plate is

Biting the plate

1 Lower the plate gently into the acid bath. In the parts of this process when your fingers are likely to be in contact with the acid, it is wise to wear rubber gloves.

2 As the acid begins to act on the metal, you will see bubbles forming on the plate. Brush them away gently with a feather.

then returned to the acid to etch the remaining lines more deeply. A detailed image may require many different stages of grounding and biting. It is difficult, though not impossible, to rework bitten lines cleanly through a new ground. The addition of tone and texture may, however, alter the effect of the initial line work, and decisions about reworking should be made on the basis of proofs that have been pulled at different stages.

THE ACID BATH

The bath to contain the acid solution can be a glass, porcelain or plastic dish, or tray – obviously the material must not be susceptible to the corrosive effect. Ideally it should be sited under an extractor hood; at the least it must stand in a well ventilated part of the studio. When checking a plate in the acid, do not stand over the bath for too long, because you will be breathing in fumes.

It is essential to work carefully and steadily when handling acid bottles and mixing solutions. Acid and water generate heat when combined, so the acid must be added to the water, never vice versa. The solution for the acid bath, which varies from a 1:1 ratio to about 10:1 water to acid, depending upon the purpose, is safer to work with than full-strength acid, but you should still take precautions like wearing rubber gloves, and if any of the solution splashes on your skin, rinse it off with clean water.

For copper and zinc plates, nitric acid can be used. The solution is made slightly stronger for copper, which bites slowly, and the reaction with the metal gradually turns the acid blue. On zinc, the acid bites quite quickly and produces bubbles on the plate surface. These must be removed with a soft brush or feather; otherwise the bubbles form a sort of acid-resist and this will result in a textured bite.

Two other solutions commonly used are Dutch mordant for copper – a mixture of hydrochloric acid, potassium chlorate and water – and ferric chloride, used for copper or zinc. Be sure to get professional advice on the type of mordant to use and its strength for the job in hand.

3 When the biting is complete, remove the plate from the acid, transfer it to the sink, and wash it off with clean, running water.

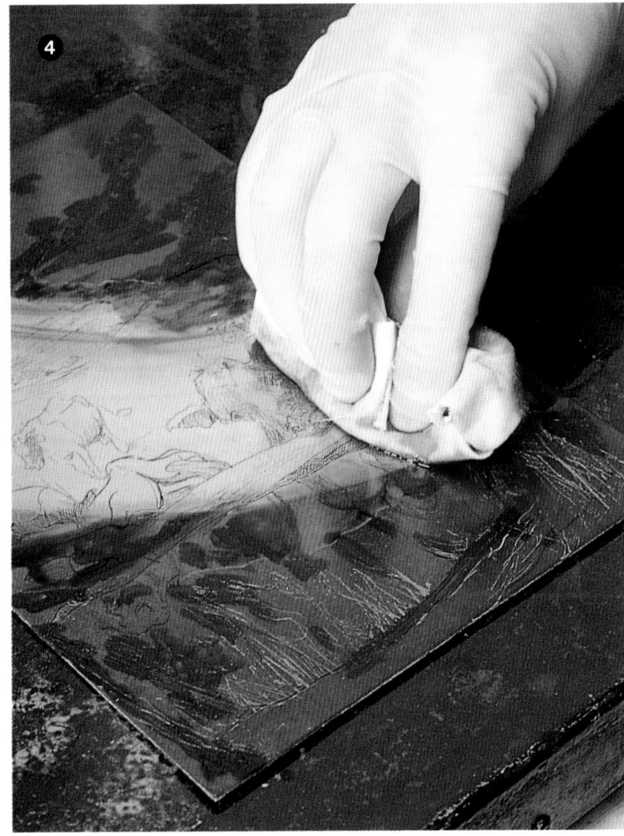

4 Return the plate to the work surface and wipe off the ground and stopping-out varnish with mineral spirit. When the plate is completely clean, you are ready to take a first-stage proof.

APPLYING SOFT GROUND

Another method of making an etching is by using the soft ground technique. A special ground is prepared for this with a higher grease content, which remains soft after application to the plate. This ground is not smoked.

It is applied to the plate in the same way as hard ground, using a roller or dabber to spread the coating evenly and thinly.

You can draw directly into soft ground with an etching needle to produce a line drawing with a softer, less precise character than that typical of work on hard ground. However, where soft ground really comes into its own is in using techniques that depend upon making an impression in the ground. Because the coating is soft and tacky, it is picked up by any material pressed down hard against it. You can draw through a piece of paper onto the ground to produce a line quality resembling soft pencil or crayon marks. All sorts of found materials leave a clear impression that etches quite accurately – woven fabrics, yarns and meshes, feathers, thin woodgrain. To make the impression, the material is laid on the plate, covered with a clean sheet of paper, and rolled through the press.

SOFT-GROUND TEXTURES

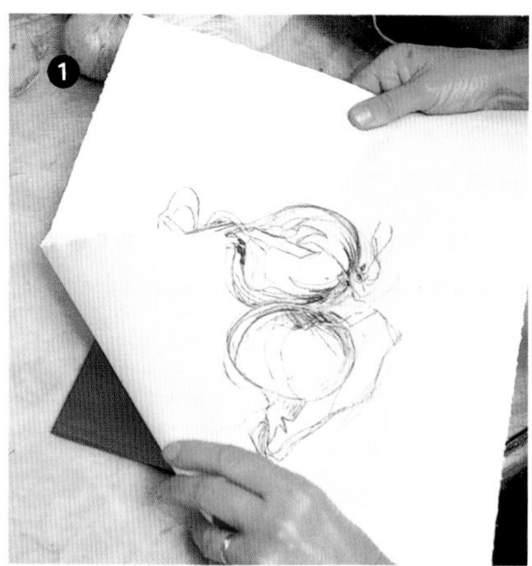

1 To make a drawing on soft ground, either work direct onto a clean piece of paper laid over the plate, or make a master drawing beforehand that you can trace over.

2 Use a hard but not sharp point to impress on the paper. Here the artist is working with a plastic knitting needle.

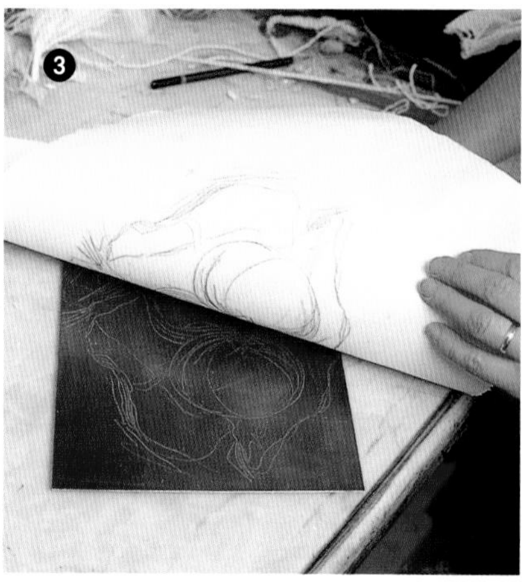

3 At any stage of the drawing you can lift the paper to check the impression on the plate, but be sure to keep one side of the paper firmly anchored, so it goes back down on the plate in exactly the same place.

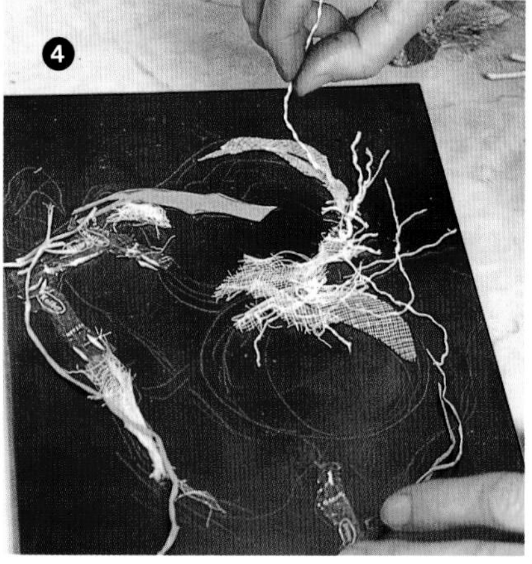

4 When using found materials to create soft ground textures, simply lay the pieces on the plate in the appropriate position.

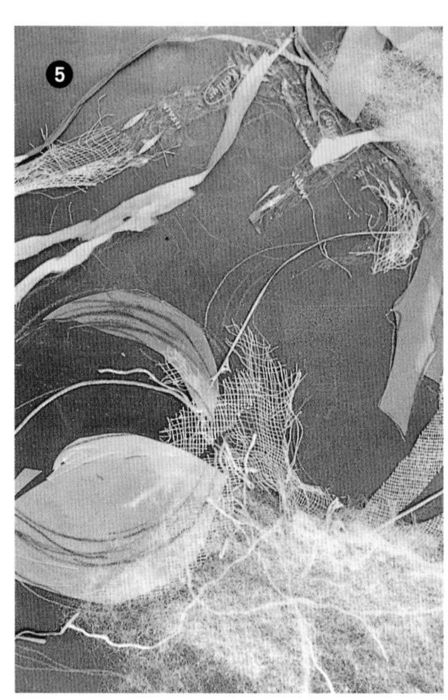

5 It is worth experimenting with all kinds of materials – some textures "take" better than others. This example shows tracing paper, scrim, cellophane, string, ribbon, wadding, and dried leaves from the onions that are the subject of the print.

6 Move the plate to the bed of the press and cover it with a clean sheet of paper. Run it through the press so that the pressure embeds the materials firmly in the ground.

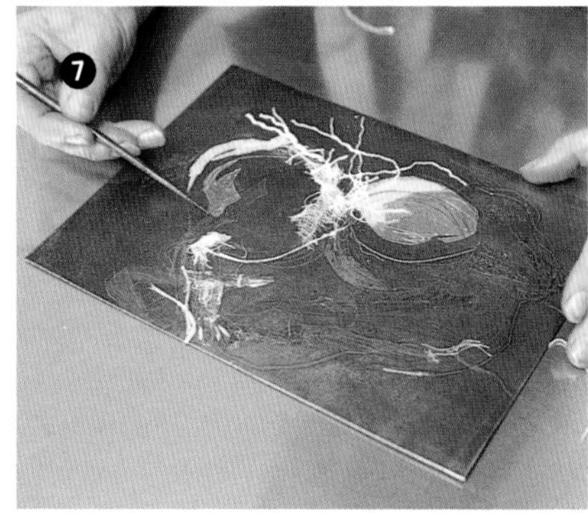

7 Lift the materials from the plate very carefully, without actually touching the ground. You can pick up paper or fibrous materials with an etching needle, or catch one end with tweezers.

8 Stop out any non-printing areas of the plate and protect the back and edges as necessary. You can now etch the plate in acid – keep checking the action of the acid bite, so that fragile textures do not break down.

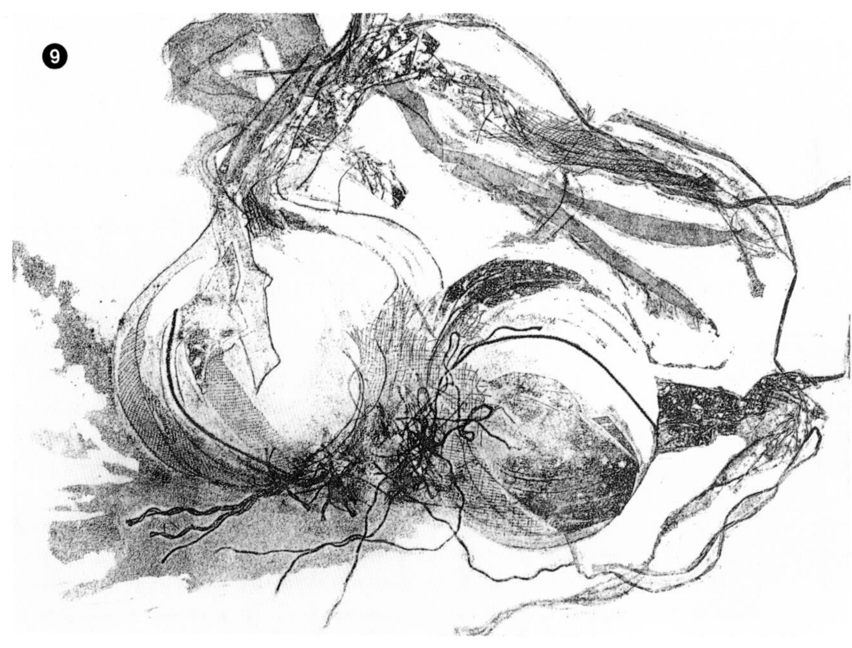

9 The final result of this print is a very pleasing combination of tones and textures. Although the materials were quite randomly chosen, they suit the subject well, and the contrast of soft lines and tonal masses gives the image weight and depth.

Aquatint

The technique of aquatint is used for obtaining tonal areas on a print. Simply explained, it means the etching into the plate of hundreds of tiny pits which give the effect of tonality. The effect is similar to that found in newspaper illustrations.

Aquatint involves laying a coating of resin dust on the plate, which is then heated, causing the resin to melt into tiny globules. On removal from the heat, these harden and when the plate is etched the acid eats into the pits between the globules to produce a fine, all-over intaglio texture. Tonal variations are made by successive stages of stopping out areas of the plate and biting the exposed shapes in the acid, gradually etching the pitted surface more deeply. To check the tones, the resin must be removed with solvent before proofing the plate, so you cannot rebite into the same texture after proofing.

TOOLS AND MATERIALS

A dense, even aquatint tone is best achieved by using a purpose-designed aquatint box. This is fitted with bellows or a revolving paddle worked from outside, with which you agitate the resin dust in the box so that it flies up in a thick cloud. The plate is then inserted face up and the dust allowed to settle on it.

A more random alternative is to apply the resin direct to the plate with some kind of shaker. Various devices can be used – a cheesecloth bag; a salt shaker; a jar with cheesecloth stretched across the top; a fine sieve.

BITING AN AQUATINT

Appreciable variations of tone occur in minutes, even seconds, as you go through successive bitings. At the first stage, you stop out the areas of the plate to remain white, and also cover the back and edges of the plate with varnish. The acid solution should not be too strong, or it may eat sideways under the resin rather than etching down evenly into the pitted texture. After the first biting, remove the plate from the acid, rinse, and dry it. Then stop out the next lightest tone and return the plate briefly to the acid.

This process is continued until you have as many tones as you require. The accumulated time that the plate is in the acid may be less than an hour overall, but you need time in between for stopping out. The varnish must cover the aquatint grain thickly and cleanly and be allowed to dry completely before the plate is rebitten. Be careful not to leave the plate too long in the acid on the final bite, or it may break down the resin ground, resulting in a foul-bitten, irregular texture.

Laying an aquatint

1 The easiest and most reliable way to lay aquatint is in a purpose-made box, fitted with a revolving paddle. The box contains a large amount of resin which, when the box is not in use, settles in the bottom of the drum.

Cyclamen (etching) by Trevor Price
This is an aquatint using a technique that imitates the effects of the mezzotint process. The aquatint was laid over the whole plate and etched in acid to produce a very dark tone.

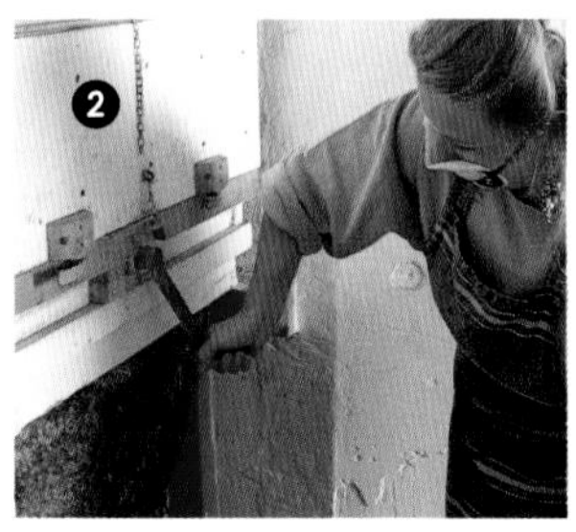

2 Close up the front of the box and turn the handle vigorously. This turns the paddle which agitates the resin dust and causes it to fly up inside the drum.

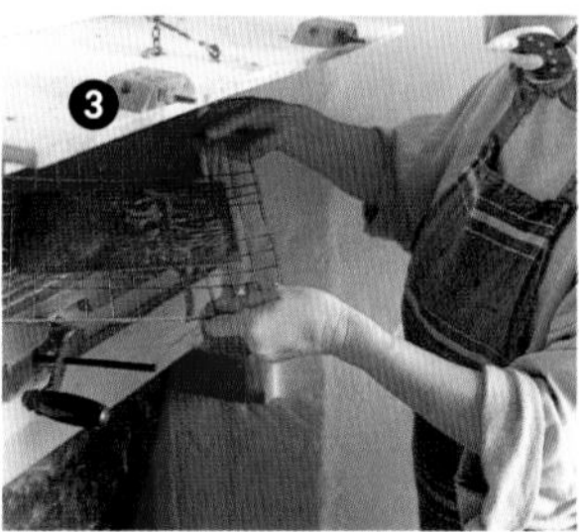

3 Lock the handle in the position where it keeps the interior paddle horizontal. Put your etching plate on a wire tray and insert it in the box. A face mask prevents you from inhaling any dust that drifts out. Close up the front of the box again.

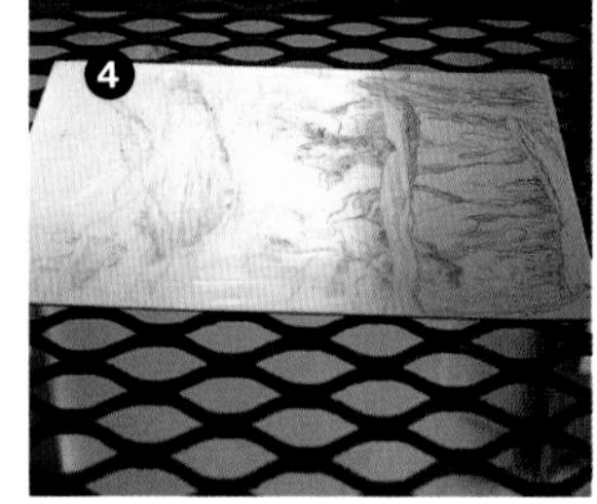

4 After a few minutes, check that an even coating of resin has fallen onto the plate, then remove the plate from the tray and transfer it to a metal grid. Use a small blowtorch or Bunsen burner to heat the plate from underneath.

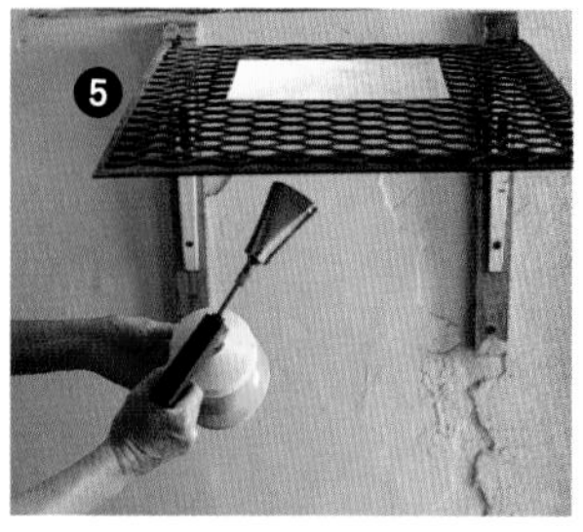

5 Keep the heat source moving gently underneath the plate so that it does not scorch the resin. The whitish, powdery coating gradually melts and turns yellow. When this color has spread right across the plate, allow it to cool.

1 In this line etching the vitality of the drawing is evident. The tone will be added using aquatint.

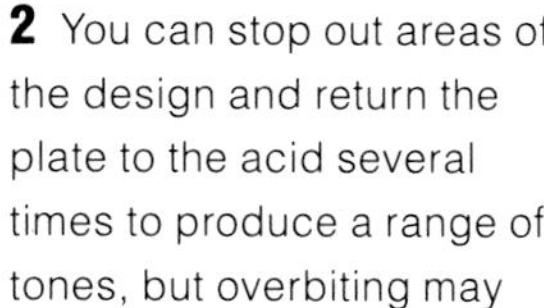

2 You can stop out areas of the design and return the plate to the acid several times to produce a range of tones, but overbiting may break down the aquatint. In this example, there are three grays – pale, mid-toned, and dark – and the heavier black. Pale gray might require only seconds in the acid, black several minutes in all. The tonal modeling can considerably alter the character of the print.

SUGAR-LIFT PROCESS

This process is generally associated with aquatint, but it can also be used to expose areas of the plate for open biting. (This term simply means exposing a broad area of the plate surface to acid, as compared to line work or the grainy texture of aquatint.) Usually, when you use stopping-out varnish to protect unexposed areas of the plate, you are painting it on as a negative surround to the shapes that will be bitten. The sugar-lift process is a resist technique that enables you to etch any shape that you have painted positively, from a solid, flat area to a textured brushmark.

You paint your design on the plate with a sugar solution colored with ink or gouache, allow it to dry, and cover it with diluted stopping-out varnish or liquid hard ground. You then immerse the plate in warm water, and the sugar gradually dissolves and lifts the varnish, leaving the acid-resistant coating in place around the painted marks. You can then choose to aquatint the exposed areas or etch them as they are.

1 Paint your design with the sugar solution on a clean, degreased plate. The solution used here was one part sugar to four parts water and one part ink. Heat the water to dissolve the sugar grains.

2 Allow the sugar painting to dry completely – this can take some time especially if the atmosphere is humid, as the sugar reabsorbs moisture. When dry, cover the whole plate with a thin coat of stopping-out varnish diluted with mineral spirit.

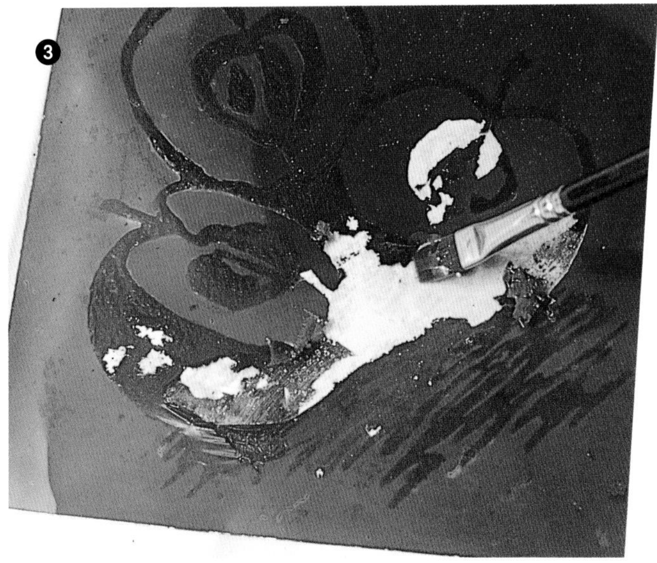

3 When the stopping-out varnish has dried, immerse the plate in a bath of water. Leave it until the sugar begins to dissolve and the varnish lifts.

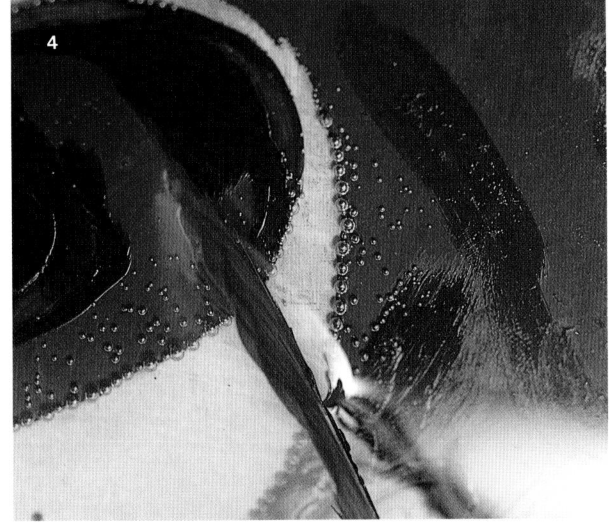

4 When the sugar coating has all lifted, leaving the design exposed in the varnish layer, place it in acid to bite as required (apply aquatint over the varnish if preferred). This plate is open biting – the bubbles show the fast action of the acid on the exposed metal.

5 The resist technique retains the fluid, calligraphic quality of the original painting. Open biting typically produces the strong outlines visible in this print, especially if the plate is etched quite deeply. After the first bite, parts of the image were stopped out and the plate returned to the acid for further biting, resulting in the production of the darker tones in the outlines and small shapes.

ETCHED TEXTURES

Etching provides a far greater range of surface effects than any other intaglio process. All the techniques previously described can be combined on one plate, and there is plenty of room for experimentation. For example, stopping-out varnish floated onto water breaks up into fascinating marbled textures that can be transferred to the metal simply by holding the plate face down on the water surface.

There are also many variations that can be obtained using different materials to impress a soft ground, or by applying stopping-out varnish to a clean plate using standard painting techniques such as dry brushing and spattering. The strength and depth of the acid bite can also be exploited to vary the tonal quality and detail.

You need to plan carefully so that your composition does not become overloaded with busy textures, but since the marks that result from different processes are all etched into a single surface, they generally cohere very well when printed.

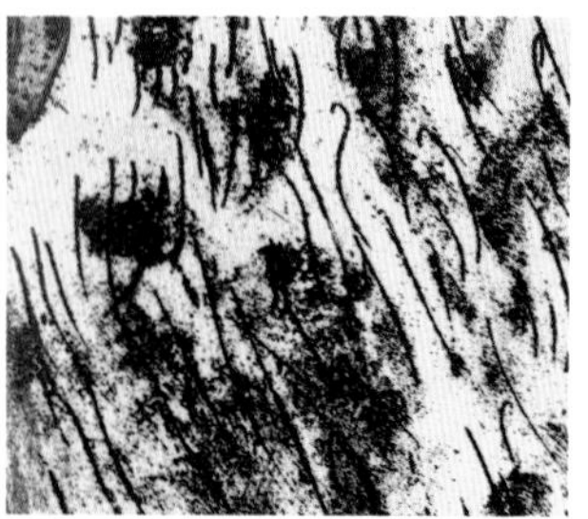

Drawing and impressing
The lines were drawn in the hard ground with free, quick strokes of the etching needle. The rounded smudges are fingerprints, made by pressing on the ground with a fingertip dampened with mineral spirit.

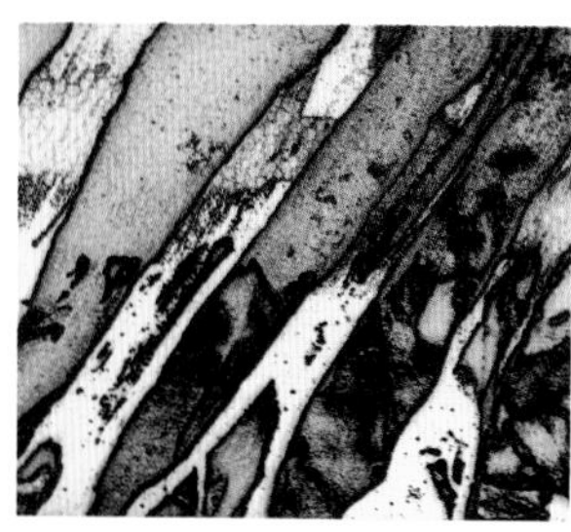

Marbling
Stopping-out varnish floated on water picks up on the surface of the plate and etches into this rich pattern. The striped effect is caused by open biting between strips painted with the varnish. The white areas represent the unetched plate surface.

Combined textures
The grid is composed of lines ruled in hard ground, the smoother tonal areas are shallow, open biting applied to areas exposed by wiping the ground with mineral spirit on a rag. The scumbled texture was rubbed into the ground with wire wool. The "bird's wing" detail was made by drybrushing into the ground with a brush dipped in mineral spirit; the resulting marks were allowed to etch a long time without feathering.

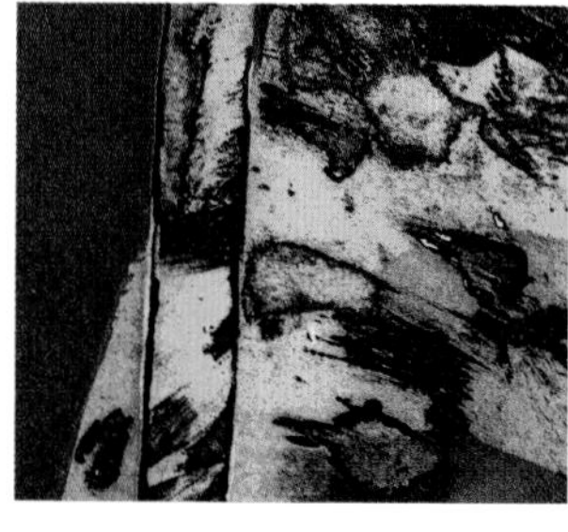

Open bite and aquatint
The spotted pattern was formed by spattering mineral spirit onto hard ground and blotting with a rag. The dark background is aquatinting; the orange color is a coating of ink rolled over the plate surface.

Etching and drypoint
Various areas of etched open bite and linear textures produced an interestingly atmospheric print, but lacked strong contrast. The darkest tone was supplied by raising a burr with a drypoint needle on the zinc plate.

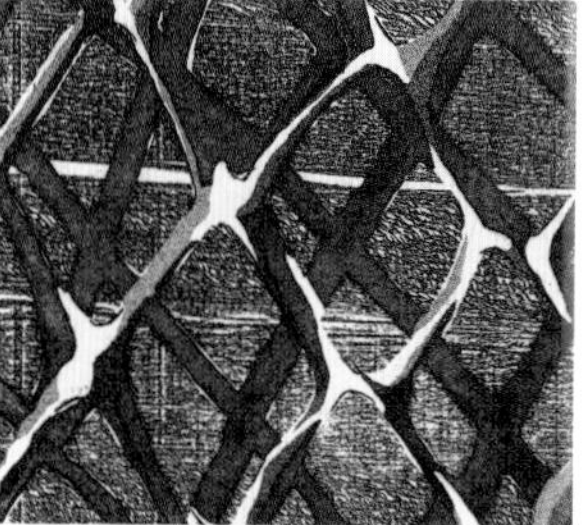

Soft ground and aquatint
The wood-grain effect was achieved by impressing a thin wood veneer into the soft ground. The criss-cross wire pattern was fully stopped out while the wood texture was etched, and was later aquatinted to achieve the tonal variations.

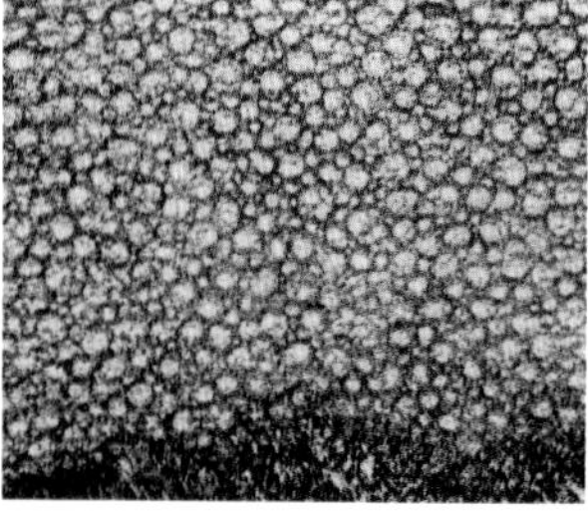

Rough open bite
This exposed area of the plate was left in the acid for a long period. The bubbles building up on the metal due to the action of the acid formed a resist. The bite worked around the bubbles to produce this texture.

Mezzotint

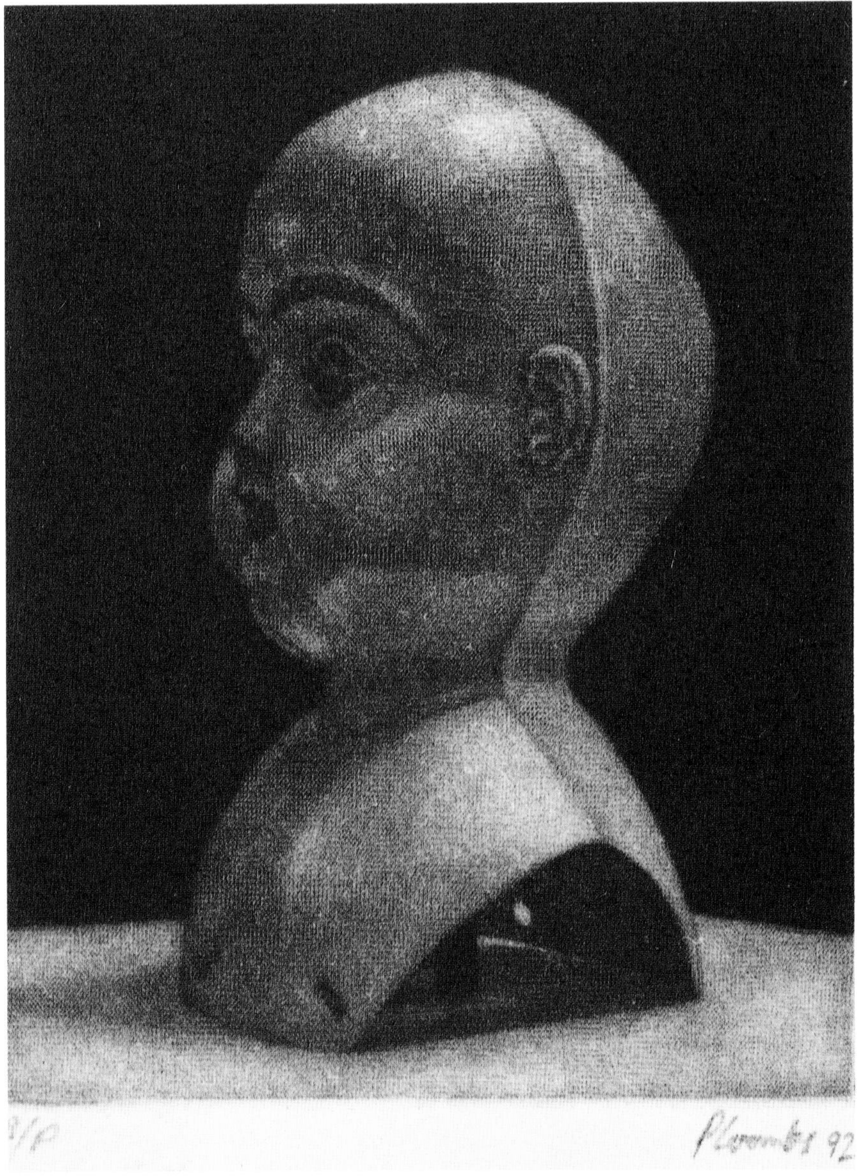

Mezzotint is an unusual intaglio process in two respects. Preparation of the plate requires quite intense physical labor; and the image is worked light out of dark, a reversal of typical approaches in drawing and printmaking. Before any creative work can begin, the plate surface is systematically roughened to produce an overall texture that prints as an even, dense black. Mid-tones and whites are retrieved by smoothing out this texture to varying degrees.

The tonal emphasis gives mezzotint prints a soft, often atmospheric quality. The technique was invented primarily as a reproduction process that would provide a more painterly effect than line engraving, allowing fluid gradation of tone.

▲ *Doll's Head* (mezzotint) by Philip Coombs
The graded tones of mezzotint have an almost photographic quality when applied to heavily modeled shapes. The strong black of the fully rocked texture, as seen in the background of this image, has a rich, velvety intensity.

TOOLS AND MATERIALS

Copper plate is used for mezzotint, and the tool for creating the rough ground is the mezzotint rocker, a broad chisel-like implement with a curved, toothed blade. The teeth indent the plate surface and throw up a burr. To achieve a consistent texture, the rocker has to be moved gradually all over the plate in all directions, and a rocking pole is often used to assist the action. Rockers are made in several sizes with teeth differently spaced – fine, closely set teeth give the most consistent tone; a coarse rocker creates more burr and therefore provides the densest blacks, but with a less even texture overall. If you wish to try out the effect of mezzotint without having to do the hard work of preparation, you can obtain pre-rocked plates. These are mechanically prepared, with an even texture, but they are expensive.

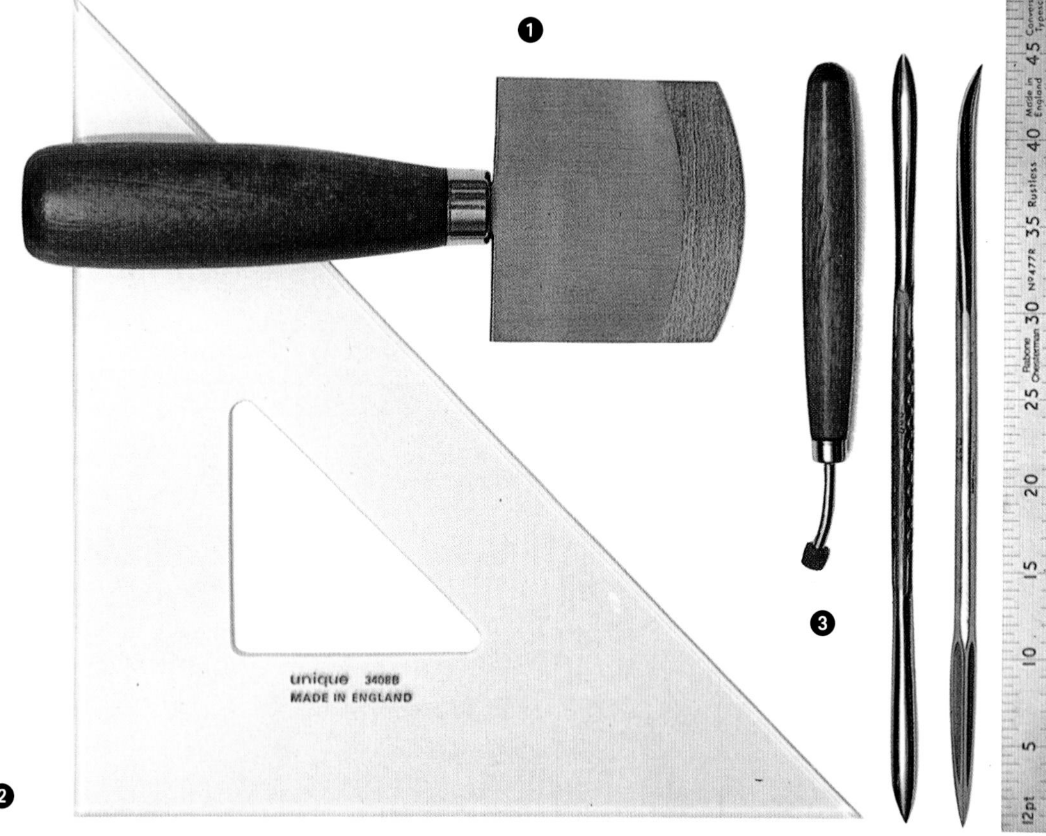

Mezzotint equipment
1 Rocker; **2** set-square;
3. roulettes; **4**, **5** burnishers;
6 ruler.

ROCKING THE PLATE

The reason why rocking the plate is such a laborious process is that it must be done quite consistently in several different directions – first at right angles to the sides of the plate, then along diagonal paths from the edges. The time that this will take depends partly on the size of the plate in relation to the width of the rocker; a very large plate may take days to prepare.

A grid of parallel lines is drawn up to guide the tool, which is held upright on the surface and rocked from side to side on the curved blade, at the same time moving gradually forward along the lines. When the rocker is hand-held, the movement comes from forearm and wrist rather than just the hand. A weighted rocking pole can relieve some of the strain of this action by contributing a consistent pressure and keeping the tool on a straight path.

DRAWING ON THE PLATE

The process of "drawing" on the plate – bringing back the lighter tones – involves removing or smoothing down the burr using a scraper and burnisher. To rework an area where you have taken out too much of the tone, you can use a roulette – a small, serrated wheel set in a handle, which can be rolled across the plate to enhance detail or repair the ground. Roulettes are available in different shapes and sizes.

In many ways mezzotint is an extension of aquatint, being concerned mainly with tones. It became used for the reproduction of paintings, but fell out of favor with the invention of photography.

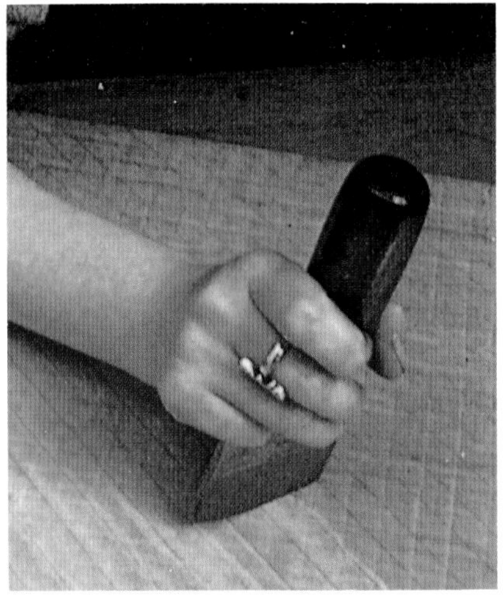

The plate must be rocked in many different directions to obtain a dense texture, indicated by the grid lines visible here.

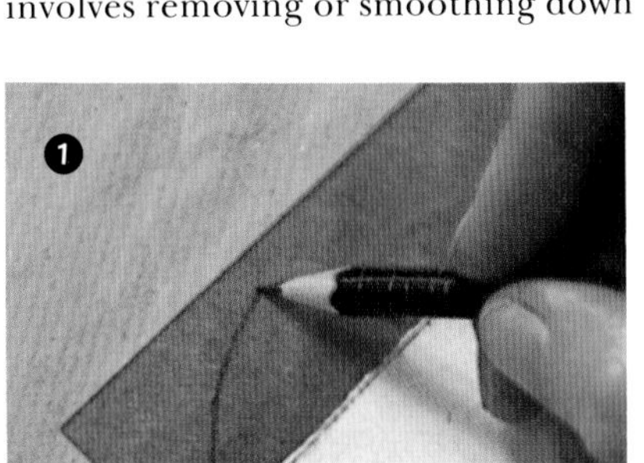

1 When the rocked texture is complete, draw the design on the plate with a soft pencil. This can be erased in the same way as an ordinary drawing if necessary.

2 Work over the drawing with a metal point to inscribe the lines lightly into the plate.

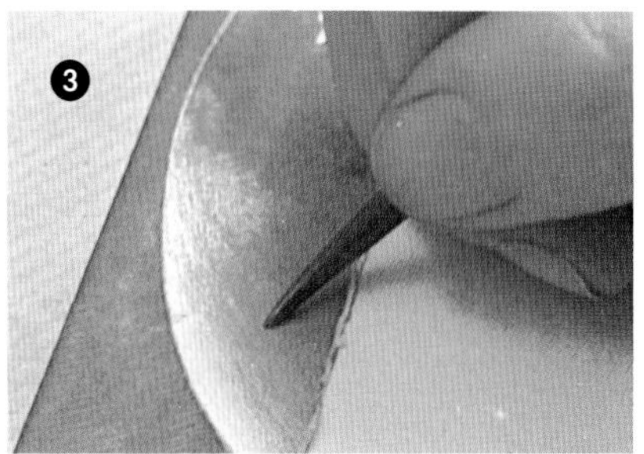

3 Rub the plate with a burnisher to create different tones, varying the pressure to form a range of gray and white highlights. The plate prints black so you work from dark to light.

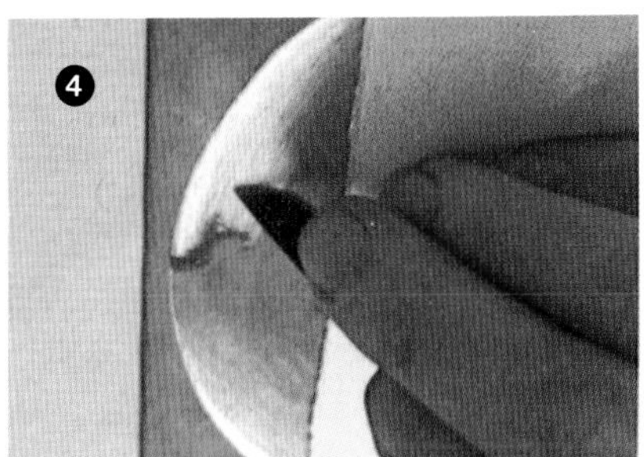

4 Alternatively, a scraper may be used as a drawing tool to remove fine layers of the textured metal. The use of a scraper or burnisher is a matter of personal preference.

Photo etching (intaglio)

A discussion of intaglio techniques is not complete without an introduction to the photo etching of intaglio plates. Photographics are accepted as part of printmaking especially in silkscreen or serigraphy.

For intaglio photo etching a transparent positive of the image on high contrast film is necessary – either a line positive or a halftone positive. The halftone positive which represents a tonal design, is associated with modern magazine or periodical illustrations, where tones are represented by dots of varying sizes, small in the highlight tones, large in the darker ones.

TOOLS AND MATERIALS

The necessary equipment includes photo resist, photo resist developer, exposure light and vacuum frame, and the transparent photographic positives bearing the image.

COATING THE PLATE

The plate, which has to be scrupulously clean, is coated with a light-sensitive solution.

If you allow the plate to dry naturally it will take about 20 minutes. If you use a hairdryer you will save time. The transparent positive is then put emulsion side down on the plate and a sheet of very

Power and Beauty no. 3 (Car)
by Colin Self
A photo etching made in 1968.

clean plate glass placed on top for good contact. Some workshops might have vacuum frames for this.

The next step is to expose the coating on the plate through the positive. For this a light source with high ultraviolet content is necessary. The length of exposure will depend on the output of the lamp. It could be a photo flood or sun lamp, or even bright sunlight. A carbon arc lamp, however, is best.

After exposure the plate is placed in a dish with the resist developer for approximately four minutes. This washes away the lines and dots of the image, as on the positives these were opaque and so were not hardened by the light. The non-image areas carry the hardened solution which is acid resisting. After development the plate is washed under running water and dried. The plate is then carefully checked for scratches and spots, and in these areas is painted out with stop-out varnish. The plate can now be etched and printed using the normal intaglio technique.

PREPARING THE PAPER

High-quality watercolor papers are often chosen for intaglio printing, particularly hand-made or mold-made papers with deckle edges which look good when framed without a mat. They are also used as they contain little or no gelatin and need less soaking because of this. It is important that the weight and texture of the paper suits the style and complexity of the image, so that fine marks are picked up accurately where appropriate, and the qualities of the print do not compete with that of the printing surface.

Intaglio plates are printed on damp paper, which gives more flexibility for pressing into the intaglio without the paper splitting or failing to pick up all the ink. The paper is prepared beforehand by soaking in clean water. It is then drained and blotted, interleaved with blotting paper, pressed between boards, and left until needed.

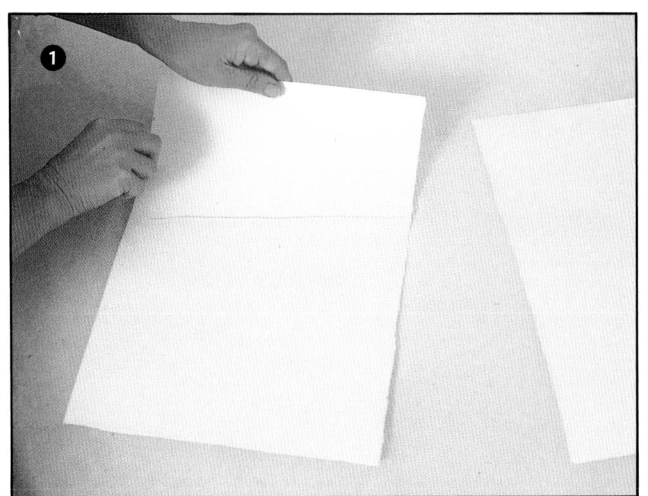

1 Put the paper to soak in a bath of clean water. The amount of time it needs to soak depends on the weight and texture of the paper – it must become fully damp right through the fibers.

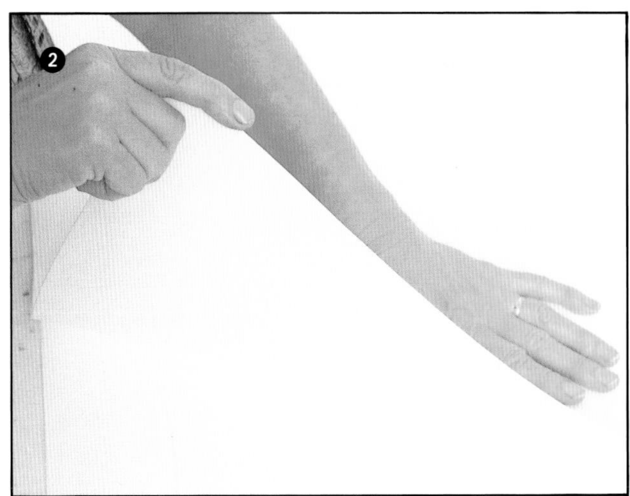

2 Lift the paper from the water bath and let it drain. Lay it on a sheet of blotting paper and cover it with a second sheet. You can build up a stack of paper layers in this way. Lay a board on top to press it so the paper sheets remain flat and moist.

INKING AND WIPING

Before you start to take a print, make sure the plate is completely clean and free of any traces of ground or varnish. Check that the edges are cleanly beveled; if they have been damaged during the etching process, file them smooth again.

The inking process requires a heavy fist application of ink, which must be rubbed well into the plate so that it is pushed into all the intaglio marks. The plate is then wiped carefully and thoroughly to take off all surplus color. This is easiest to do if the plate is warmed slightly on a hotplate, but heating is not always essential. It is important that there is no "loose" ink left on the surface after wiping, as this will prevent the true tones of the intaglio being seen, and make it impossible to produce identical prints.

The ink can be applied with a ready-made dabber or simply with a pad of coarse cheesecloth, called scrim or tarlatan. The same cheesecloth is used for wiping, with a slightly finer fabric sometimes chosen for later stages. The final wipe, which polishes the white areas and cleans the pale tones, is done with the heel of the hand, dusted with French chalk, or with pieces of tissue rubbed flatly over the metal surface. Drypoint plates are not hand-wiped, because the burred texture is abrasive.

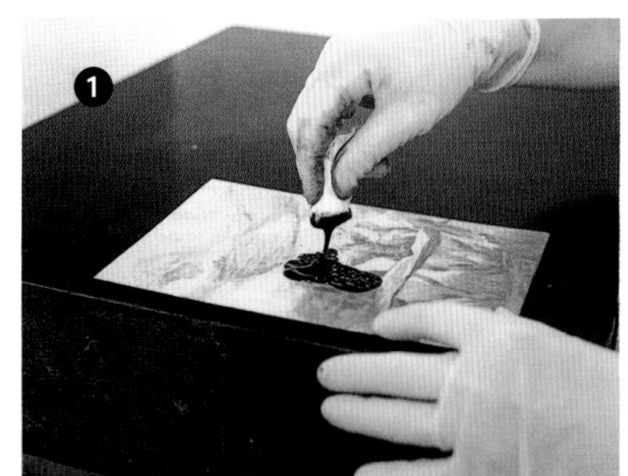

1 Let the clean etching plate warm through on the hotplate. Twist a small piece of wiping canvas (scrim) to make a dabber – a little firm pad with a "stalk" that you can hold it by. Pick up ink on the pad and dab it on to the plate.

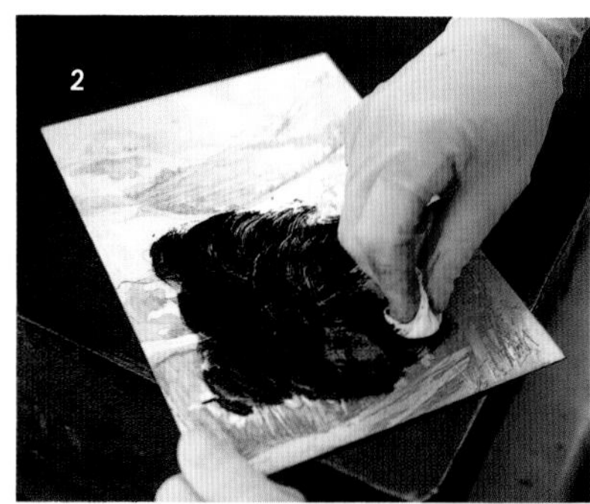

2 Work the ink into the intaglio all over the plate surface. Use a generous amount of color, and push it firmly into any deep lines and heavily bitten areas.

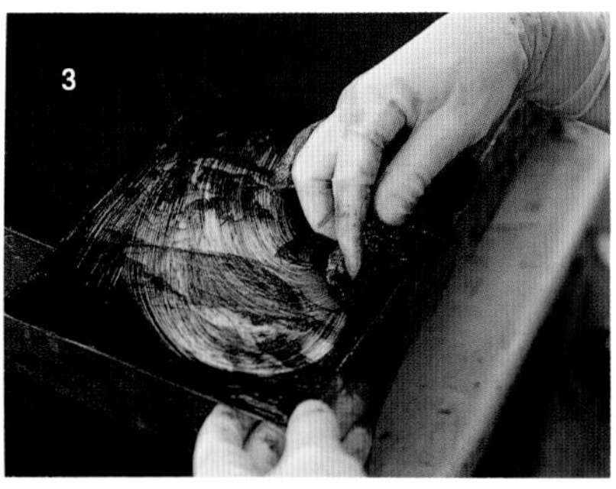

3 Fold a large piece of wiping canvas into a pad and briskly wipe the surface to remove excess ink. Keep the pad traveling flatly across the plate to clean the smoother textures and lighter tones – do not dig the ink out of the deep intaglio.

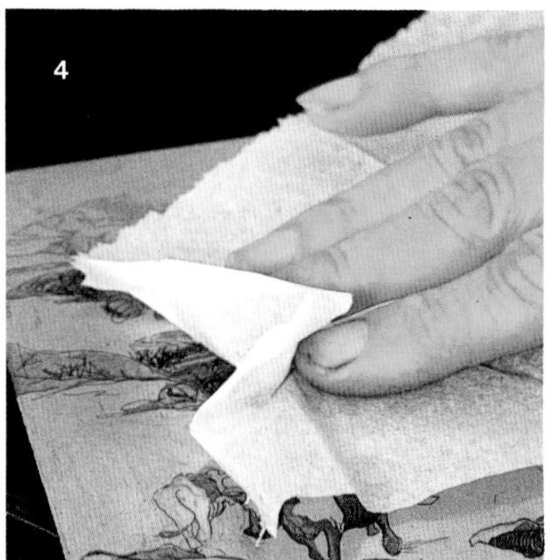

4 When you can see the design clearly, continue wiping with a clean piece of canvas, working lightly and consistently so no obvious smears of ink are left on the surface. To polish the light tones and obtain a clean tonal range from the aquatint areas, go over the plate with a piece of tissue. Spread your fingers flatly on the tissue and rub with a circular motion.

TAKING A PRINT

This process is very simple. The plate is positioned on the flatbed of the press and the damp paper laid over the top. Felt blankets are spread over them, between two and five layers, with a lightweight felt next to the plate and a heavy, napped blanket next to the press roller. The handle of the press is turned to run the bed between the rollers.

To make sure that the impression is taken square on the paper, with even borders, you can lay a base sheet of paper on the bed of the press with the outline of the plate marked on it. When the printing paper is placed on the plate, the edges can be aligned to the base sheet, working from one corner. Alternatively, you can stick masking-tape guides for both plate and paper onto the bed of the press.

1 Make sure the blankets are in place on the press, fed in under the roller but turned back so the bed of the press is clear. Lay the inked plate on a clean sheet of paper on the bed.

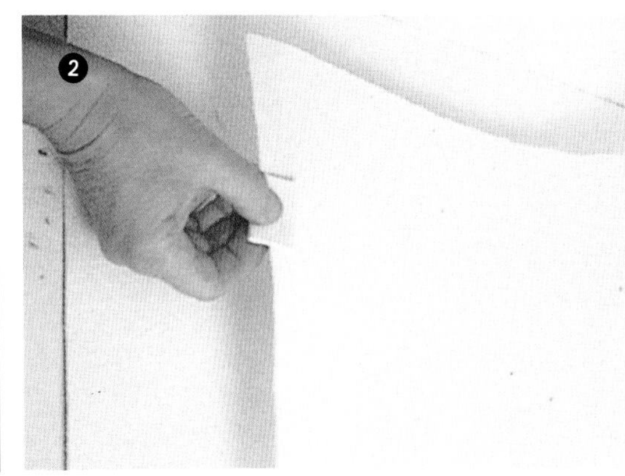

2 Turn back the board on the paper stack and lift out one sheet of damp paper. To keep the edges clean, hold it between small paper folds.

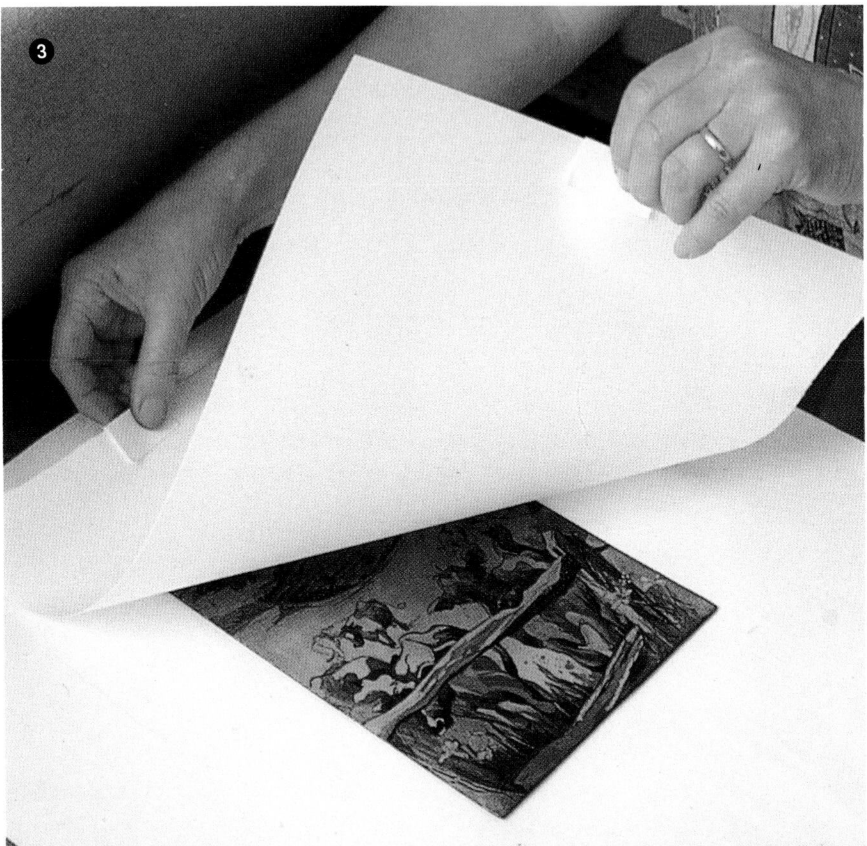

3 Position one corner of the paper on the press in relation to the inked plate. Gently lower the paper and smooth it down on the plate.

4 Pull the blankets down onto the bed of the press one by one, smoothing them carefully in place over the plate and paper.

5 Turn the handle of the press to pass the bed between the rollers. It should turn easily, though a slightly greater effort is required as the thickness of the plate moves through, as the pressure of the rollers does need to be quite heavy.

6 Take the bed through far enough to release both the plate and printing paper from beneath the rollers. Turn back the blankets and peel the print up gently from one corner. The finished print is the example shown in full on page 83.

COLOR PRINTING

There are several ways of introducing color into an etching, even when you are working on only one plate. One method is to ink up the intaglio in one color, usually black or a dark color such as blue or sepia, then use a roller to lay down a flat coating of a second color over the plate surface. Any areas required to print white can be masked off with paper before the color roll-up.

You can also ink the intaglio in more than one color, using separate dabbers for different parts of the plate. This is not absolutely precise, as color areas will merge or overlap slightly in the process of inking and wiping, but it can produce very expressive and atmospheric results.

PRINTING FROM THREE PLATES

A more complicated technique involves producing a separate plate for each color. The plates have to be identical in size and a key drawing is made, which can be transferred to each for registration of the image. Each color print is then run through the press separately. Between the printing of each color, the leading edge of the printing paper is held between the rollers, together with the blankets. The lightest color is usually printed first, then the next plate is registered on the bed, and the paper and blankets carefully lowered in position so that another print can be taken. The process is continued until all plates are printed. Speed is essential for this method as the paper must remain damp during printing. Ink all plates before printing so as to save time between the printing of each color.

1 The plate may be printed in more than one color by dabbing colored inks separately into different areas. Use a clean cheesecloth dabber to ink the first section of the plate.

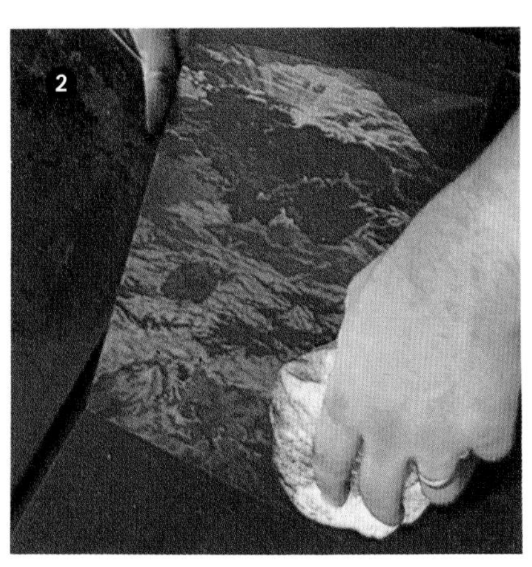

2 Wipe off the excess ink with scrim to prepare the surface for printing. Wipe away from those parts of the plate which are still clean.

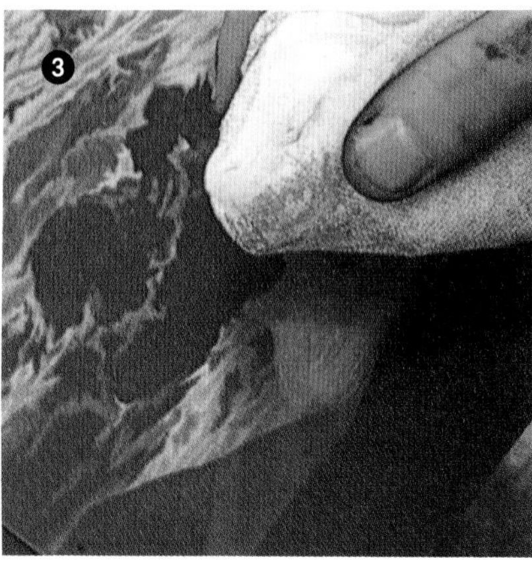

3 Dab in another color with a clean dabber and wipe with scrim as before. Several colors can be applied in this way, but be careful not to wipe one color over another.

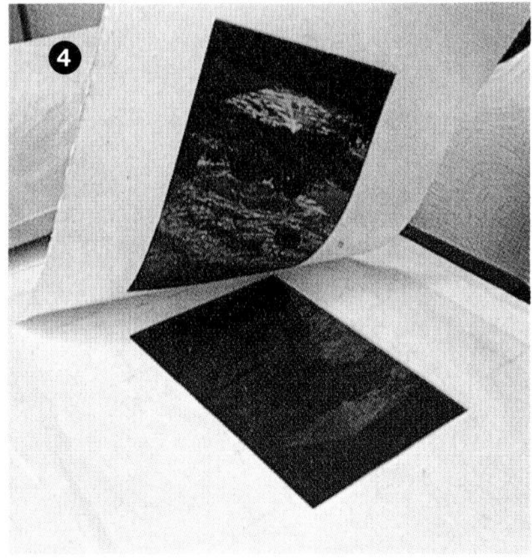

4 Take a print of the plate on damp paper in the usual way. The colors will bleed into each other a little but the separate areas will show a clear change of hue.

Drooping Ash
by Alfred Hartley
This color print was taken from three separate plates. The three stages can be seen in these three illustrations. The first plate was made as an aquatint and was used to print the color beige. The second plate was also made as an aquatint and used to print the green. The last plate was made as an aquatint and an etching and then printed in brown. The result can be seen in the finished illustration.

CHAPTER FOUR

LITHOGRAPHY

Lithography is in one respect an ideal introduction to printmaking because the image is created by standard drawing and painting techniques, put onto the printing surface in exactly the same way as drawing or painting on paper. You describe the image positively, and the marks you make hold the ink for printing. Monochrome lithographs are comparable in tone and texture to crayon or ink line-and-wash drawings. Color lithography involves preparing an individual plate for each color that is to be printed, but you can build up beautifully wide-ranging effects of both surface texture and color by overprinting.

The process depends on a simple chemical principle – the mutual antipathy of grease and water. The image is drawn with greasy materials on a grease-sensitive surface, with the non-printing areas treated with water-based materials to keep them clean. When printing ink is rolled on, it adheres only to the sensitized, greasy marks. The inked image can be printed on paper either by direct contact or by offsetting, that is, taking up the ink from the plate onto an intermediary surface and laying it down separately on the paper.

Although lithography is such an expressive, painterly medium, the chemical processing can seem initially tedious and difficult to grasp. However, it is carried out in simple stages, all designed to "set" the image on the lithographic plate.

▲ *Old Breakwater* (lithograph) by Joy Brand
The gentle tones and textures that can be achieved with lithographic painting techniques enable the artist to produce a very delicate and subtle effect of light on water. The rendering is sparing of detail and effectively employs the limited palette to develop the spacious, atmospheric feeling of the view.

◀ *Burnet Moth* (lithograph) by David Koster
There is a strong linear quality to this composition which creates both visual texture within the print and a sense of the natural textures in the subject. The artist draws in lithographic ink, using quill pens and brushes, to prepare the black plate, which forms the key design for additional color plates.

Lithographic equipment

1 Lithographic stick ink; **2** lithographic crayons; **3** pencil and graphite sticks; **4** lithographic drawing ink; **5** printing ink; **6** expandable sponge.

TOOLS AND MATERIALS

Originally, lithographic images were prepared on large blocks of limestone and printed by direct contact. This method is still practiced, but is now more common to use metal plates – zinc or aluminum, depending on which is more easily available. Metal plates can also be printed direct, but are particularly adapted to offset printing. The stone or plate has an even grain which contributes to the characteristic textures of lithographic printing. After printing, the surface can be cleaned and resensitized to be used again, but after a few uses it must be completely regrained. There are specialist services for this.

For drawing up the image, you can use lithographic crayons and pencils, and ink (tusche), brushed on full-strength or as diluted washes.

Lithographic drawing materials must contain grease or soap in the form of fatty acids in order to function on the plate. Traditionally they are pigmented with black (carbon). Many materials can be adapted for lithographic drawing – wax crayons, oil pastels, candles, shoe polish, and Chinagraph pencils are only a few you can use.

All these materials are black, but once you have drawn and processed the plate, the image can be inked up in any color for printing.

Inks for color lithography are composed of finely ground pigment, specially selected and combined with oils to operate in conjunction with the water used in the lithographic process. These inks are basically transparent; they can be made more so by using a special medium; made opaque by adding white; mixed, stiffened, or made fluid, according to requirements. A wide range of colors are available from printing ink suppliers and art stores.

Sharp knives, burins, and razor blades are also needed to scrape negative areas. Watercolor or oil painting brushes can be used to apply the ink.

PREPARING THE PLATE

The plate is treated with a number of chemicals in the processing stages. The undrawn plate is first sensitized with a liquid preparation known as "counter-etch." This solution may be a commercial chemical solution, or a saturated solution of alum and water with a few drops of nitric acid. Gum arabic is used to protect non-printing areas while you draw on the plate or to seal the plate surface between stages of processing and printing. The image is "fixed" on the plate by applying a caustic etch solution, such as a dilute acid mixed with gum. The term "etch" is confusing if you are already familiar with the physical process of etching on metal – in lithography the etch solution does not eat into the plate surface; it simply helps to set the greasy marks.

At all stages of processing and printing, the plate is frequently dampened and dried off. Sponges are common equipment for lithography, and a hairdryer or fan is essential for drying stages – unless you are prepared to wait hours, or even days, to move on to the next step.

1 Hold the plate under running water and allow the surface to become fully wet. Drain off the excess water but keep the plate damp.

3 Hold the plate under running water and rinse off the solution thoroughly. Drain off the excess water.

4 Dry off the surface of the plate completely. A hairdryer is valuable studio equipment, as the need to dry the plate recurs throughout the lithographic process.

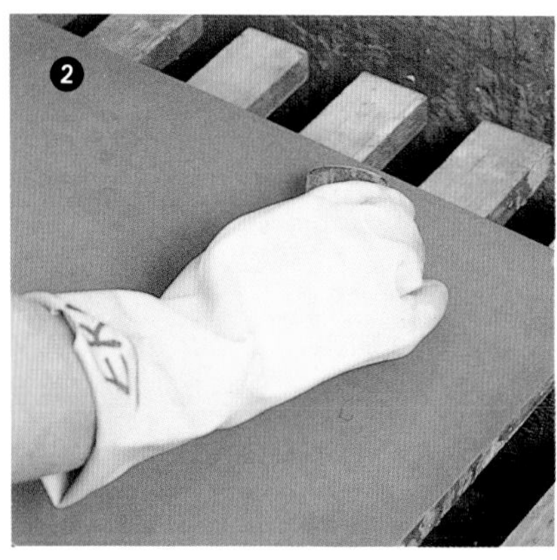

2 Pour on the counter-etch solution and use a sponge to spread it evenly over the whole surface of the plate.

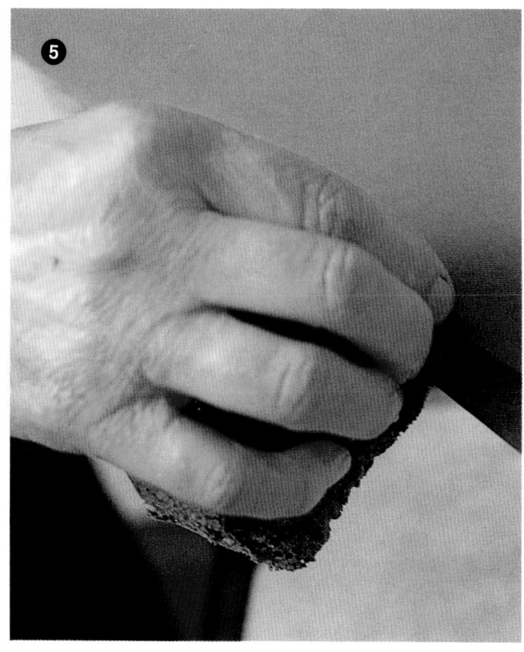

5 Sponge gum arabic around the edges of the plate to make a border for the image area. Allow gum to dry.

Drawing on the plate

Working study

The lithograph shown in this demonstration is to print in only two colors, so the artist has prepared her idea of the image quite carefully beforehand in a sketch and more detailed color study. This gives her guidelines for the basic shapes in the composition, the balance of tones, and the interaction of line work with broader areas of color. However, as the image is allowed to develop freely as the plates are prepared, the finished lithograph will be different in character and detail.

DRAWING FOR MONOCHROME

Once the plate surfaces have been prepared, you can sketch out a composition onto the plate using non-greasy materials such as charcoal or chalk, or trace down over a chalky transfer paper. Remember that the plate is sensitive to any greasy materials – even fingerprints – so pencils or crayons cannot be used for guidelines not intended to appear in the final print. Use a piece of paper as a bridge to rest your hand on when drawing, to keep the plate clean.

You can apply the full range of drawing and painting techniques – line drawing with crayon, brush or pen, free liquid washes, sponged, spattered, and drybrushed textures. It is also possible to make erasures at this stage to correct any errors.

Any areas you intend to leave white can be painted out at this stage with gum arabic solution using a fine watercolor brush. The gum should have dried thoroughly before you proceed. Only use turpentine-based inks in conjunction with gum; water-based inks penetrate the film, depositing grease.

DRAWING FOR COLOR

A separate plate is required for each color in a color lithograph. The

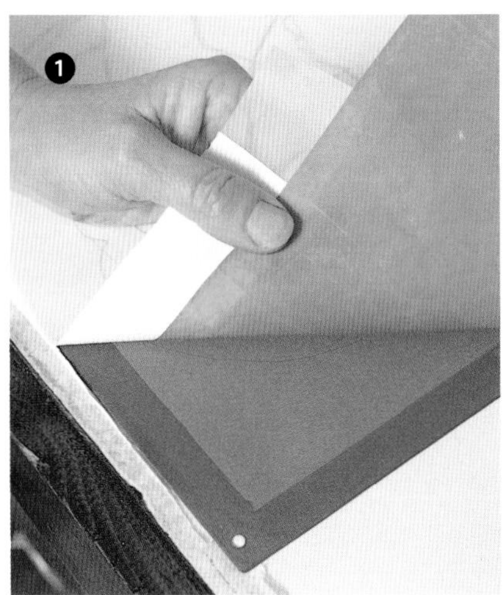

Drawing on the plate

1 If you wish to transfer the guidelines of a working drawing to the plate, you must use a non-greasy transfer paper so the lines will not appear after processing of the image.

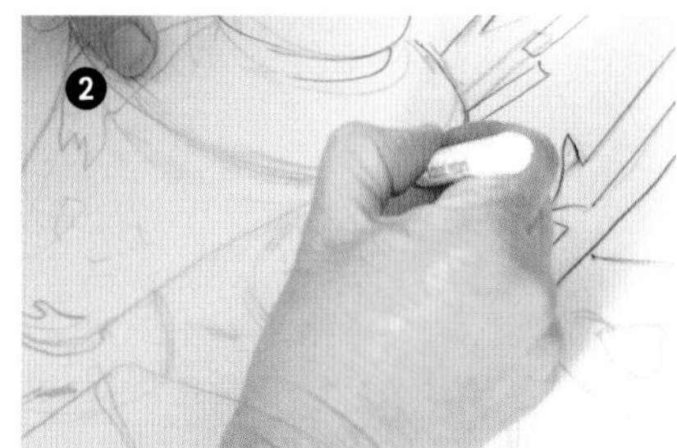

2 Place your drawing over the transfer paper and work over it with a pencil or pen to press down the main lines of the image onto the plate.

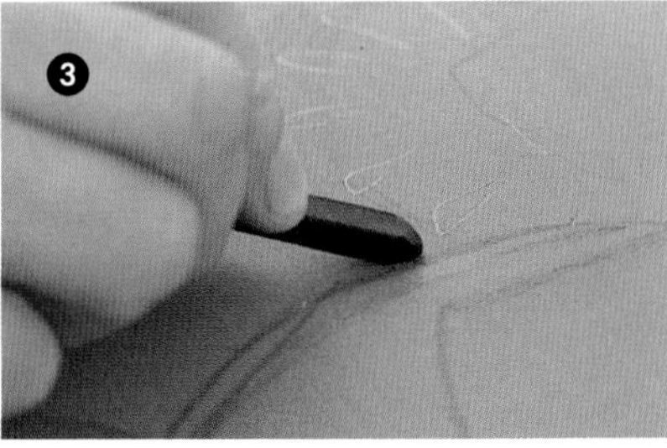

3 Start to draw directly onto the plate with a lithographic crayon or pencil. You can work exactly as you would with chalk or pencil on paper.

process is fairly complicated and most artists begin by producing single-color prints before attempting more complex compositions. It is a good idea to make a series of color sketches to help decide which colors to use and where the color areas will be.

The plates are drawn individually but must print in sequence on the proofing paper, in overprinted as well as juxtaposed colors. Some lithographers prefer to see each color proofed before they draw the next; others draw a series and have them proofed as a group.

It is important to state each color sufficiently. For example, a plate which will be printed in lemon yellow must be emphasized when it is drawn, so that the color will show up well in relation to the others in the proofing sequence. Even though the image will be drawn on each color plate in black, the artist must bear in mind the eventual color and try to anticipate the desired effect.

All colors must fit together correctly and consistently. A simple method of registering involves tracing the outline of the image (same size) on grained film or strong tracing paper with a technical pen or fine ball point. Make two crosses on either side of the drawing to act as registration points. Place the tracing in position on the plate and secure it at the top edge with a piece of tape. Insert a sheet of lithographic tracing paper between the tracing and the lithographic surface chalk side down, and follow the line of the drawing with a fine stylus or ball point pen, pressing firmly. This will deposit a non-printing red ocher line onto the plate, which can then be used as a guide for the lithographic drawing. Repeat the operation for each plate. Do not forget to draw in the registration marks on each plate and do not use carbon paper for tracing – it is greasy and will print.

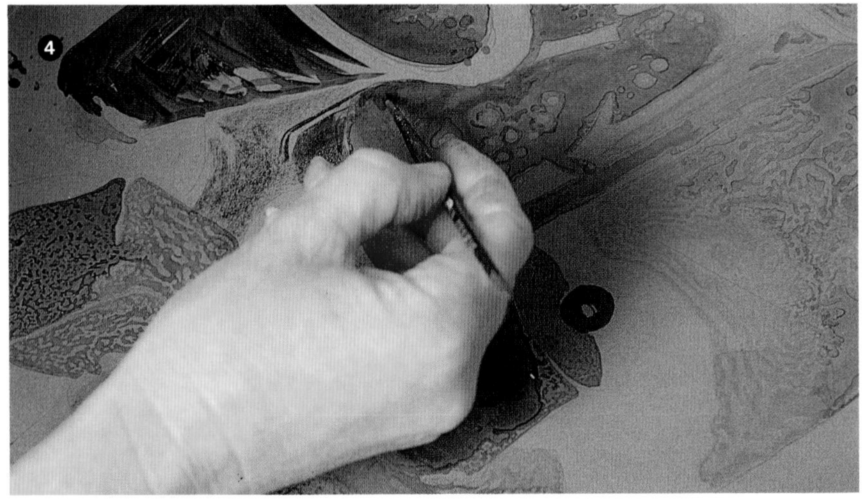

4 Apply the lithographic ink with paintbrushes, again working as you would on paper. You can use the ink at full strength or diluted with distilled or tap water.

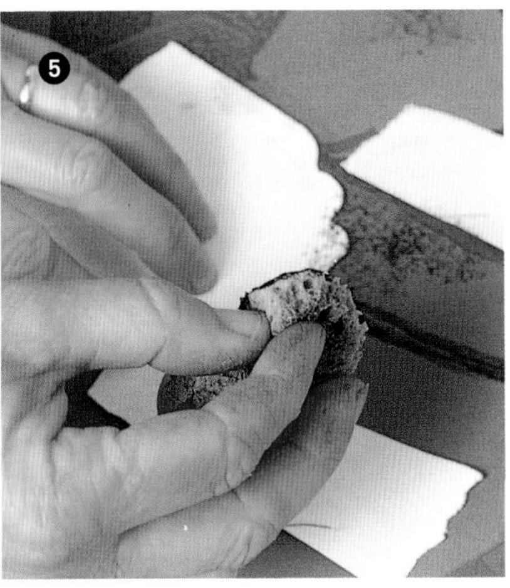

5 You can apply ink with a sponge, as here, or with a rag or other applicator to vary the textures of your drawing. Here, paper masks are used to contain the sponging.

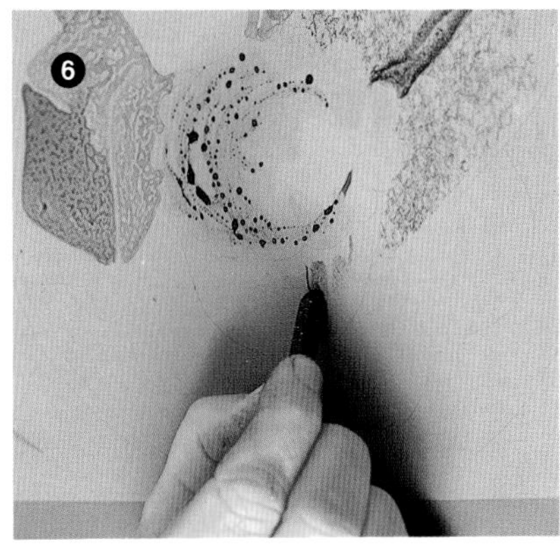

6 Continue working until the image is completed in as much detail as you require. Keep in mind that this image will print uniformly as tones of one color.

PROCESSING THE IMAGE

This stage is a second "etch" that strengthens the effect of the greasy marks on the plate surface. It is very similar to the preparatory stages, except that this time the drawn image is washed out and the marks are treated with asphalt or printing ink. This makes the color appear different, but as you take out the original drawing and put color back in you have the opportunity to check how effectively the marks have set into the grain of the plate. This is where you begin to see the real appearance of the image for print and can judge how well the textures have developed. Again there is an opportunity for correction, using an erasing fluid.

When the image is satisfactory, it is rolled up with ink as if for printing, gummed, and left to stand.

PRINTING PAPERS

There are two kinds of paper used for lithographic work: paper made by hand on a traditional frame and paper manufactured mechanically known as moldmade. Handmade stock is ideal for direct printing; its deckled edges and various textures have many devotees. It is made from linen rags or cotton linters and has only a little sizing added. Waterleaf is perhaps the best quality, but this is a matter of personal choice.

Handmade paper is not always suitable for color printing because it has a tendency to stretch, giving problems with registration. For this reason it is advisable to use moldmade paper, manufactured from the same materials but produced mechanically. Moldmade paper comes in a variety of surfaces, colors, weights, and sizes. For early attempts at proofing and printing, using good quality white cartridge paper is often the most economical solution.

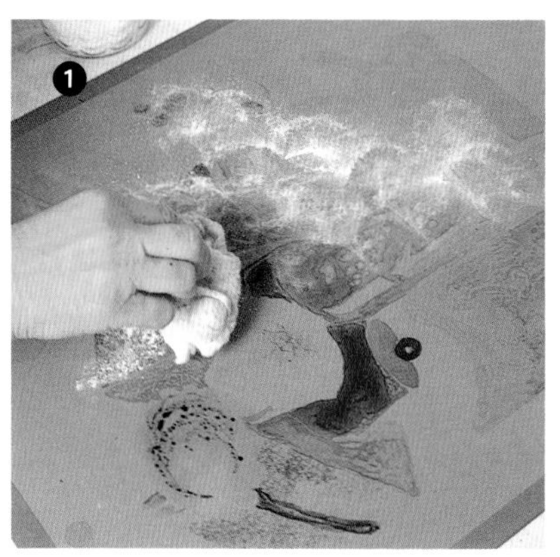

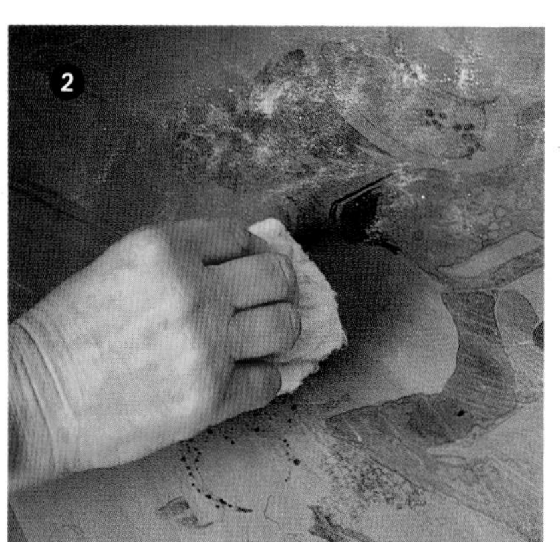

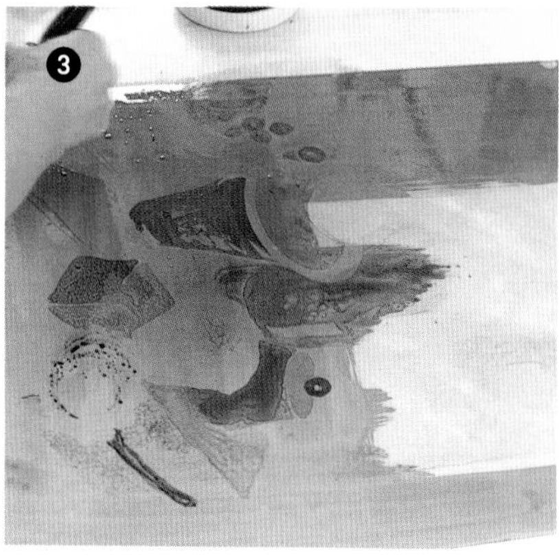

First-stage processing

1 When all the ink drawing is completely dry, dust over the plate with French chalk, spread with clean cotton wool or a soft cloth.

2 Repeat the dusting, this time with powdered resin. These dry materials temporarily counteract the greasiness in the image, so it will accept liquid processing in the next stage.

3 Brush on the liquid-etch solution, covering the whole surface of the plate evenly and generously. This helps to "fix" the drawn image on the plate. Leave it on for just a couple of minutes.

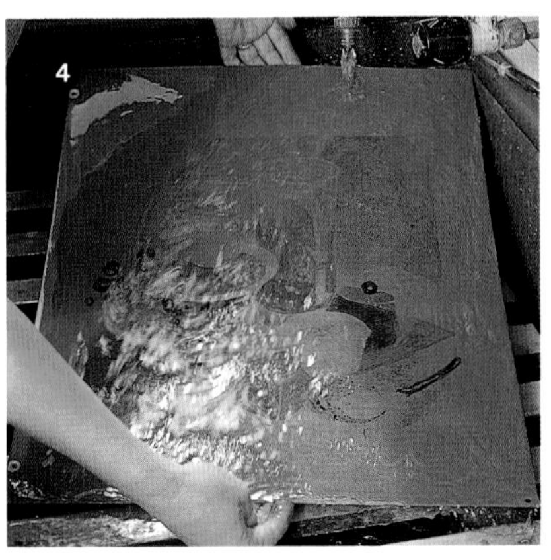

4 Put the plate under running water and rinse off the etch solution thoroughly. Use the hairdryer to dry off the plate completely.

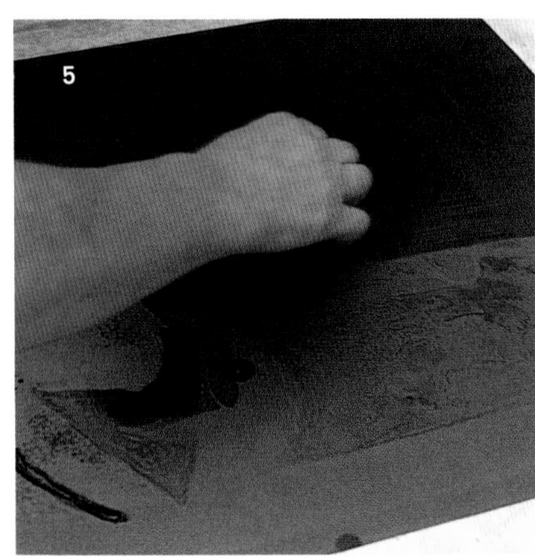

5 Sponge a thin layer of gum arabic over the whole plate surface and allow it to dry. Leave the plate overnight before continuing the processing.

SECOND-STAGE PROCESSING

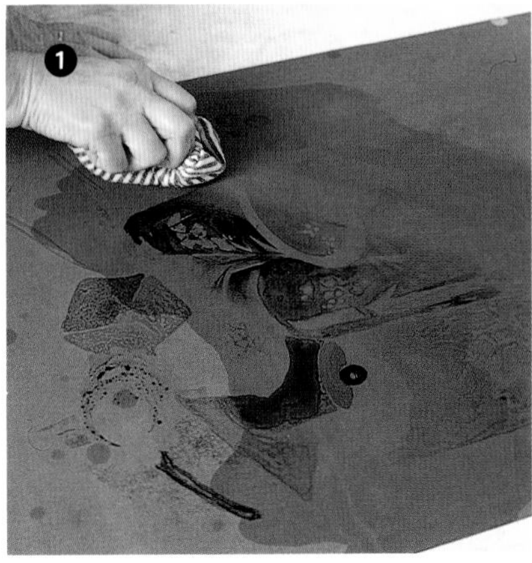

1 Use mineral spirit and a clean rag to wash out the drawn image from the surface of the plate. All the black disappears, but you can still see the marks as a greasy "shadow" on the plate. The gum is unaffected by mineral spirit and continues to protect undrawn areas of the plate.

2 Rub in a thin layer of printing ink. This helps to reinforce the image and preserves delicate wash effects. Alternatively you can use asphalt which strengthens the textures and is better suited to a heavier, more dense drawing.

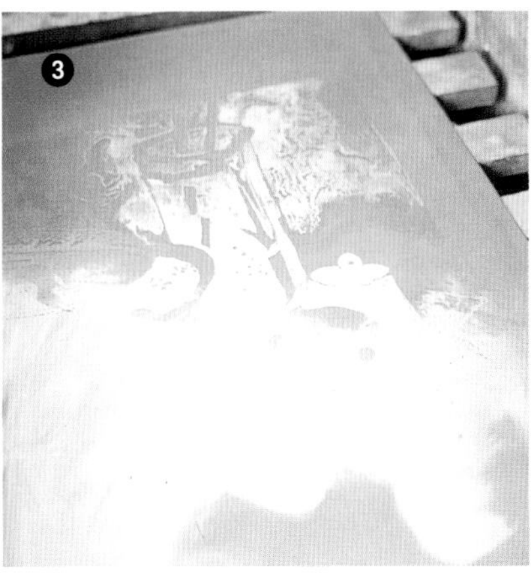

3 Wipe out the ink with mineral spirit then wash off the plate with water to remove the gummed layer still surrounding the image.

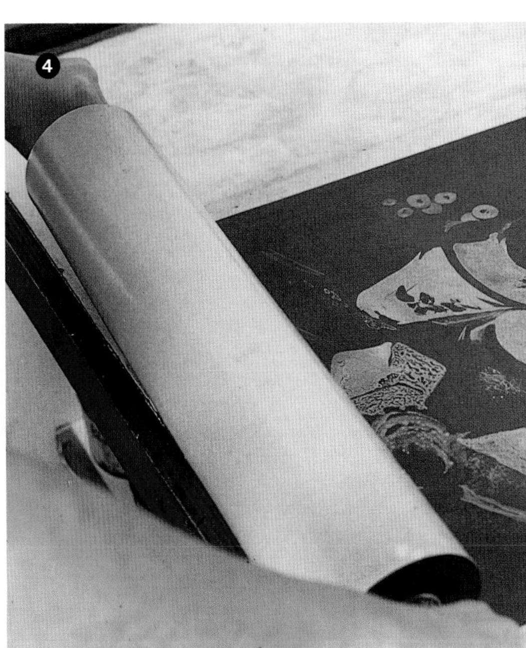

4 Roll up the damp plate with printing ink. The image now appears as it will print. Dry off the plate and cover the surface with gum. Let it stand for at least half an hour.

Proofing

DIRECT METHOD

Today, most lithography is done on hand-proving presses by a method known as the direct method. These presses vary in design but are similar in principle. Very basically, the bed of the press holds the tone or plate, supported on a metal block constructed for the purpose. This is then inked up, and the selected proofing paper is placed on top of the inked image. Several sheets of soft backing paper are then laid over it. A side lever lifts the bed of the press so that it comes into contact with the printing pressure and the plate is then drawn through the press by hand-winding or by motor traction.

OFFSET METHOD

There are many different types of offset lithography machines, some operated by hand, others by machine, or electronically. The main difference between this and other printing methods is that the plate has to be wetted before any ink is applied and kept damp while it is rolled up. The water protects the clean, non-printing areas of the plate but does not affect the ink's adherence to the greasy printing areas.

Generally, a lithography plate is inked with a large, wide roller that covers the width of the image area in one pass, giving an even, consistent coverage of color.

OFFSET PRINTING

1 Mix up a quantity of printing ink and roll it out evenly on a glass slab. Use a large roller that will cover the image area. The artist is working here with a gradated tone of pink; she has mixed three tones of the same color and rolled them out together.

2 Use a wet sponge to remove the gum arabic from the plate. Position the plate on the bed of the offset press. Keep it damp throughout the rolling-up process.

3 Roll the color over the image area on the plate firmly and evenly. As necessary, wipe the surface with a damp sponge to remove any ink residue that may float on the non-printing surface.

4 When a sufficiently heavy and even color layer has adhered to the image, dry off the plate completely. If it remains damp, moisture will be picked up on the press roller and spread onto the printing paper.

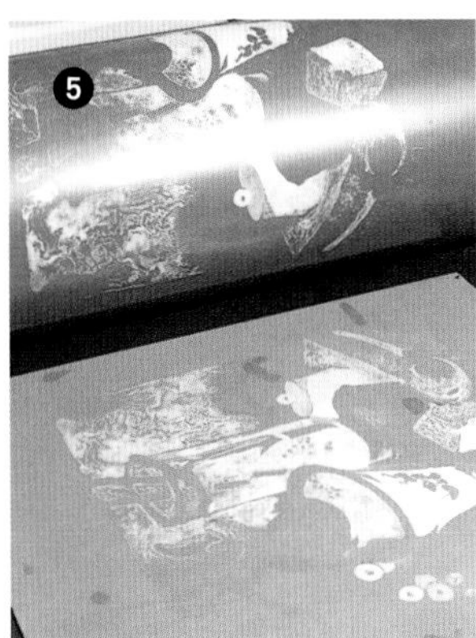

5 Roll the press roller back and forth over the inked plate until the image is clearly picked up on the roller "blanket" (the rubber covering). Mechanisms for presses vary; at this stage the roller is not making contact with the area where the paper lies on the press bed.

6 Position the paper on the bed of the press adjacent to the plate. The press has grippers to keep the paper flat and in place. Take the roller over the plate and back to pass over and make contact with the paper, laying down the inked image.

7

7 In the first printing, the main shapes are all in place within the image but the tones and textures are very delicate. The artist has to visualize how the imposition of a second color will add the depth and detail needed to sharpen and complete the rendering.

COLOR PROOFING

Color lithography is similar to painting in many respects, but a great deal of patience and concentration is required to achieve the right quality. Progressives, or sequence prints, are an essential aid, helping you to understand the anatomy of the work, and are useful as a guide to color balance and image registration. Prints can be affected not only by these factors, but also by the order in which the colors are imposed. Sometimes first attempts will work, but re-proofing is often necessary to formulate an idea correctly and, if a proof is to be editioned in quantity, professional help may need to be sought. Such work requires expertise and the use of machines not often available to the amateur. But if only a small quantity is required, there is no reason why, with proper preparation, editioning should not be attempted by the individual.

When printing in two or more colors, the basic procedure for each one is the same, but you need to register them accurately on the previous printing. There are various ways of registering, but most presses are equipped with grippers and stops that enable you to position the paper correctly in relation to each plate. In this example, the second color is first printed on an acetate sheet attached to one end of the press. The print of the first color is positioned underneath the acetate, aligning the color areas. The stops are then set to the edges of the printing paper so that further prints can simply be slipped into place.

Registering the second color

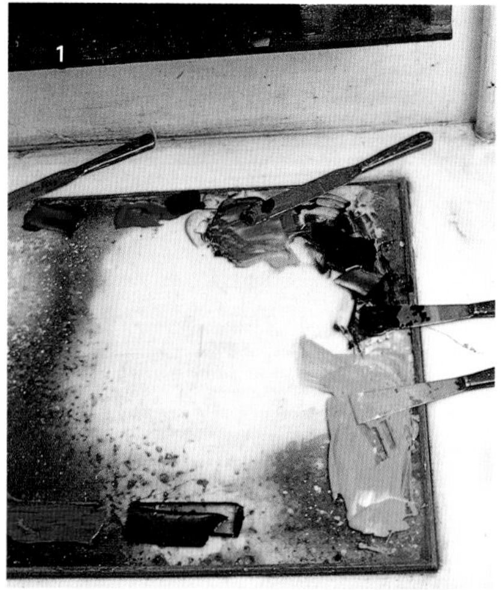

1 The artist has planned this print so that both colors are gradated, giving tonal variation across the whole image. She lays out the three mixed tones of the second color on the mixing slab.

2 The large roller is used to work the ink evenly back and forth on the glass slab, until the three colors merge together smoothly.

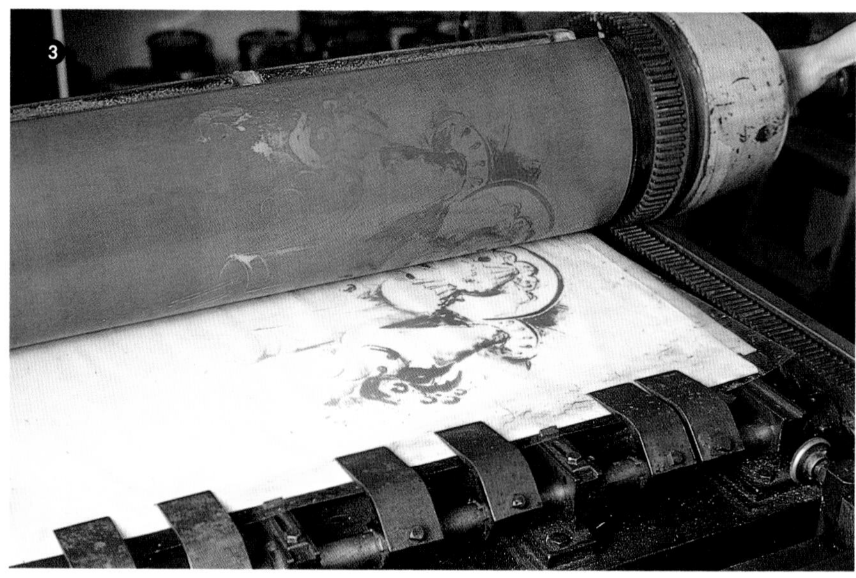

3 The plate is put in place on the press and inked with blue. The first print is taken, by the same technique as previously, on a sheet of acetate anchored at one end of the press.

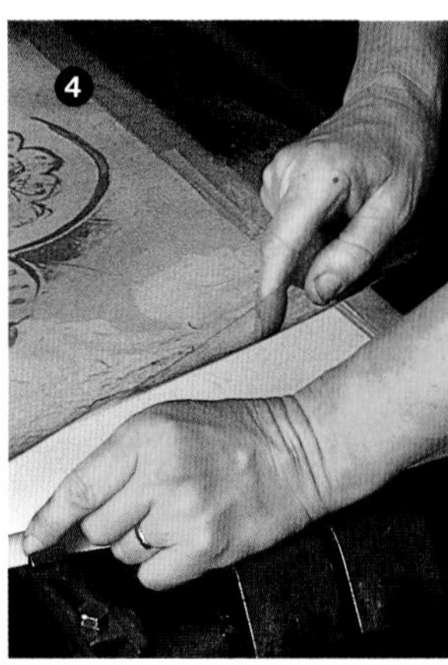

4 A print from the first plate is positioned under the acetate and moved until the image areas register exactly.

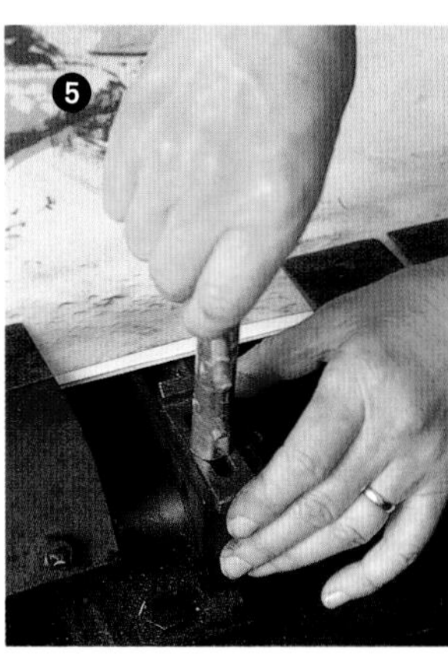

5 Carefully keeping the print in place, the artist adjusts the stops on the press that butt to the side and bottom edges of the printing paper. Methods of registering and marking the position of the paper may vary, depending on the press model.

6 The second color is printed onto each of the pink prints, each time positioning the paper against the fixed stops, and holding it in place with the grippers. As before, the roller is taken across the press over the plate, then back to lay down the blue image on the print.

7 In the final print, the strength of the blue tones emphasizes particular shapes, as does the greater amount of linear drawing included in this image. But the two colors integrate convincingly to give the still life depth and form.

CHAPTER FIVE

SCREENPRINTING

The principle of screenprinting is somewhat different from that of the other printmaking processes in that the print is taken not by the direct impression of one surface upon another, but by printing through an intermediary surface – the screen mesh. The images of screenprints are formed by various kinds of stenciling techniques, based on blocking out areas of the mesh either with sheet materials such as paper or stencil film or with liquids that fill the mesh.

As well as being a fine-art process, screenprinting has a direct association with commercial and industrial printing processes, being used extensively in graphic, ceramic, and textile design. It is a colorful, versatile medium which you can adapt to the context of your work.

◀ *Russian Tea Room* (screenprint) by Beryl Cook
This print, created from a combination of photographic and handmade stencils, was produced and printed from an original painting by the artist, who oversaw all stages of its production.

◀ *Papillon* (screenprint) by Moira Wills
Using mid- to light-toned colors and an informal pattern of freely drawn shapes, the artist creates a bright, painterly image with much attractive detail. The textures and edge qualities are cleverly varied by using a combination of stencil techniques.

TOOLS AND MATERIALS

The basic equipment required for screenprinting consists of the screen – a wooden frame with a fine-mesh fabric stretched over it – and the squeegee. This is a rubber blade set in a handle, with which the screen ink is pulled across the mesh. The mesh transmits an even coating of ink which adheres to the paper below the screen.

The stencil, whatever its form, seals certain areas of the screen so that the ink cannot pass through, thus creating positive and negative color areas. The stencil can be a material as simple as thin paper that will adhere to the underside of the mesh – for example, newsprint, tracing paper, or greaseproof paper. Commercial stencil film is a gelatinous material on a plastic backing that can be cut with a sharp craft knife – when soaked with water it softens and is pressed into the mesh before the backing is removed. A similar effect can be obtained with self-adhesive plastic film applied to the screen, and you can also use adhesive tapes.

Screenprinting equipment
1 Squeegee; **2** screen; **3** screenprinting inks; **4** solvent brush to remove stencils; **5** palette knife.

OILS AND SOLVENTS

Oil-based Inks. Most fine art prints are made using oil-based inks. These are usually matte-finished, fairly scuff-resistant, and of high pigment quality. The consistency and drying time of the ink can be controlled by the type of thinner used – fast, standard, or retarder. Fast and standard thinners are used when printing at speed with, for example, a semi-automatic printing machine, requiring a correspondingly short drying time. For hand-printing, a retarding thinner allows a slower rate of printing and time to check each print without the ink drying into the mesh.

The consistency of the ink relates to the mesh count. For an average mesh (62, 77, 90), the ink should resemble engine oil; if the count is lower, it should be slightly thicker, like molasses, and if it is higher than the average it should be thinned to the consistency of light cream.

Finishes. You can overprint oil-based matte colors with glossy or silk varnishes to produce different surface qualities. But silk- and medium-gloss finishes are usually obtained by using solvent-based or cellulose inks. For a really glossy effect, an oxidization ink or varnish should be used, bearing in mind that they dry by chemical reaction, which requires 24 hours in the rack, and they cannot be dried in a tunnel dryer.

Metallic powders may be added to varnishes to produce silver, gold, and bronze – in fact, almost any mineral powder will work with these bases. There are also a number of special-

▲ *Cranes* (screenprint) by Yuriko
This contemporary Japanese print based on traditional imagery uses modern glitter inks to express the reflective quality and movement of the splash of water. Today there is a wide range of inks to help the artist achieve the precise effect required.

◀ A glimpse of the range of hues and textures (note the gold glitter ink on the left) is seen here. Indeed there are many brands and types of inks used for different styles of printing and for a wide range of effects.

effect inks on the market; these include pearlized, expanding and glitter inks.

Water-based inks, as used in schools, have an inherent disadvantage in that when printed on paper, the stock changes dimension by absorbing the water. However, concern with the environment will inevitably force ink manufacturers to develop new products that will solve these problems.

The advantages of water-based inks are that they are easily diluted with water and are much less trouble to clean up than the oil-based inks, as they dissolve in water.

THE FRAME

The frame is the support over which fabric is stretched; together they make up the screen. At its simplest, a frame can be made from a thick cardboard rectangle with a smaller rectangle removed from the center, covered on one side with a coarse organdy fabric that has been stuck to the cardboard. This would be perfectly adequate for printing Christmas cards, or small images up to 6 x 8 inches.

Wooden Frames. The most readily available type of frame and the one chosen by most beginners is a wooden one, either homemade or custom manufactured. Making the frame yourself is not difficult, but requires some basic carpentry skills. An advantage of the homemade frame is that you can choose the size you require – 16 x 24 inches is a good size to start with. Cedar is often used by commercial manufacturers as it is water resistant, rigid, and light to handle. Make sure the weight of the wood is appropriate for the size of screen being made, as the fabric exerts a considerable tension when stretched. But the frame should not be too heavy to handle easily. The corners take the strain of the tension and should be properly glued and jointed (not simply screwed or nailed). Finally, all wooden frames should be coated with a protecting finish that is ink and water repellent, such as polyurethane varnish or French polish.

Ready-made Frames. If the cost of the artist's time is taken into account, it is probably more economical to buy a ready-made frame, unless you possess an adequate tool kit and enjoy making things. The advantage of the manufactured frame over those made at home are that it will be made of the correct material, with the right ratio of cross section to frame, and with properly jointed corners.

Wooden frames can be purchased in 6 inch incremental sizes from 5 x 8 inches to 108 x 76 inches as standard, and any other size by negotiation. The frame should always be the largest size that is practical, since small images can be put in a large screen, whereas obviously a large stencil will not fit into a small one.

Metal Frames. Most professional printers use metal frames; they are more durable and, if correctly stretched, they make it easier to

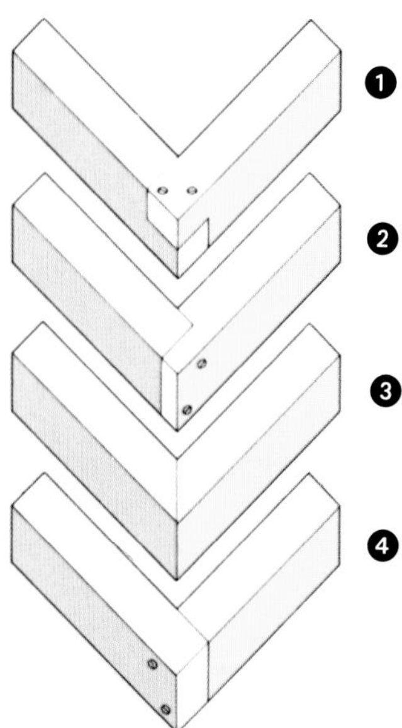

Wooden frames
Wooden frames can be homemade or purchased from suppliers of printing equipment. The corners take the strain and therefore need to be glued and jointed properly. Illustrated here are four strong joints: **1** end-lap joint; **2** rabbet joint; **3** miter joint; and **4** butt joint.

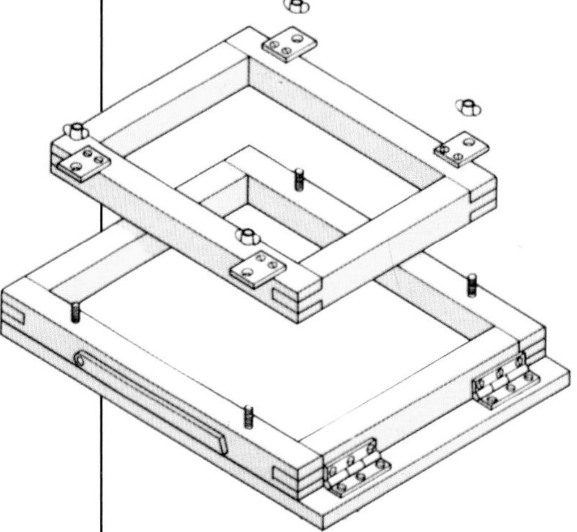

Master frame
A master frame into which different frames can be fitted makes it easier to remove the printing frame for cleaning.

SILK FABRIC WEAVES

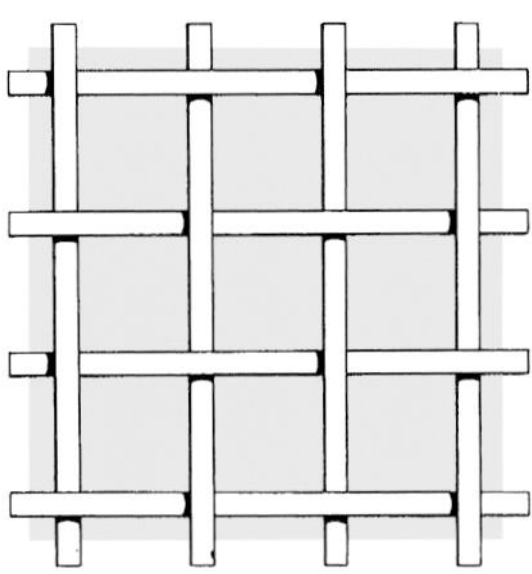

1 The basic taffeta weave is a weave which has strength and durability.

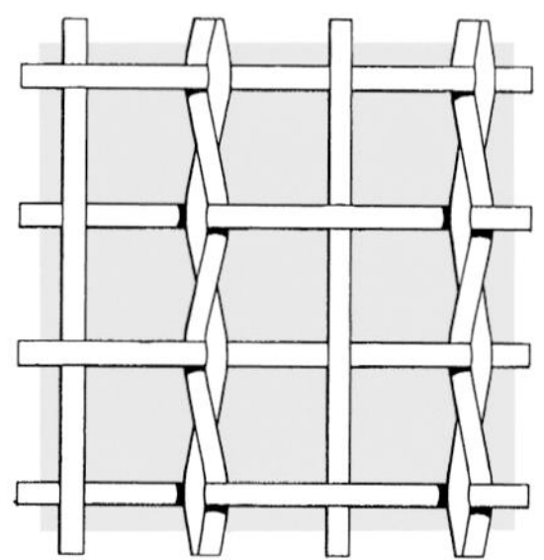

2 The half-gauze weave has an extra thread added to every other strand to give added strength.

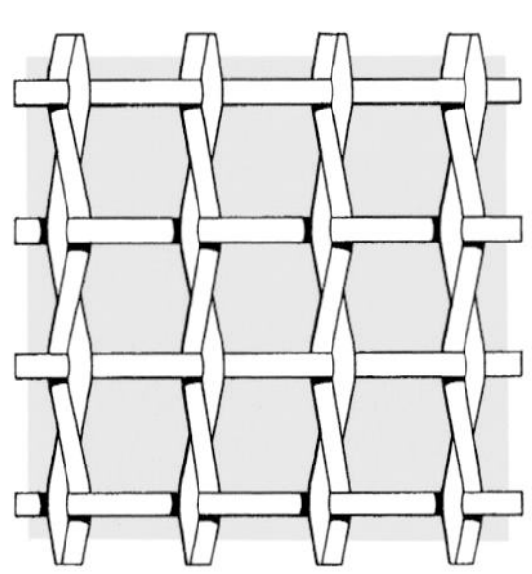

3 The full gauze weave is the strongest weave: an extra thread is added to every strand.

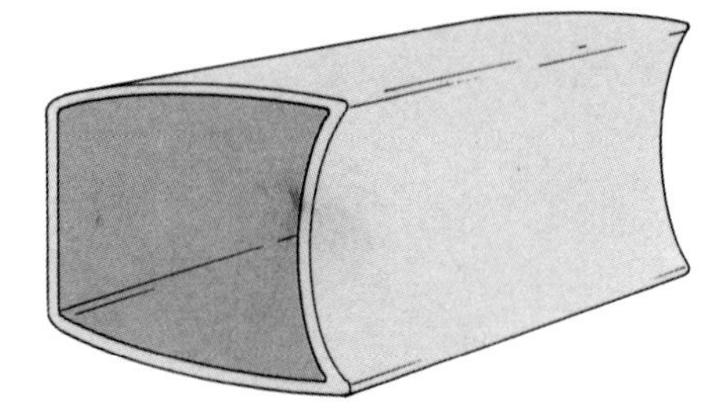

Metal frames

Metal frames are durable and are unlikely to bow under fabric tension. There are two cross-section profiles: **1** the box frame; and **2** the seriframe.

register prints correctly as they do not warp or bow under fabric tension. Wooden frames, even if they are professionally manufactured, will eventually flex and warp, causing stencils to distort.

Metal frames are made either of aluminum, which is light to handle but subject to distortion if clumsily attached to the printing table, or steel, which, if coated with baked-on preserver, is the strongest and most durable material available. There are two main cross-section profiles: the box, which is rectangular, and the seriframe. If a homemade print table is being used for printing, a box section frame is best because it is more easily attached. If a professional printing table is used, the seriframe is stronger, more resistant to fabric tension and, because of its inside profile, easier to clean.

STRETCHING THE MESH

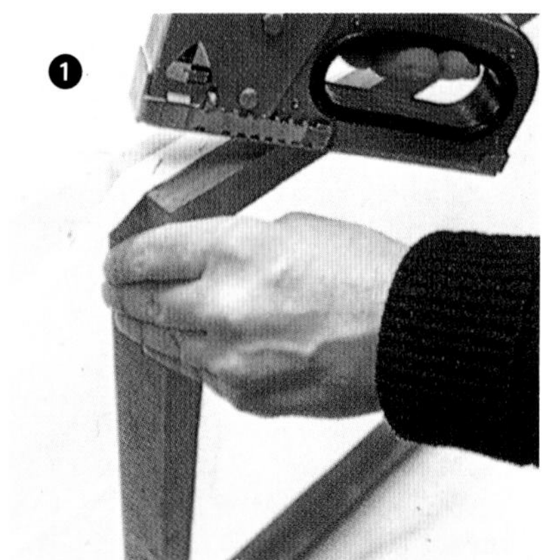

1 Cut fabric to size allowing a 1 in overlap on each side of the screen. When attaching the fabric, staple through a thin strip of card to avoid tearing the mesh.

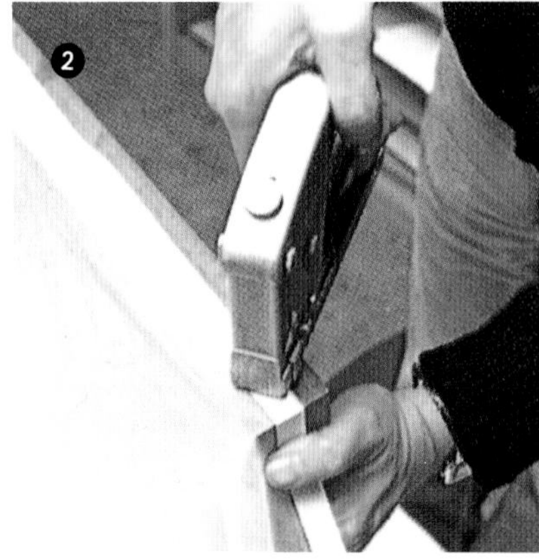

2 Staple from the center of one side of the screen towards each corner, pulling the fabric taut as you work. Put in the staples at an angle across the side of the frame.

MESHES AND FABRICS

The amount of ink which is deposited onto the print is governed by the coarseness of the mesh and type of material used. Care must be taken to choose an appropriate fabric.

Silk was the original fabric used in the silk-screen process, hence the use of the word serigraphy as an alternative, meaning literally "silk drawing". Silk bolting cloth and taffeta weave silk are still in use because of their ability to withstand heavy printing, their good tensile strength and the uniformity of the mesh.

All silks used in printing are classified by a number indicating the number of threads per linear inch, and a code which relates to the weight of the fabric. Many manufacturers employ their own coding systems so a check is essential before buying. Various other fabrics have come into service now and the wide range includes nylon, terylene, polyester, metal-polyester, copper, and stainless steel.

TYPES OF MESH

Organdy is the least expensive mesh to use but it has the disadvantage of being unstable. It tends to shrink when wet and then slacken off as it dries out. Good dressmakers' organdy or cotton organdy made for screenprinting with a mesh count of 90 threads per inch is suitable for beginners.

Synthetic Meshes are differentiated by the letters S, M, T, and HD. The S gauze is widely used and is a thin thread weave. M is medium weave, T gauze is a twilled weave and is used if the screen is to be exposed to strain. The HD gauze is heavy duty.

Nylon is produced in finer grades than silk. It consists of a smooth monofilament thread with a taffeta weave and it is resistant to attack by chemical solvents and acids. It is elastic as well as extensible, and stretching should be carried out in two stages. It has the disadvantage of being slightly unstable. This limits its use for precision work.

Polyester is slightly less resistant to chemical agents but less extensible than nylon. It has the added advantage of being unaffected by moisture, and comes in a wide range of mesh sizes. Its strength and stability make it popular for high precision work.

Metal Polyester is a very stable fabric requiring minimum stretch. It is extremely durable, and indirect stencils adhere well to it.

3 Repeat the process along the opposite side of the screen so that the mesh is tightly stretched across the width of the frame. Secure the third and fourth sides in the same way.

4 Use a large pair or scissors to trim off any surplus fabric around the edges of the frame.

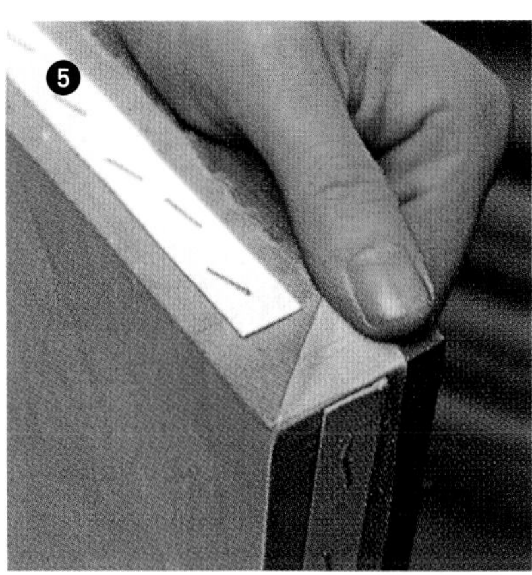

5 Fold the fabric around the corners of the frame keeping tension on the stretched face of the mesh. Secure the folds with staples.

Metallic Screen Meshes made of bronze, copper, or brass have all been used, but stainless steel is now used increasingly because of its excellent durability and resistance to abrasion and caustic inks. It has the advantage of being woven very finely and uniformly. It is used particularly in printing on glass and can reproduce fine detail. The disadvantages of this material are its high cost, a smooth surface inhibiting stencil adhesion, and the difficulty of removing the stencil at the end of the run.

Deckled paper

The edge of the paper is said to be deckled when it has a rough finish. On handmade paper, the deckle is on four sides; on moldmade paper, on two sides.

VARIETIES OF PAPER

Although paper is not the only stock on which limited editions or fine art prints are printed, it is the most common. And although screen inks adhere to the majority of papers and boards, it is good practice to test a new paper by printing on it and checking the ink for scuff resistance and adhesion.

As there are such a variety of papers available, it is useful to look at the characteristics of papers in general. There are three main types of paper, handmade, moldmade, and machine-made, varying widely in price and usage.

Paper Surfaces. The three characteristic surfaces of paper are "hot pressed and callendered" (HP), which means that the finish is smooth; "rough," meaning textured rather like watercolor paper; and "cold pressed" (NOT) surfaces, which has a texture between HP and rough.

The way paper has been sized, which is part of the manufacturing process, determines its degree of absorbency. The greater the absorbency of the paper, the greater the tendency of the ink to spread, possibly blurring detail. The most absorbent is "unsized" or "waterleaf." Many screenprints, however, are made on paper that is "internally sized" because it is fairly dimensionally stable and absorbs only a small quantity of ink, thereby holding detail.

Grain. The grain of the paper, determined by the direction of the fibers, also has an effect on the quality of the print. In handmade papers, the fibers adopt random directions, producing a strong, light-fast paper which provides excellent color resolution. The grain of mold-made paper, unlike handmade paper, has definite direction, determined by the machine on which it was made. In long-grain paper, the grain runs parallel to the long edge of the paper and in short-grain paper, the grain runs parallel to the short edge.

Other Distinguishing Features. The natural deckle is the rough finished edge of the paper. On handmade paper it is on four sides, whereas on moldmade paper it is only on the two outside machine edges. Natural deckles run parallel to the grain; imitation or torn deckles run at right angles to it.

Weight and Size. The weight of the paper should be taken into account when making prints. If a sheet is large, it also needs to be heavy to enable it to be handled successfully. Papers come in a huge choice of weights, but the heavier the paper, the more difficult it is to handle.

Acidity is produced by impurities or bark in wood pulp; rag papers should be acid free. The presence of acid makes the paper brittle and causes deterioration and discoloration. If prints are interleaved with tissue for storage, this should also be acid free, as acid can spread through stored prints and harm them.

Stencils

Screen process printing is a stencil process and is based on the principle of blocking out areas of mesh in order to prevent color passing through while leaving clear open areas which do allow ink through. There are two basic types of stencil: direct and indirect. Direct stencils are made on the mesh, while indirect stencils are processed separately and adhered to the mesh at a later stage.

INDIRECT STENCILS

Hand-cut Paper Stencils. Using newsprint or tracing paper for your stencils is ideal for the beginner in one respect – it enables you to experiment inexpensively. However, remember that a paper stencil is naturally less durable than film. You can draw direct on paper or trace from an original drawing and cut with knife or scissors. The paper pieces laid on the screen bed adhere to the mesh with the first pass of squeegee and ink, so you do not need to have links between all the shapes. "Floating" pieces must be positioned carefully at the start, but will then become self-adhesive.

Even if you keep to a fairly simple design you can create exciting variations by trying different ways of inking. Color blends and variegations are easy to form on a screen. This demonstration also shows the use of talcum powder to obtain a mottled texture: the talc is pressed into the mesh at the first inking and forms a block in the same way as a sheet material or liquid filler.

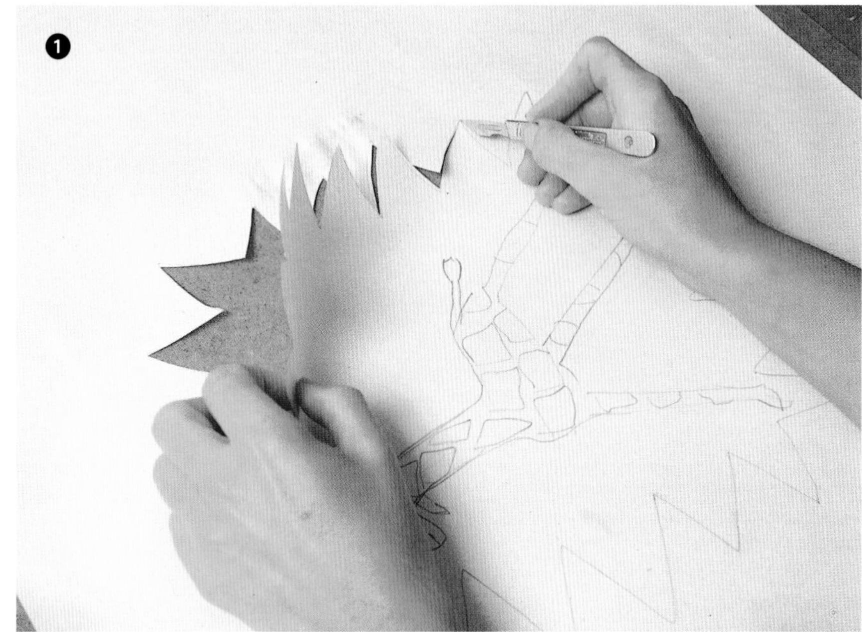

1 A simple design is freely cut from newsprint – a starburst with an animal figure inside. You can use freestanding shapes within a paper screen stencil, as each piece individually adheres to the screen mesh.

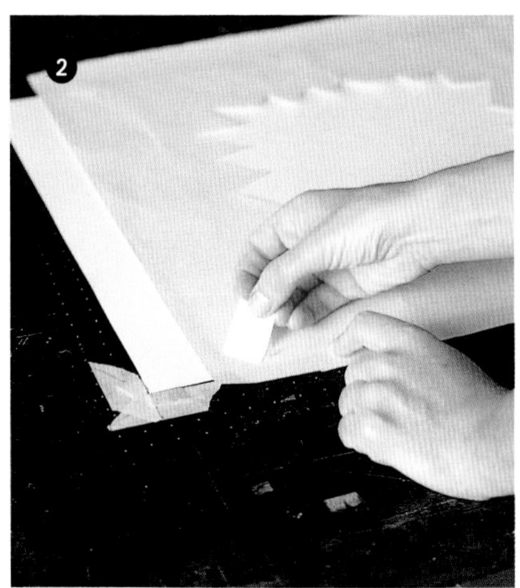

2 Position the printing paper on the screen bed and mark the corner. Lay the paper stencil over it in the required position. You can put pieces of double-sided tape at the corners to help the stencil attach to the screen.

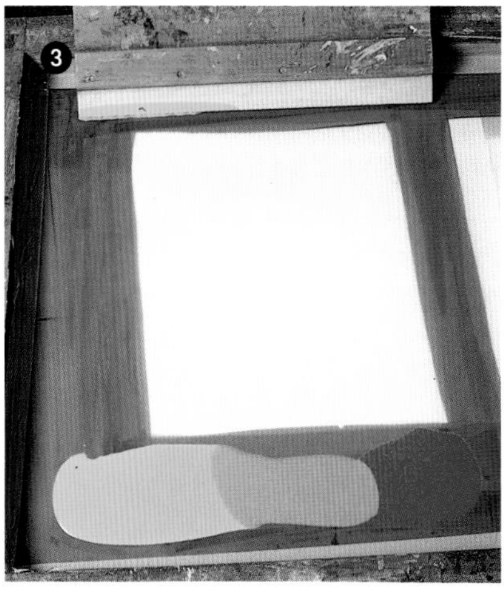

3 Lay out the ink along the bottom of the screen. To make a blend of colors, pour a small pool of each color and let them flow gently together.

4 Lift the screen and flood the color back into the mesh by pushing the squeegee upward. Then lower the screen and pull the other way to make the print.

5 The starburst shape and the cutout of the giraffe can be seen sticking to the underside of the mesh, while their silhouettes are clearly printed on the paper in the warm color blend.

6 To add texture using talcum powder, make a paper stencil outlining the shape to be printed and attach it to the screen. Shake talc freely but loosely onto the print.

7 Lower the screen and print the required color in the usual way. The movement of the squeegee presses the talc into the screen mesh, acting as a block to the ink. This forms a random, lacy pattern.

8 It is easy and economical to experiment using these techniques. This example has been printed using the discarded section cut out of the previous stencil. The giraffe appears this time as a positive image, while the starburst is the negative shape.

Hand-cut Film Stencils. The advantage of using hand-cut stencils is that all the elements of the printed image are prepared away from the screen. If you get something completely wrong, you can remake the stencil. When cutting film stencils, you can see through the material, so it can be placed over a working drawing to guide the cutting.

When you plan the image, you must take into account that paper or film stencils give you hard-edged, graphic shapes. Each color to be printed requires a separate stencil. If the ink is fairly transparent you can obtain color "mixtures" by overprinting one hue on another, and build up quite complex effects of pattern and form by varying the shapes and details of each overprinting.

1 Stencil film has two layers: the colored stencil and a clear backing sheet. Use a fine scalpel to cut lightly into the top layer. Here the artist is using a working sketch slipped under the stencil as a guide.

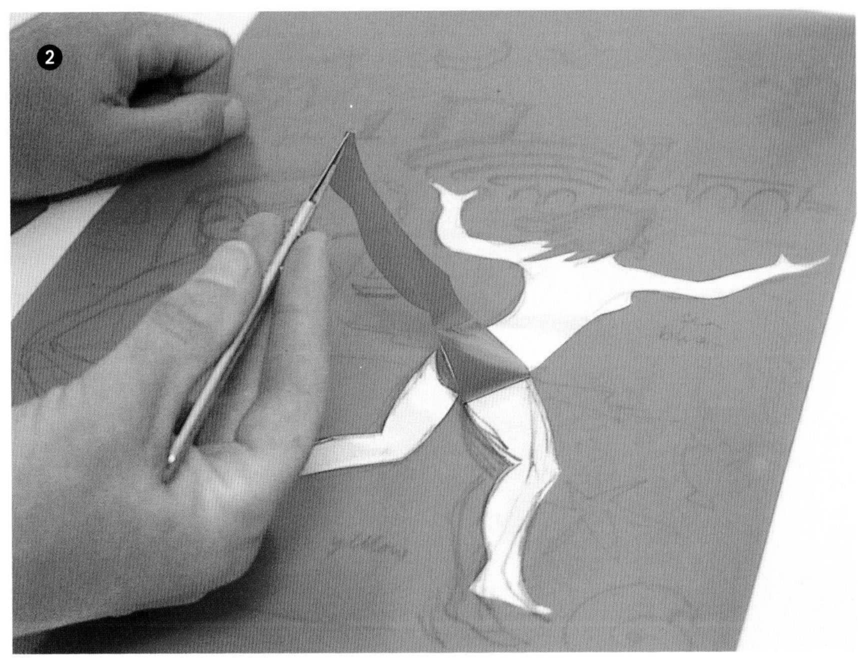

2 When you have cut a shape in outline, use the point of the knife to lift one edge or corner, then peel back the cut shape.

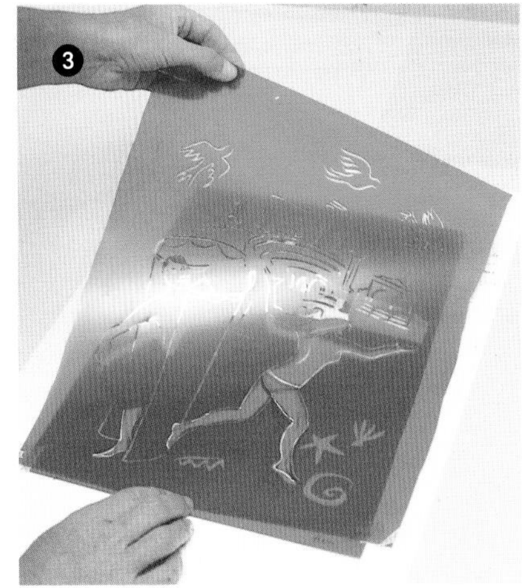

3 Prepare stencils for each of the colors you are to print and check that the shapes align by overlaying them one on another. In this demonstration, six colors are to be printed: pink, yellow, light blue, red, mid-blue, black.

4 Position the stencil under the screen mesh. Because a large screen is used here, and the stencils are relatively small, the artist is placing three stencils side by side on one screen.

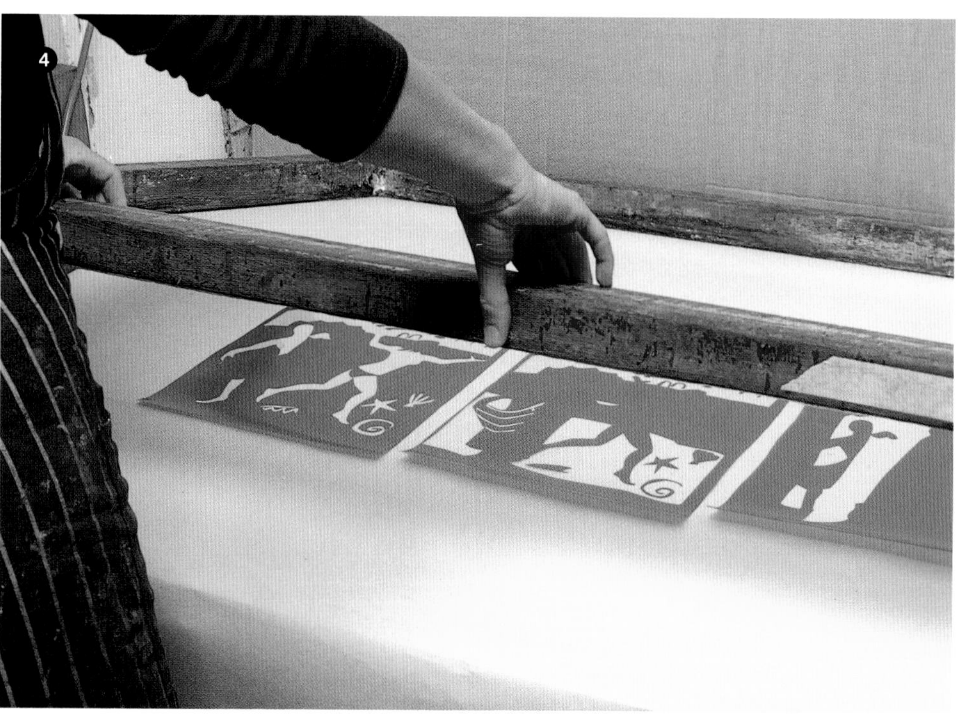

5 Lower the screen so the mesh lies flat on the stencil and spray clean water on the mesh. This softens the stencil material so it will adhere to the screen. You must move quickly to the next stage.

6 Lay a clean piece of newsprint over the screen and blot firmly with your hands, creating pressure that sticks the stencil to the mesh. Because this has to be done quickly, if you are putting more than one stencil on the screen, do each in turn rather than all together.

7 When all of the stencils adhere to the screen, allow them to dry out completely. You can speed up the process by using a hot-air dryer.

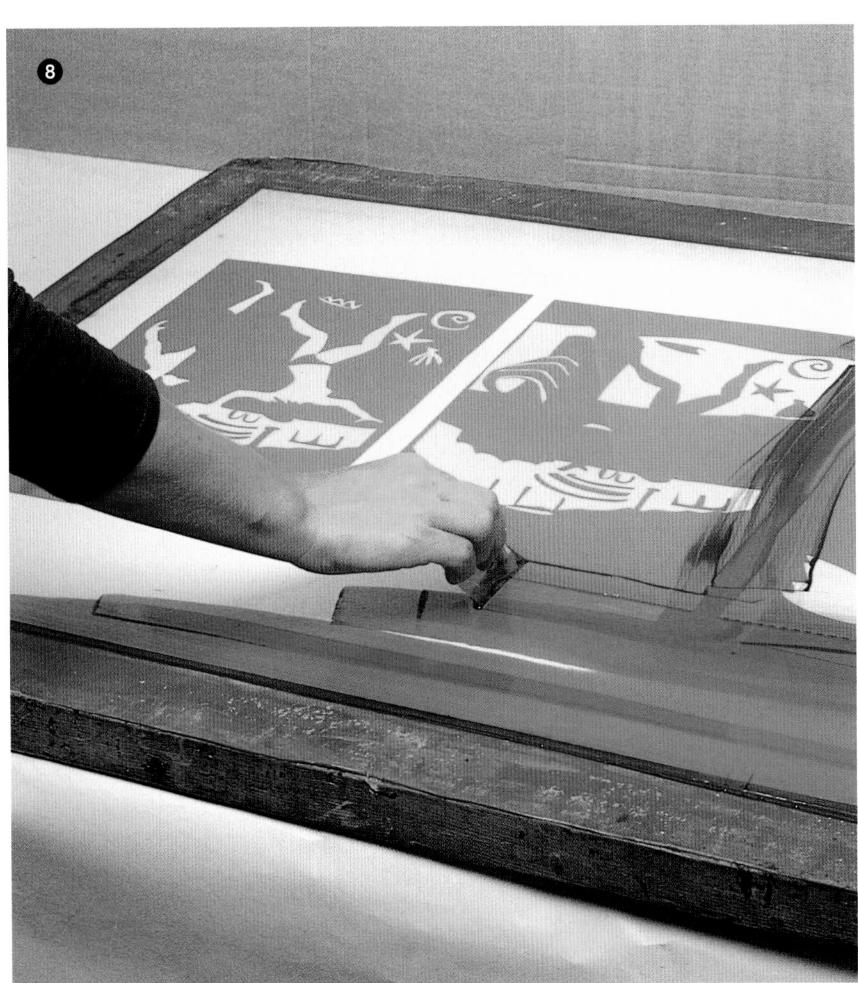

8 To block out the open areas of the screen mesh surrounding the stencils, turn the screen upside down and spread a liquid filler around the borders. The simplest way to do this is to use a small piece of card to pull the liquid across the mesh.

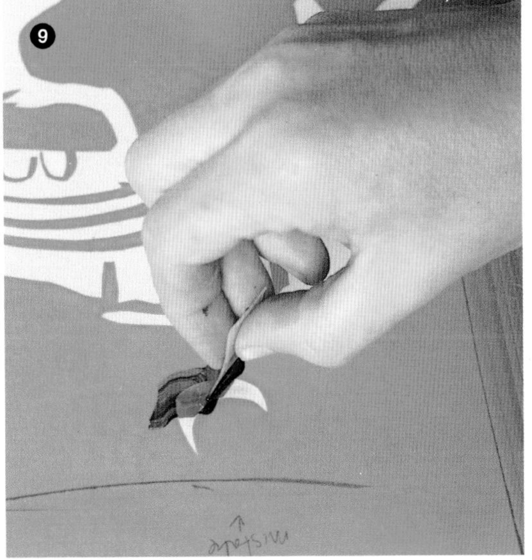

9 Any errors on the stencil can be blocked out in the same way. Here the artist fills in a shape that is not intended to print.

Direct stencils

Stencils have been painted onto the screen using filler since the end of the last century. It is probably the most common form of stencil-making.

Stencils made with filler usually require the artist to work negatively, that is, if a brush mark is painted on to the screen, it will appear as a negative when printed. To make the process easier, the design can be outlined on the mesh with a soft pencil to determine the areas which will need to be painted. Sharp edges or lines can be masked off using tape and filler applied with a small piece of cardboard. Fillers are usually either water soluble (for use with oil- or solvent-based inks) or spirit based (for used with water-based inks).

Red, Green, and Blue Fillers. There are three types of water-soluble filler. Red flash-dry filler, as its name suggests, dries instantly. Its main uses are for pre-masking and edge-filling stencils made of other materials, and for repairing or spot-filling leaks in stencils while the print is being printed. Green filler is a moderately fast-drying fluid, which has a high viscosity and elasticity that makes it ideal for masking, painting, or retouching stencils and spot-filling stencils before starting to print. Blue filler is the most useful material for making handmade stencils: it dries slowly and can be thinned extensively to enable it to be used for painting, spraying, and stippling on screens.

If water-based inks are to be used, filler made from a mixture of shellac flakes and denatured alcohol (French polish) should be used. This filler, though more difficult to remove when dry than its water-soluble equivalent, is suitable for fine brushwork and dries very quickly.

Whatever kind of filler you choose, it is important to match the thickness of filler to the mesh of the screen. The thinner the filler, the finer the mesh required; very coarse meshes may not be suitable for filler stencils as there is a risk that the resulting images will "saw tooth." In some cases, it maybe preferable to apply several thin coats of filler rather than a single thick coat.

Filler stencils can be applied with brushes, cardboard squeegees, sponges, or fabrics to produce textures. Spray guns (which produce negative dots) can be loaded with thinned filler and sprayed on to the screen. Contact prints may be taken from any surface which has previously been coated using a roller with the filler. Whatever method of production is used, it should be on a mesh that is capable of retaining the detail of the mark made.

MAKING A STENCIL EDGE WITH RED FILLER

1 First, rule a line on the mesh with a soft pencil to show the area that needs covering. Apply filler first to the underside of the screen starting at the corner closest to you, using a card squeegee to spread the filler parallel to the frame.

2 After two minutes to allow the filler to dry, invert the screen and treat it in the same way. Prop the frame to stop the underside sticking to the table.

USING FILLER

1 When painting the filler directly onto the screen mesh, you may find it easiest to place a working drawing or sketch under the mesh as a guide, as shown here.

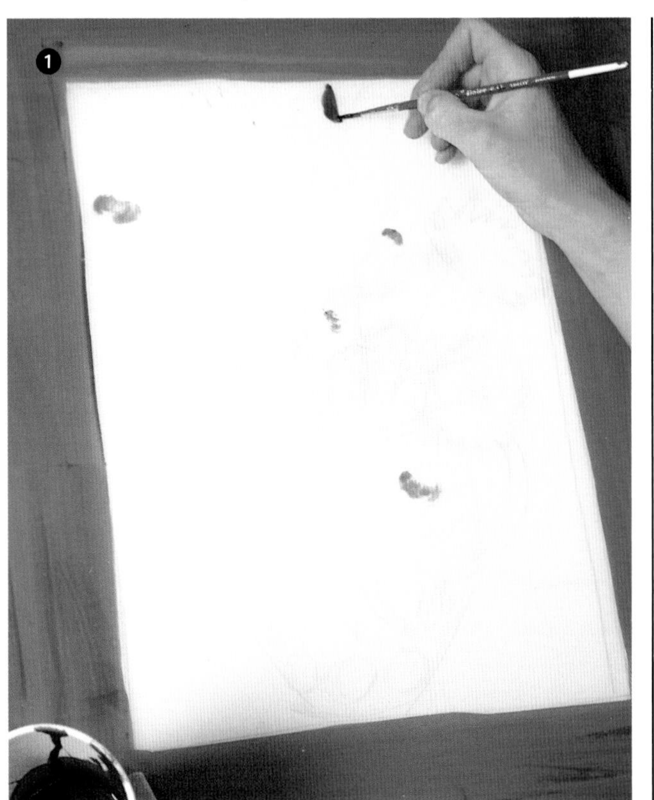

2 In this example, the artist begins with a stencil that will print blue. To allow for overprintings that will form mixed hues, only the flowers and outline pattern on the vase are blocked out.

Cellulose Filler is another type of filler which can be exceptionally useful when changes need to be made to existing stencils. Because it is neither oil- nor water-soluble it can be used to change or re-work stencils made from other materials, which are then printed. When the image has been printed, the filler can be removed using cellulose cleaner and the stencil returned to its original state. Another use for cellulose filler is when a reverse image of the stencil is required. Use a water-solvent stencil to print the design, then apply celulose filler to the stencil with a squeegee and allow it to dry. Finally the original stencil is removed with water, leaving a new reversed stencil in its place.

Stage proofs

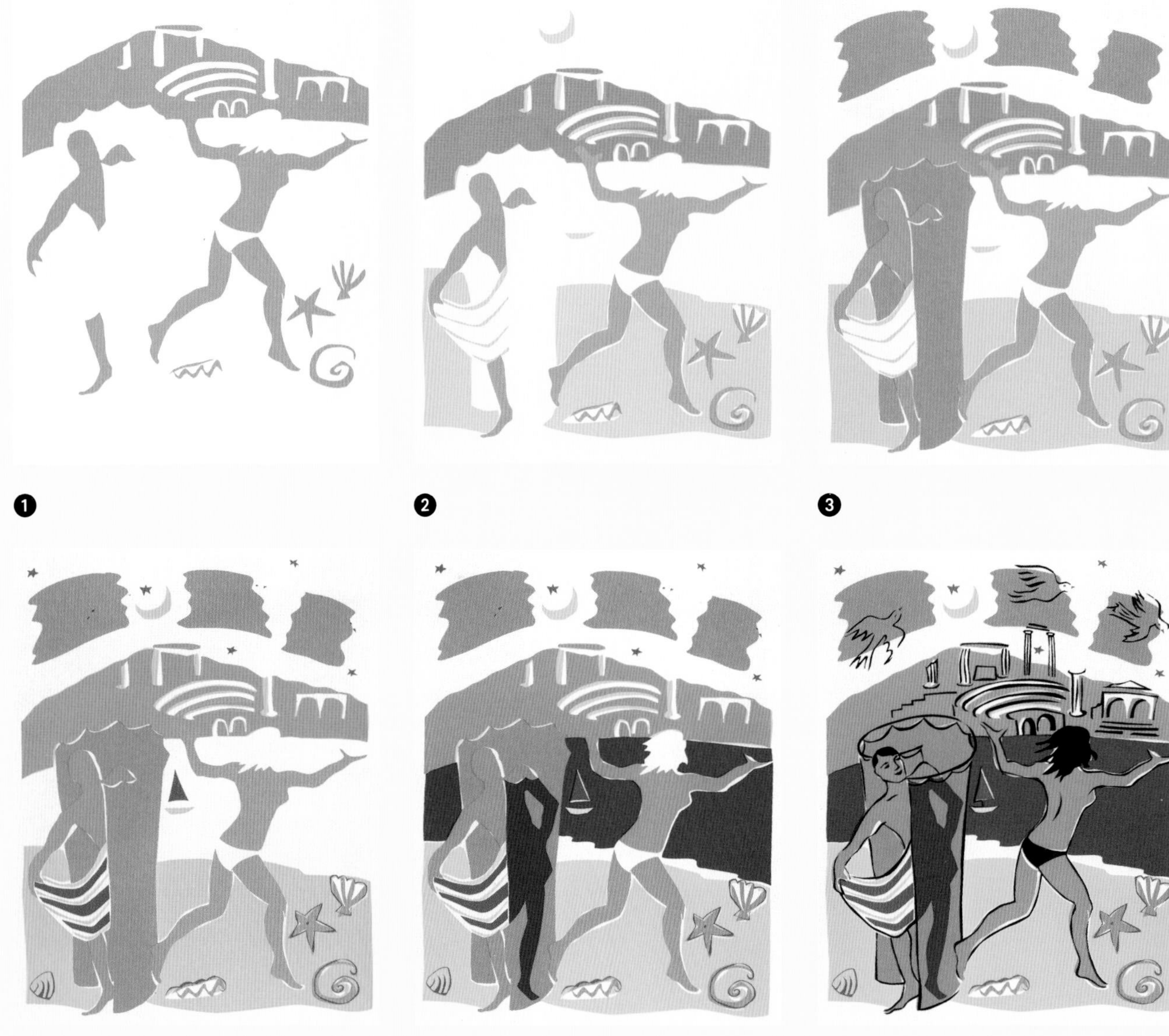

This sequence shows how the image develops new form and depth with each color printing. Notice, in the second stage, that the overprinting of transparent yellow on pink has produced a "mixed" color – a warm orange. Although each stencil image consists of hard-edge shapes, the artist has successfully achieved a free, lively style of image by using small shapes and patterns to break up the broad color areas. She keeps the final, black printing very linear, to sharpen the detail.

PAINTING ON THE SCREEN MESH

Painting on the screen mesh with liquid filler is a direct way of working, enabling you to produce more free and painterly effects. The drawback for the inexperienced printmaker is that the design has to be worked out negatively – the brushmarks create the non-printing areas. However, because you can see through the screen mesh, you can place a working drawing underneath to guide you as you paint the stencil image; then it is only a matter of concentration.

This demonstration sequence shows how effectively you can utilize overpaintings of semi-transparent colors. The artist uses the process printing colors – cyan (blue), magenta (red), and yellow – with a final overprinting in white. She achieves dark tones such as green and purple, as well as tints of pale blue and pink. This is the same principle as applied in commercial printing, where combinations of the process colors achieve an almost infinite color range – the color photographs in this book are printed using only cyan, magenta, yellow, and black.

3 The second color to be printed is red. Only those areas to remain pure blue are blocked out. The artist applies a sponged texture to the foreground area.

4 The background will remain blue and is fully blocked out, leaving the shapes of the flowers, vase, and tabletop to print in red.

5 The same process is applied to preparing and printing the third stage of the image – the transparent yellow layer.

6 White ink will be used in the last stage, to vary the tones and enhance the textures. The artist prepares the final stencil exactly, by working to the existing print, placed underneath the screen.

7 The white ink is flooded onto the screen and the print is pulled by drawing the squeegee downwards.

Stage proof: one
The first printing shows broad areas of fairly solid, uniform color with little detail visible at this stage.

Stage proof: two
Where the red has overprinted on the original blue, a rich, deep blue-purple is formed that gives depth and weight to the image. Flashes of the white paper remain where the mesh has been blocked out on both stencils.

Stage proof: three
The yellow overprints on both the blue and red, producing green and scarlet respectively. This completely transforms not only the color balance of the image but also the description of the shapes.

Stage proof: four
The white ink creates paler tones of all the original colors, and where it is printed over red and blue, it makes a neutral, warm gray. Using only four colors, the artist has produced a wide range of hues and tones, and some fascinating textures.

Tusche

The method of preparing stencils by the tusche method is similar to the filler method, but there is one crucial difference – this is a resist technique which produces a "positive" stencil. The image is drawn up with tusche (drawing ink) and/or lithographic crayon, both of which are oil-based materials with a greasy texture.

The finished drawing on the screen mesh is coated with gum arabic and is allowed to dry. This acts to block the mesh, as does blue filler, but does not adhere to the tusche. The image is then washed out with mineral spirit, but the gum arabic, being water-soluble, remains in place. The open areas of the stencil are now those marks that you originally drew and painted, so that the printed image is a positive reading of what was first applied.

Using tusche

1 Work directly on the screen with tusche, using any typical painting techniques. This picture shows spattering applied with a toothbrush between paper masks, after parts of the image have been drawn with a paintbrush.

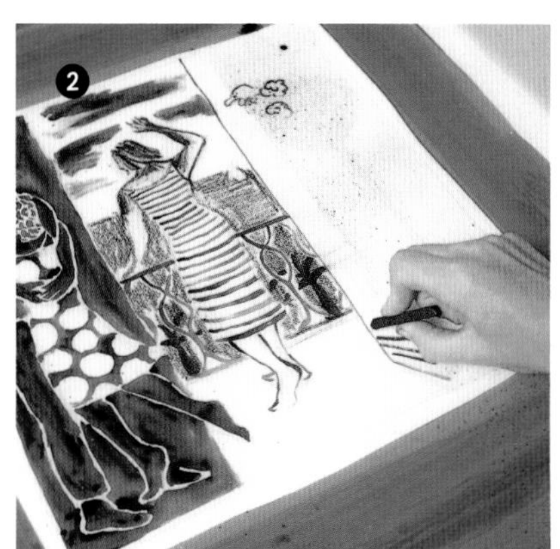

2 Lithographic crayon can also be used to give a different quality of line. Technically, it acts on the screen mesh in the same way as the tusche. To make the first stencil you can draw

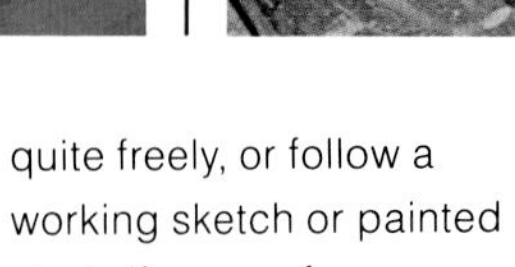
quite freely, or follow a working sketch or painted study if you prefer.

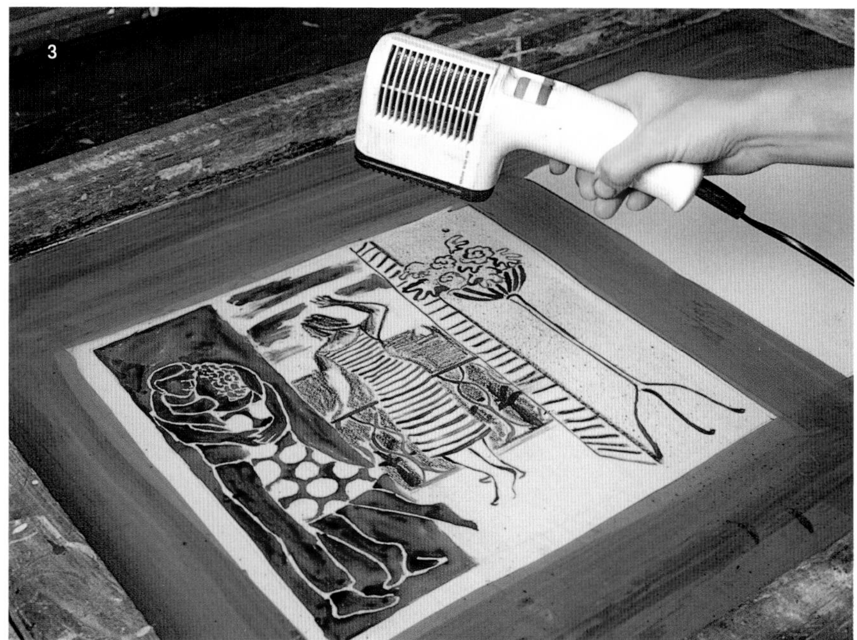

3 Allow the painting on the mesh to dry out completely before moving on to the next stage. To save a long wait, you can use a hairdryer to speed up this process.

4 Spread a thin layer of gum arabic over the whole image area. Use a small rectangle of card or plastic to help coat the mesh quickly and evenly. Allow the gum to dry.

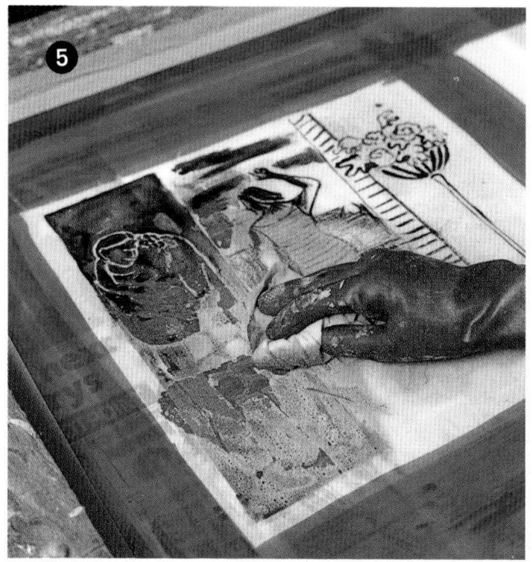

5 Wash out the tusche image with mineral spirit applied with a rag or sponge. This has no effect on the gum arabic, so you are left with a gummed stencil consisting of the negative areas of your drawing; therefore the positive marks will print.

Stage proof: one

The first printed image has a fresh, painterly quality with interestingly varied textures. The rough shading of the sea was made by a frottage technique, placing the mesh over a board, then rubbing over it with the lithographic crayon.

Finished print

Second or subsequent colors can be printed by preparing stencils in the same way, using the original print or your working sketch as a guide. The mid-toned green and pale flesh tint applied here maintain a bright, airy quality appropriate to the subject, while overprinting on the left-hand side introduces an effect of deep shadow.

Inking and printing

The process of registering color printings on the screen bed is quite simple.

Where color areas are to be butted together, you should allow a very tiny overlap when cutting the separate stencils for each color, as otherwise you may get a white line between them as you print the colors individually. This demonstration sequence shows the basic methods of inking and printing. The simple technique of laying out ink and pulling the squeegee across the mesh is standard however the screen stencils are prepared.

1 This demonstration shows printing on a screen frame attached to a vacuum-bed printing table. The screen is securely locked into the frame. The lowered screen does not quite lie flush with the bed – a small gap, known as "the snap," allows for the "give" in the screen mesh when the squeegee passes over.

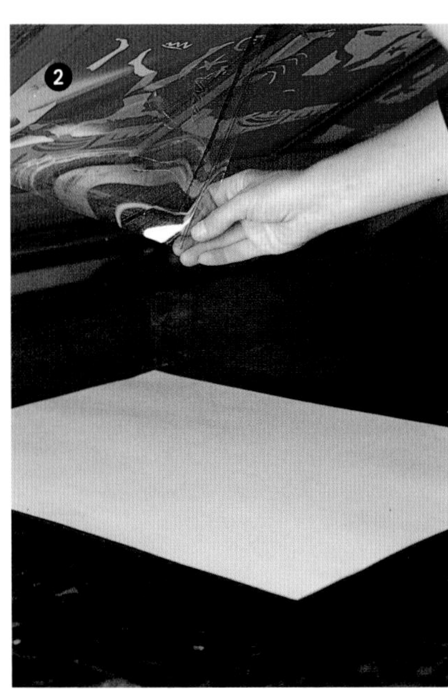

2 The plastic backing on the stencils must be removed before they can be used to print. Take hold of one edge, and peel the backing off smoothly.

3 Tape the edges of the screen all round to form a reservoir for the ink and ensure that no color bleeds under the mesh where it joins the screen frame. You can use gummed paper tape or self-adhesive tape.

4 If you have more than one stencil on the screen, use paper to cover those not printing at this stage. This keeps them clean and prevents ink bleeding through beyond the borders of the first stencil.

5 You need to put registration marks on the screen bed so the image is correctly positioned on the paper. The artist uses the original working sketch to locate the printing area.

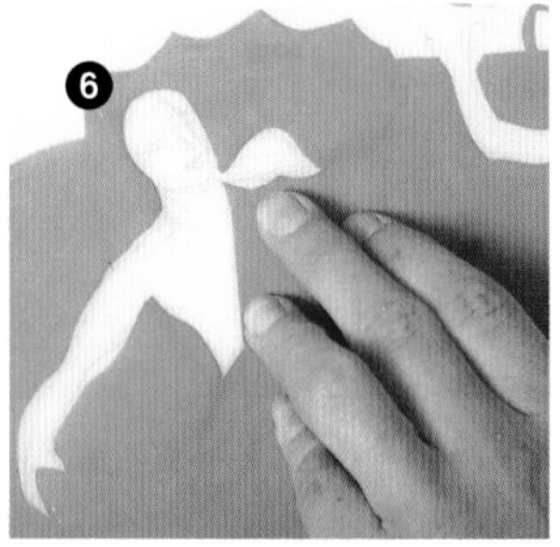

6 The sketch is moved around until it is accurately aligned with the stencil image. This picture showed the screen lowered and the artist checking the alignment through the mesh.

7 When the paper is in the correct position, the left-hand lower corner and edge are marked with pieces of masking tape stuck to the screen bed. The printing paper will be positioned against these guides each time the first color is printed.

8 Mix your ink colors in sufficient quantity to allow for the required number of prints. Screenprinting ink is a thick liquid and is commonly mixed in waxed-paper cups; any leftovers can be stored this way.

9 Pour the ink in an even flow across the bottom border of the screen, below the image. It puddles outwards but, because it is viscous, does not flow into the stencil area.

10 Lift the screen slightly and use the squeegee to push the ink back across the mesh, flooding the color into the image area.

11 Position the clean piece of printing paper on the screen bed, aligned to the register marks previously taped in place. Lower the screen over the paper.

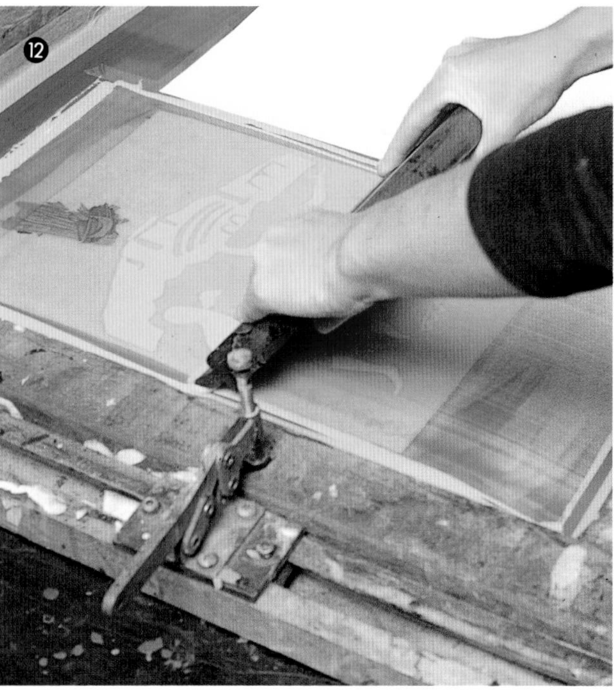

12 Place the squeegee in the layer of ink at the top of the screen and pull it firmly and evenly across the image area. You must use a squeegee that covers the whole width of the stencil, and keep it firmly horizontal as you pull.

CLEANING THE SCREEN

After you have finished printing you must clean the screen. It is advisable to wear rubber gloves for protection, as some solvents can irritate the skin. A spatula or piece of cardboard can be used to scoop up any excess ink and replace it in the container. The squeegee should be held in a vertical position above the container and carefully scraped with the card or spatula, allowing excess ink to be saved. The frame can be detached from the hinges and cleaned outside by placing it on a pile of newspapers and pouring on the appropriate solvents.

Turpentine substitute will remove oil-based inks, and those preparations containing toluene and ethylacetate will effectively dissolve most screen inks. Stubborn, hardened inks will be easily cleaned by the use of universal screen wash. Most solvents are highly inflammable, and cheaper types are highly toxic and should not be inhaled for long periods. If the screen remains on the baseboard, first place old cardboard or newsprint underneath and rub the inside with rags impregnated with solvent, replacing the newsprint as necessary until very little color is left. Use a clean soaked rag on the underside of the screen in a counter-movement with the rag rubbing the inside mesh. Repeat until no trace of color remains on the rags. Care must be taken in rubbing the underside as this is the surface to which the stencil adheres.

1 Between each printing, you must clear the screen of ink. Use the squeegee to collect excess ink into a puddle, then pick it up on a palette knife.

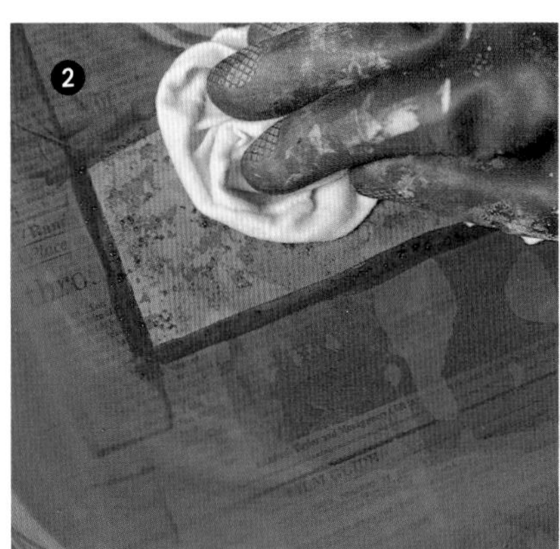

2 Wash the ink out of the stencil with the appropriate solvent. In this demonstration, oil-based ink is being cleaned off with mineral spirit.

3 When printing from one stencil is complete, it can be cleaned out of the screen mesh. Here, water-based filler is flushed out with a spray jet: the screen stands upright in a purpose-made trough. Stubborn traces of filler can be scrubbed with a soft brush.

CHAPTER SIX

PHOTOCOMPOSITION

The photostencil freed the screenprint from its early coarseness and enabled prints of great detail to be printed hundreds of times without serious deterioration of the image. Anything which can be made acceptably opaque can be used as a positive and made into a stencil that can be printed.

Before discussing photostencils in detail, it may be useful to differentiate between the terms positive, photopositive, autographic positive, and photostencil.

A **Positive** is any image, usually on a transparent or translucent base, that is opaque enough to prevent ultraviolet light from reaching photostencil material when it is placed in contact with it. Examples of materials used to make positives include black paint or photographic opaque on tracing film, red lithographic tape or masking film on a transparent base, amber cut stencil film, a sheet of Letraset, torn black paper, soft black crayon on tissue paper, any opaque object, and any high contrast photographs or photocopies which are on transparent film as opposed to paper. It may be slightly confusing to learn that a positive is always positive, even when the image is negative. This is because whatever constitutes the opaque element of a positive is what will eventually print.

Photopositives (as photographic positives are known) are generated in the darkroom by enlarging existing negatives or transparencies, or by photographing artworks onto film.

Autographic Positives are drawn, painted, sprayed, collaged, frottaged, or otherwise handmade with an opaque medium on transparent or translucent material.

Photostencils are the means by which all of these types of positive can be made into printable images. This is done by placing the positive in direct contact (preferably in a vacuum frame) with photostencil material and exposing both to ultraviolet light through the back of the positive. The resulting stencil is then applied to the screen. As for other types of stencil, the screen has to be selected for mesh count and prepared, before a photostencil can be applied to it. The photostencil has to be dried, masked, and spotted before being printed.

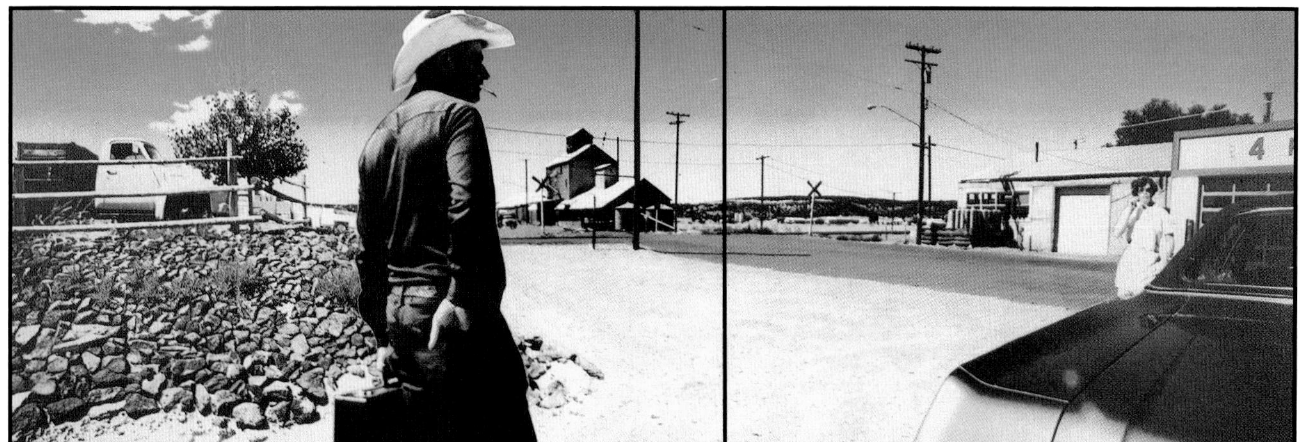

Passing Through
(photomontage)
by Boyd and Evans
Created from photographic elements with four-color separation. The sky color was applied as a blend and there are hand-worked areas.

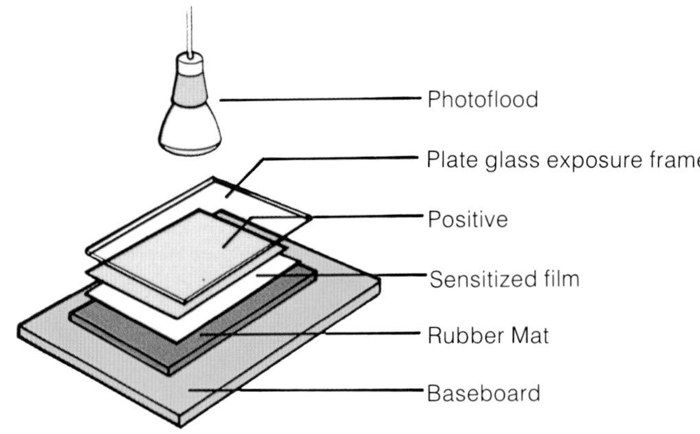

▲ A homemade light source using a photoflood.

TOOLS AND MATERIALS

There are four types of photostencil material for making screenprint stencils: direct, indirect, capillary, and direct/indirect.

Direct Photostencil film is the least expensive of the photostencil films and is relatively easy to process. It must be used if water-based or textile inks are required.

Indirect Photostencil film comes in the form of a roll of light-sensitive film, supported on a transparent backing sheet. The process for making an indirect photostencil is similar to that for a direct photostencil except that it is made away from the screen and attached to it after it has been developed. Capillary film is also used for the indirect method as it provides accurate registration and is very sensitive to detail. It also has the advantage over all indirect films in that it can be cut to the required size.

Direct/Indirect Photostencils. The direct/indirect stencil film is bonded to the mesh with photostencil emulsion, which is applied with a soft, rounded squeegee to the ink side of the screen. The method of application is the same as for the capillary film.

WHICH FILM TO USE

All photostencil films have advantages and disadvantages so it is important to experiment to find out which is the most suitable for any individual printmaker. The indirect film is the most consistent in quality and has the ability to produce fine detail. It has the added advantage that it is ready

▼ Photostencil materials

There is a wide range of photostencil materials suited to all types of printing methods. Some are designed to bond well or to stand up to long print runs, while others are particularly well-suited to fine line or half-tone work.

for exposure and does not require elaborate equipment, as only the stencil is exposed and washed out, rather than the screen. Indirect stencils are also easier to remove from the screen when printing has been completed.

LIGHT SOURCE

A light source is needed to expose the stencil film and the type of source will affect eventual quality of the stencil.

The best source is the metal halide lamp which is available in 2 and 5 Kilowatt models. (The latter can be switched to 2 Kilowatt for use with materials such as daylight film.) However, a fairly efficient homemade light source can be made using a photoflood. But make sure it is correctly wired using the manufacturer's recommended components.

MAKING PHOTO STENCILS

Direct Photo Stencils. There are many effective forms of direct photo stencil emulsion now available. When you are using this form of stenciling, the mesh on the frame is coated with the photo-sensitive emulsion and, after drying, is exposed to a light source which passes through a positive transparency. The areas of the positive which are opaque and which are to be represented in print protect the emulsion so that it remains soft and can be washed away later in the process. Those areas which are exposed to the light are hardened so that they become impervious to the printing ink.

PREPARING A DIRECT PHOTOSTENCIL

1 Fill a coating trough with light-sensitive emulsion. Draw the trough up the screen at an angle to lay an even coating of emulsion on the mesh.

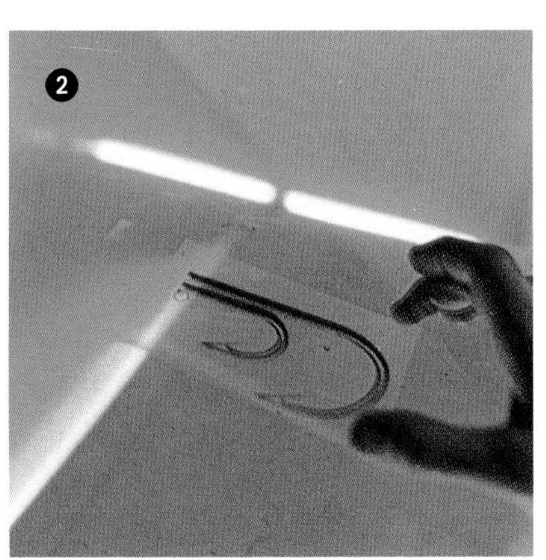

2 Dry off the coated screen in a dark room. Place the photopositive on the exposure unit with the image reading the right way round as you look at it.

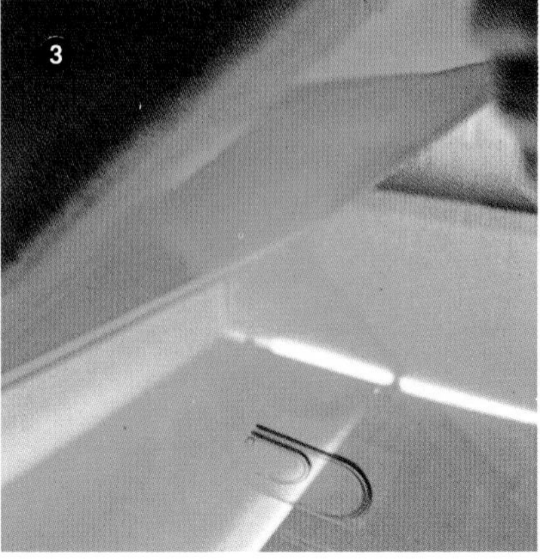

3 Position the light-sensitive screen over the positive. Close the exposure unit and expose the screen to ultraviolet light for the right length of time.

4 After exposure, wash the screen out with water. The emulsion has been hardened by the light but those areas protected by the positive image are washed away.

Indirect Photo Stencils. Indirect stencils are so-called because they are made away from the screen and attached to the screen after they have been exposed and developed. They are mostly quick and convenient to process and are capable of reproducing sharp detail and very fine textures, particularly halftones. A further advantage of indirect stencils is that there is a wide range of products available designed specifically for a whole variety of printing requirements. Whichever type of indirect stencil product you use, the technique of application remains essentially the same. The stencil is usually manufactured in the form of a two-layer film. One of these layers consists of emulsion of the sort used when doing direct photo stencils. The other layer is a transparent backing sheet which is removed after exposure. The emulsion side of the positive is placed in contact with the backing sheet. The film is then exposed to light which is directed through the positive and onto the film. The film is then usually developed in a solution of hydrogen peroxide or in a developing solution provided by the manufacturer. This process of developing further

PREPARING AN INDIRECT PHOTOSTENCIL

1 To make an indirect photostencil, the roll of light-sensitive film, supported on a transparent backing sheet, is cut to the right size, allowing at least 2 inches extra around the positive.

2 Now the film is placed in the printing frame on top of the positive, with the backing side down on the emulsion side of the positive.

3 Here the printing frame is being released into the vertical position prior to exposure. The vacuum has now been switched on to hold the two films hard against each other to prevent the light scattering.

4 After exposure, some films at this stage need to be processed for one minute in a bath of hydrogen peroxide (20 vol). This further hardens those areas of the film exposed to the light.

hardens the areas on the stencil which were exposed to the light.

The stencil is then washed, to remove the soft areas, the shapes of which will print in color. The screen is then lowered onto the stencil and any excess water removed by blotting. Further drying can be done with a cool fan. When the stencil is dry, the plastic backing can be peeled away, gently.

Direct/Indirect Stencils. This method combines both the previous methods. The advantage of this technique is that the durable quality of direct photo emulsion is combined with the accuracy and fine detail of indirect photo stencil film.

The method of application is relatively simple. The screen mesh is laid down on top of the stencil film which is itself laid emulsion side up. A transfer medium is then squeezed through the mesh and onto the film. By doing this, the mesh is impregnated with the film. With the ordinary indirect method, the film is attached only by the drying process. When the transfer medium is dry the backing sheet can be removed and the screen is then ready for exposure. The screen is now processed in the same manner as a direct photo stencil.

5 The film is rinsed with hot water until the areas of emulsion that were covered by the opaque positive, and therefore not affected by the light, have been thoroughly removed. A final rinse with cold water returns the film to its original size and washes out any residual stencil material.

6 Having checked that all particles of the unexposed emulsion have been rinsed from the stencil, it is carefully positioned on the underside of the screen.

7 The stencil is bonded to the screen by laying a sheet of newsprint over it and rolling it gently but firmly with a roller to squeeze out the moisture, and force the stencil into the mesh.

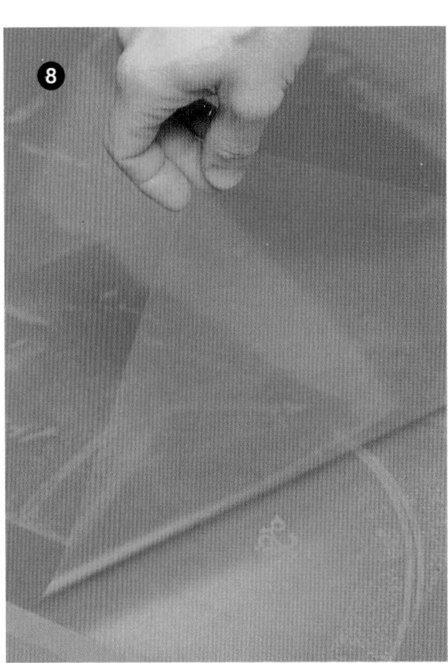

8 Drying can be assisted by a warm hairdryer from the printing side. Once dry, the transparent backing sheet can be removed from the stencil film.

AUTOGRAPHIC POSITIVES

Autographic positives are handmade by the artist with opaque materials on transparent or translucent backings. It is the modern equivalent of the serigraph. The marks made by the artist are accurately translated by the stencil to create a printed image which is a true reflection of the artist's work.

The autographic stencil can be made in any number of ways such as painting with opaque ink on to tracing film; by spraying with an airbrush or spray gun onto film; by drawing directly on film with soft black crayons (toothed tracing film is available which is rather like drawing on a lithographic plate); by taking rubbings with black waxy crayons to produce textures (frottage); by collaging discrete forms to produce an amalgamated image; stippling with a sponge or fabric; or simply coating objects with black ink and contact-printing them on to tracing film. Pre-worked screen stencils can be printed onto transparent sheets, with any color that is UV safe – black, red, amber – and re-worked to produce new stencils.

PHOTOPOSITIVES

The potential range of photopositives is so vast, that to effect even an introduction to it requires a minimal photographic knowledge. Before attempting to make photostencils, the artist should understand about the timing of exposure, aperture opening, depth of field, grain size relative to film spread, and have a rudimentary knowledge of developing and printing photographs. The most basic photopositive can be made by placing opaque objects on a sheet of high-contrast (lithographic) film, which is then exposed, developed and fixed. But the simplest truly photographic image can be made by enlarging 35mm black and white negative film on to (lithographic) film. Incidentally, if a high-contrast photographic print or photocopier print is coated with liquid petrolatum on the back, the paper becomes transparent enough to use as a positive. This does not work with resin-coated papers.

PHOTOGRAPHIC IMAGES

Film positives provide the opportunity to combine photographic and autographic images. There are two types of photographic image: continuous tone, and line. A continuous tone film is familiar to anyone with a camera – it is the "normal" type of film which reproduces all tones from black to white. The implication of continuous tone is that every possible tone from black to white (or color) is on the negative. If the negative is magnified, however, it will be found to be made up of tiny, similarly-shaded particles, which are more concentrated in the dark areas than the light Line film reduces the image to black and white, like a silhouette.

Frottage

The artist intends to include a textured area like knotted wood as part of an autographic stencil. A sheet of thin tracing film is placed over a piece of pine and the texture is picked up by rubbing over it with a soft black waxy crayon (right). This frottage may then be used as an autographic positive with a photostencil (below right).

Anonymous Portraits 5 and 6 (autographic screenprints) by Terry Wilson
These autographic screenprints were made by drawing and painting onto the stencils. The paint was applied using a range of techniques – flicked with a paintbrush and splattered with a toothbrush.

CAMERAS AND ENLARGERS

To make a photopositive, first the image is photographed with a camera. The image may be some artwork or a painting or simply a person or landscape. This image is developed onto continuous tone or line film which is then enlarged onto photostencil film.

There are many different makes of camera and enlarger which will produce reasonable positives. The range of 35mm, 2¼ inches square, 4 x 5 inch and 8 x 10 inch formats are all usable with any of the films mentioned in this section. The only thing to bear in mind when purchasing equipment for enlarging, other than cost, is that the larger the format of the negative, the higher the quality of the positive, and the more flexible the system for experimentation. It is difficult to mask or register 35mm film, but relatively easy to do it with an 8 x 10 inch film. A positive register

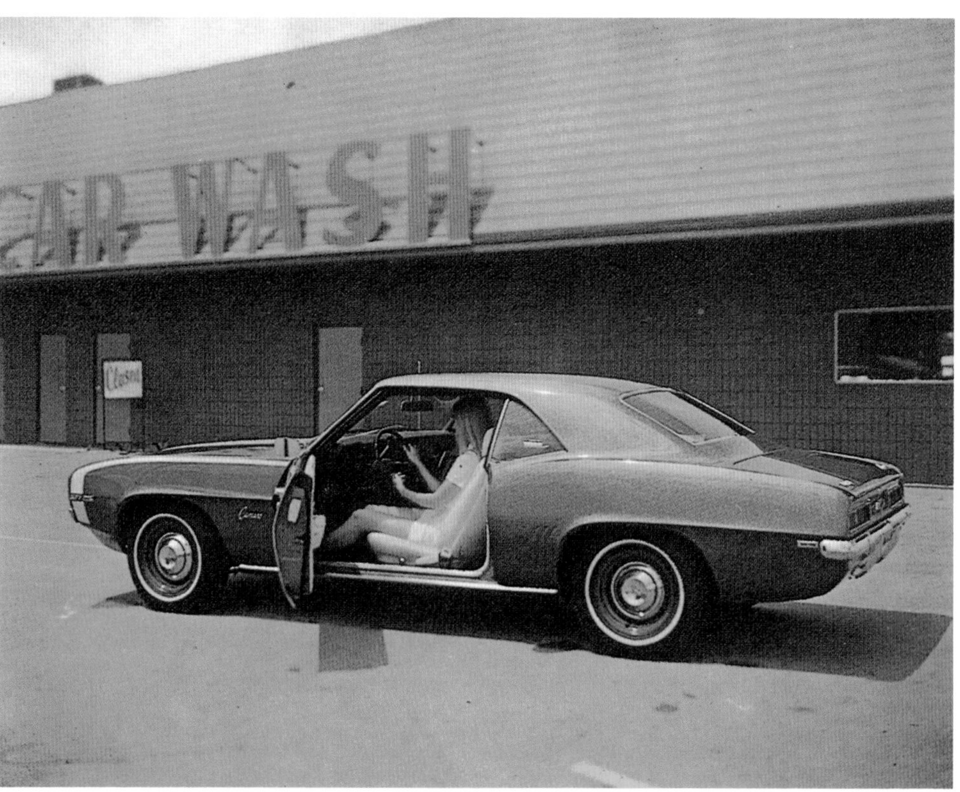

▶ *Car '68*
(photographic print)
by Allen Jones
The point of departure for this 1960s car was a photograph developed on continuous tone film, which was then enlarged onto photostencil film with a half-tone screen interposed to make the positive.

system, made by punching a set of holes which correspond to pins in the head of the enlarger, enables a number of films to be exposed in absolute registration. It is worth remembering too that an enlarger can double as a camera if it is fitted with copy lights.

HALF TONE

In printing, inks cannot reproduce continuous tone, so it has to be approximated by breaking the tonal range of the image into distinct dots or marks which are quantified – 90 per cent dots = dark, 10 per cent dots = light. The most common use of this method – known as half-tone printing – is seen every day in newspaper photographs and advertising posters.

The half-tone effect is achieved by placing a half screen in contact with either the negative in the carrier or the image on the bed of the enlarger, or by interposing a screen between the artwork and the film in the camera back, if a process camera is used. This contact screen breaks up the image into a regular dot matrix in

▲ *Iguana* (posterized print)
by Wendy Taylor
Posterizations made from a pastel drawing were printed with transparent inks from dark to light to create a continuous tone effect.

the case of a half screen and an irregular dot in the case of mezzotint. The regular dot pattern of the half-screen is very difficult to work by hand. Consequently the artist may find the mezzotint, with its affinity to sprayed dots, more useful if creative decisions are to be carried out.

Dot matrix stencils always produce moiré patterns if one of them is overprinted with another. To limit this, the mezzotint screen should be moved through at least 10 per cent each time a new positive is made from the same source material. In the case of the four-color half-tone reprographic process, the screens are moved through 30°, 15°, 15°, as the rulings on the screen for the yellow printer are angled at 45°, the magenta 75°, the black 90° and the blue 105° to any common side. If half-tone positives are applied to the mesh, they should be rotated until coinciding moiré with the mesh fabric is eliminated.

Sainsbury Centre
(photographic print)
by Ben Johnson
Here the perforations in the blinds impose their own grids of dots vying with the much smaller dots of the half-tone screen.

POSTERIZATION

Posterization is an alternative way of creating an illusion of continuous tone. This is achieved by printing a number of over- and under-exposed line film positives made from the same negative with sequential exposure. To exploit this, a continuous tone negative or transparency is projected on to a sheet of light-sensitive film and a test strip is made using a number of exposure times. A selection of these exposure times is made with the intention of producing evenly-spaced, tonal separation. Those separations are then enlarged to produce positives – the greater the number, the closer the approximation to continuous tone. If enlargements are made using positive material (e.g. color transparencies), it is advisable to work with full-size negatives as they are easier to hand work, and at any time new positives can be made by merely contact printing them; it is exceedingly difficult to re-size an enlargement once the image has been removed from the carrier. When posterizations are printed, opaque inks can be used to print from light to dark, or transparent inks can be used or printed in reverse order.

Harrison's Wharf
(posterized print)
by Gerd Winner
The technique used here is more sophisticated than conventional posterization in that negative masks were used to eliminate some areas of color.

DEVELOPING PHOTOSTENCILS

The films discussed can all be processed with the same chemicals, which are suitable for the artist or small studio. Lithographic developer usually comes in two packs, A and B, each of which is diluted 3 parts water to 1 part chemical, before being mixed together to produce the working solution. (Rapid access developers are usually sold in a single pack ready for use.) Developers have a recommended working temperature of 68°F. However, if they are slightly warmer, 70–72°F, a greater range of exposed images may be produced from the same source material such as a negative.

Photographic work should be completed in small batches because developers start to oxidize and deteriorate as soon as they are mixed. The optimum development range for lithographic materials is between 2½ and 3 minutes. It is best to consult the manufacturer's information sheet provided with each film. The state of the developer can be observed in the time it takes for the image to appear on the film. Normally, this should be between 45 and 60 seconds into the development time. If it takes longer, the developer needs renewing.

FIXATIVE

Fixative should be diluted in the ratio of 3 parts water to 1 part fixative. A rule of thumb is that film should be in the solution three times the clearing time of the anti-halation backing. So, if it takes 20 seconds for the pink backing to go transparent, the film should be left another 40 seconds. Fixative can be stored after use until it begins to take too long to clear. The fixed positive should be washed for about 10 minutes in running water and dried in a dust-free cabinet.

PRINTING

No matter which type of stencil has been attached to the screen mesh, there is a basic procedure to follow before printing.

First you must check registration. For successful registration, the position of the stencil relative to the print bed needs to be constant. A reasonable quality print table should prevent any horizontal screen movement from taking place when it is clamped into the master frame. The problem is to make sure that the paper is always placed in exactly the same place. This is achieved by using "lays," three small rectangular pieces of cardboard or plastic taped to the print bed.

Paper, however, is unstable and despite all these safety checks to ensure there is perfect color registration, there may be some distortion if the printing lasts over a few days.

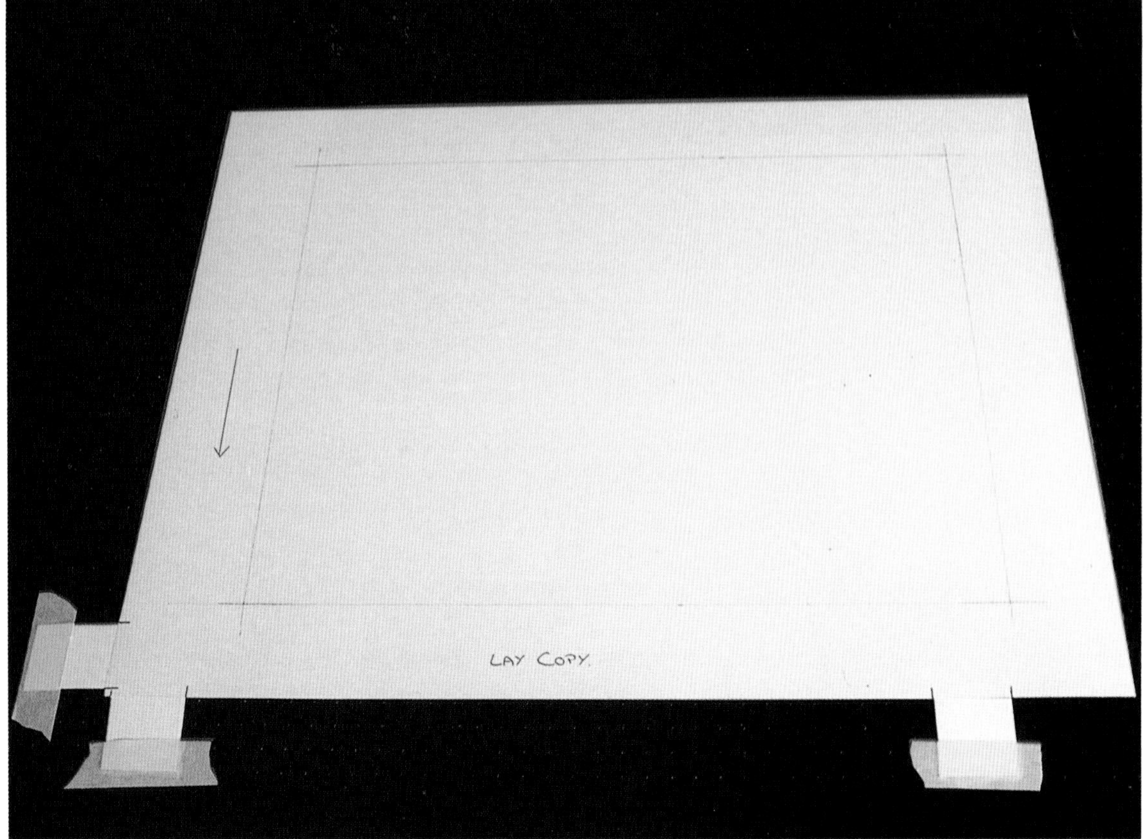

To achieve a clean, sharp print the mesh should not touch the surface of the paper when the frame is lowered into the printing position, but should have a slight clearance to prevent the wet ink from attaching itself to the screen after the squeegee has forced the color through.

The printing process is relatively simple. Raise the screen and place stock against the registration guides. Then lower the screen onto the baseboard. Pour ink into the screen at one end so that it is spread evenly from one side of the frame to the other. Position the squeegee behind the color and close to the frame. Then, standing at the opposite end, pull at an angle of about 45° towards you, maintaining a constant speed and without altering the angle of the blade. This may appear an extremely simple operation but it is, in fact, quite difficult and will probably require considerable practice. As a rough guide, a pull at angles close to horizontal gives a heavy deposit of ink, and an increasing possibility of

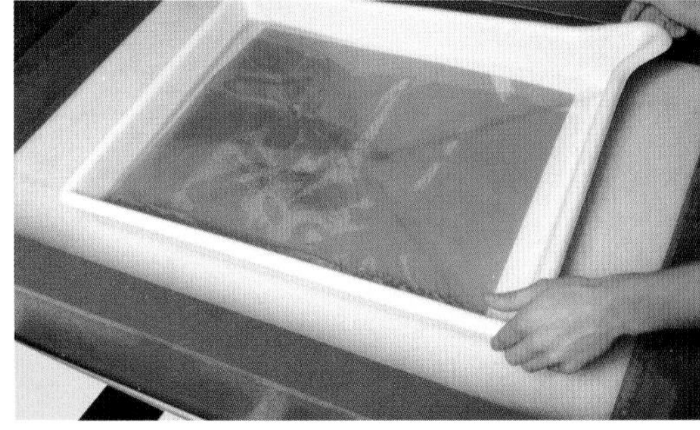

Developing the film

The photopositive film is developed in a shallow dish containing lithographic developer diluted with water as recommended by the manufacturer.

The image should appear after 45 to 60 seconds.

Registering with lays

To make sure that the paper is always placed in the same position on the print bed, lays are used. Lays can be made by sticking double-sided tape to the underside of a small rectangle of plastic in a contrasting color to the print bed and then cutting it into three rectangles, 1 x 2 inches. As can be seen, two rectangles are stuck on the table along the longest edge of the paper. With the paper tight against these two lays, the third rectangle is fixed on an adjacent corner. The two corner lays should be fixed ½ inch from the actual corner of the paper as this often gets damaged, making it difficult to register. Once the register is finalized, the lays should be additionally taped to ensure there is no movement.

the print sticking to the mesh, causing a lack of definition on the edge of the color. A pull at too vertical an angle puts down a very thin, uneven layer of color and may cause the squeegee to jump or skip.

After you have pulled the squeegee down the length of the frame, you can raise the screen, using one hand, and push the squeegee and ink towards the back of the screen with the other. This will deposit a flood coating of ink which ensures an adequate ink deposit for the next pull. Finally, remove the proof and place it in a drying rack.

Taking a handpull

1 With everything ready to print, the ink is poured with the aid of a palette knife into the reservoir.

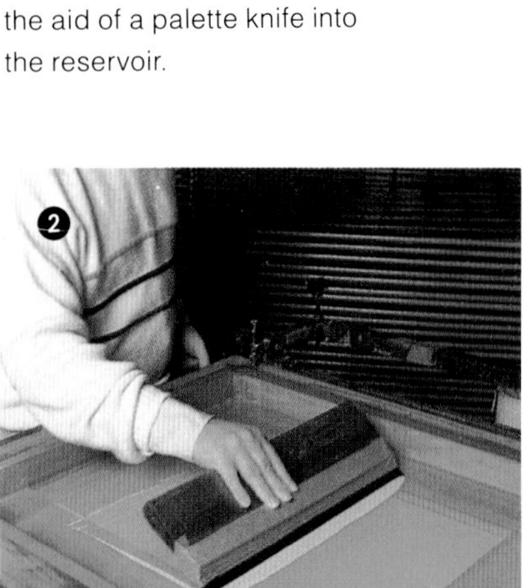

2 To charge the screen with ink, lift the front of the screen and with the other hand place the squeegee behind the ink. Keeping it at a low angle push it away from you across the stencil and about 2 inches beyond it.

3 At the end of this "flood" coat, lift the squeegee cleanly to break the surface tension of the ink.

4 Having lowered the screen, use both hands with a firm even pressure, and pull the squeegee toward you to take your print.

5 Once again, lift the squeegee cleanly off the mesh to prevent the ink from dripping.

CHAPTER SEVEN

ALTERNATIVES IN PRINTMAKING

Artists have always experimented with printmaking techniques, materials, and methods of originating images. Their desire to create certain effects has led them to make imaginative use of existing methods, to combine different processes, and try out unusual surfaces. These extensions and adaptations are an integral part of the history of the medium.

Development of a monoprint

1 Color is rolled up on a glass surface. Paper is placed over the glass and the print taken by rubbing over the back.

2 A sheet of corrugated glass is then inked in a second color and the print taken in the same way.

3 Lastly, a third color is applied to a glass surface by squeezing ink straight from the tube. The print is then taken and the final effect shows a build-up of color in patterns.

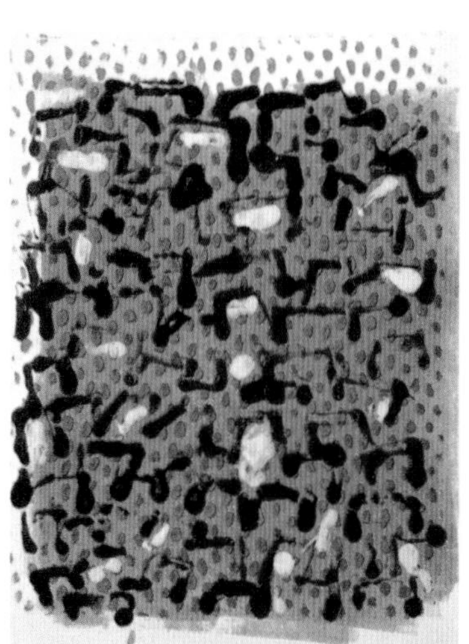

◀ *The Garden* from *Bluebeard's Castle* (3-dimensional screenprint) by Ronald King, with poems by Roy Fisher
This pop-up book is composed of nine designs, screenprinted onto specially folded and cut-out paper, assembled into book form. Each image represents one of the secret rooms in the story of Bluebeard and demonstrates how paper can be manipulated in a striking way within a book format.

Inset Wheels ▶
(multi-media print)
by Michael Rothenstein
This is a print from linoleum and metal relief, with photolithography insets. Rothenstein advocated printing from a variety of materials, either singly or in combination. He often printed his own work by hand, using an old Victorian press.

MIXED MEDIA

Today, artists have far greater access to a variety of printmaking equipment than ever before. Colleges usually offer facilities for all the main processes. Inevitably, when such a choice is available, artists come to realize that certain ideas are best expressed by combining more than one technique.

The usual combinations are screenprinting on top of intaglio or lithography; intaglio on top of relief, lithography or screenprinting; and embossing (using a relief or intaglio press) on any print. The choice of technique obviously depends on the effect that is required. Screen inks cover well and can be used to solve the problem of applying an opaque pale color to a lithograph; metallic and fluorescent inks are also more satisfactory when screenprinted. Fine line work or a three-dimensional emphasis is best achieved by intaglio.

In the sixties, Michael Rothenstein used a combination of hand-cut relief blocks, found objects and process engravings. He also used screenprinting to contrast with relief blocks.

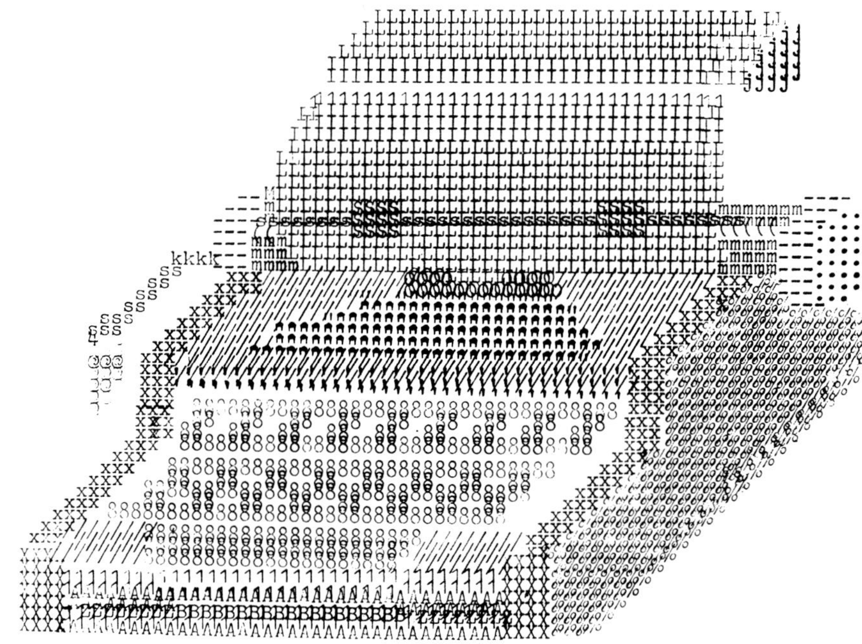

▲ *Typewriter*
(mechanically produced print) by Gary Blake
A print both representing and produced by a typewriter. This mechanistic means of creating images has fascinated many artists throughout the twentieth century and is only one of a variety of office machines which can be used for experimentation.

IMAGES ORIGINATED IN NEW WAYS

One of the differences between pre- and post-sixties printmaking was the use of imagery derived from photomechanics – the use of previously printed material which employs a half-tone screen or the use of half-tones directly on the print. Most artists today regard the camera as a tool for collecting information, much as the pocket sketchbook was to previous generations. In each case, the photograph has to be made into a printing matrix. This usually involves the half-tone screen, but other textural screens with random aquatint effects or parallel, horizontal, and spiral lines – all photomechanical screens – can also be used to create the appearance of tone. Artists have also benefited from developments in continuous tone lithography.

Many other forms of image-making technology, apart from photography, have been exploited by printmakers. The typewriter was twenty-five years old in 1898 when it was first used to make a work of art – a picture of a butterfly.

In the late fifties, typed concrete poetry became popular but many purely visual images have also been made. Initially, the compositions had to be transformed into a photo-plate or screen if they were to be replicated, but nowadays word processors can be used for that task.

The use of the typewriter naturally led on to the use of all forms of office copiers and in-house printing machines. The blueprint, dyeline, and similar proprietary processes used by architects to copy plans discolor rather quickly but are still suitable for producing work intended to be ephemeral.

Copiers now, however, have scanning devices to make photo-stencils from visual material, but the small-scale table-top photo-plate makers have caused the greatest revolution in this field. Once the four-color system became reasonably reliable, electrostatic printing systems caught the imagination of artists, and is widely used today in North America and Europe. If the artist has access to the color printing controls, some very unusual effects can be produced. A copier is not always used to produce an edition as such, but is often a means for trying out color variations for a project which will eventually be realized in more conventional ways.

X-rays, electron-microscope photographs, televison, and video-originated images have all been made use of by artists, but the tool explored with the greatest orginality has been the computer. The computer is perhaps most able at plotting the sequential changes possible in a complex shape seen from many angles and, of course, produces a print-out on paper.

Henri Chopin (mechanically produced print) by Robert Morgan
An example of typewriter art which also incorporates words – in particular the names of artist and subject. The line dividing a "print" and concrete poetry is not always clear-cut.

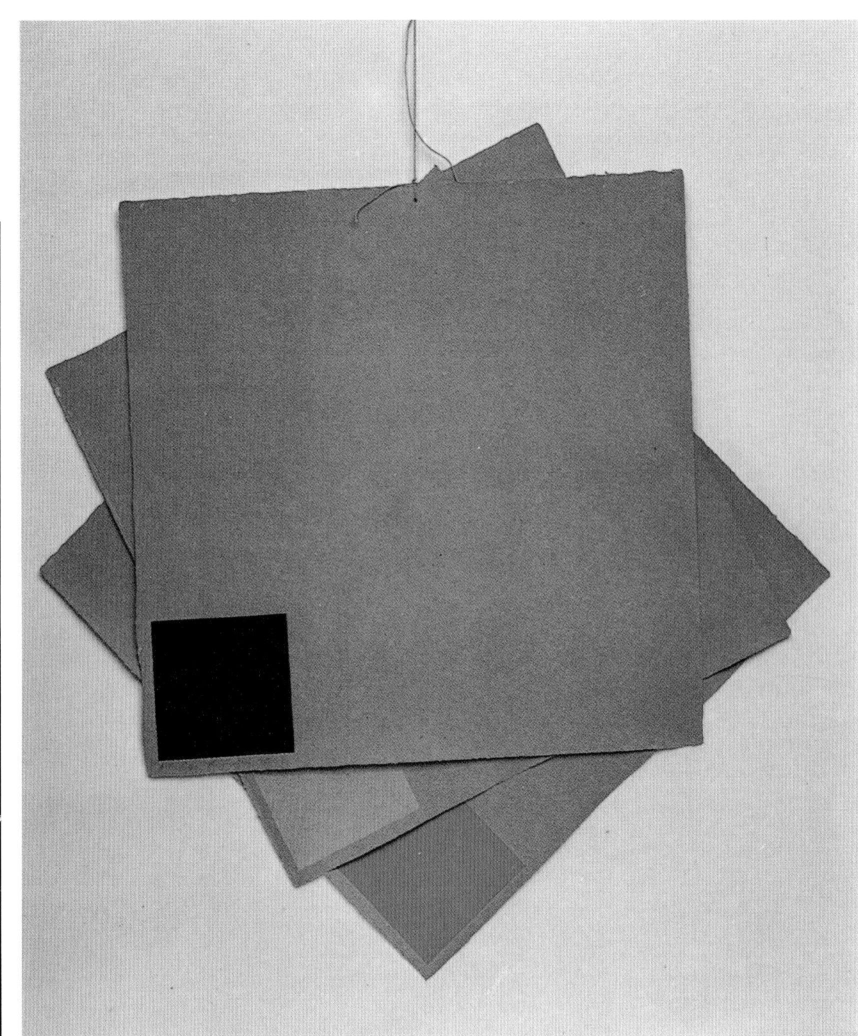

Russian II (multi-media print) by Richard Smith
Made by a combination of intaglio and collage and printed on specially made paper. This print is an example of experimentation with techniques, materials, and the way the finished print is assembled. The three sections which make up the print are joined at the top by string.

COLLAGE AND ASSEMBLAGES

Another preoccupation of the late twentieth century has been collage – particularly in printmaking, in the context of Pop Art. Many different types of objects and pre-printed images have since been glued to prints or assembled with them – paper-clips, advertisements, postcards, plastic toys, rubber bands and plastic bags to name but a few.

Many prints that feature collage do not survive for long. Untried chemical adhesives present the greatest danger; almost all of them have a disastrous effect on paper in the long term. Curators of contemporary print collections are already shaking their heads as the collages disintegrate and discolor.

PAPER MANIPULATION

A significant development in the last few years has been the revival of interest in paper. During the initial enthusiasm for screenprinting when anonymity of the printed surface was sought, characterless paper (often smooth machine-made cartridge paper) was used. Intaglio has always had a more direct and physical relationship with paper, and once the first excitement with screenprinting subsided and artists reassessed the possibilities of other printing methods, interest revived in the vehicle carrying the image.

This interest went further than the choice of a paper with character. During the fifties and sixties, handmade paper mills were closing all over the world, and in reaction, artists and craftsmen tried to preserve and revive these skills, often collaborating to produce a batch of special paper for an edition. In some cases, printmakers made (and still make) their own paper.

FRINGE PRINTMAKING

The distinct categories of printmaking are now becoming blurred as repeatable techniques are used in conjunction with variable ones. Printing is also being done on surfaces hitherto associated only with painting and sculpture. Some "prints" might better be classified as kinetic sculpture which happens to utilize

◀ In this vacuum-formed print by a first-year student at the London College of Printing, the design was screenprinted onto opaque white plastic and drawn down over wooden shapes in the bed of the vacuum frame under vacuum pressure.

▲ Color photocopying has inspired many artists to experiment with the odd color effects that can be achieved by using this process. This print by a first-year student at the London College of Printing was produced by drawing in four colors on cartridge paper with grease pastel and then printing color variations using a four-color photocopier.

print. Other artists have printed transfers or decals which are then applied to ceramics and fired. These, together with other three-dimensional works, are generally called "multiples" but are hard to distinguish in principle from other works called "prints."

Nothing is sacred in printmaking any longer. Most artists in the past had access to only one of the printing processes and consequently experienced some restrictions; without question, the range of technology available today has opened up new vistas and spurred the imagination. It is still worth remembering, however, that technique is only a vehicle for ideas and should enhance rather than dominate.

CHAPTER EIGHT

DISPLAY

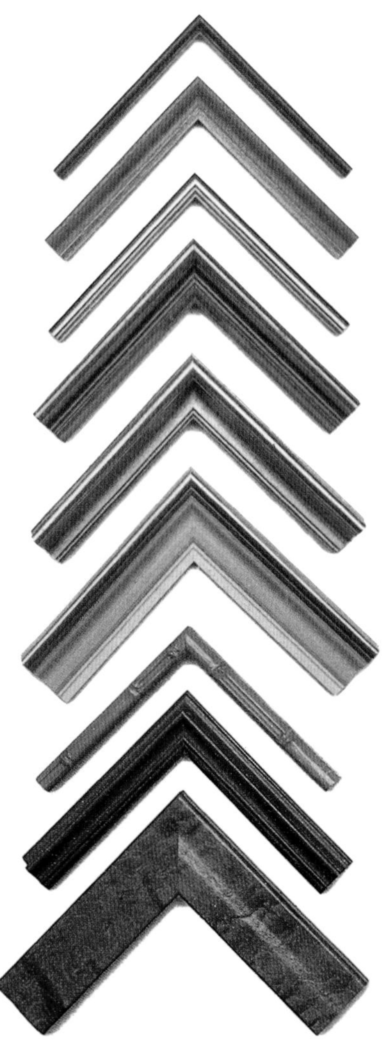

Frames today are no longer confined to basic geometric shapes but can be as large as a mural or small enough to house a miniature. They can be as flat as a sheet of paper or deep as an alcove. They can be triangular, oval, pentagonal, hexagonal, octagonal, or freely contoured, and made from any of the vast range of natural and synthetic materials now available.

The choice of a frame should be given as much thought as the choice of furnishings for your home. It is easy to go out and buy a frame to fit a print but surprisingly few people try out a variety of types to assess different effects.

Whether you choose your frame moldings to make up at home or buy or commission a specific frame from a maker, bear in mind the effect you are trying to create. Good framemakers have a selection of made-up corner pieces and colored mats, as well as finished frames, and it is worth spending time before making a final choice.

The frame you choose should be considerably larger than the print if a mat is to be used. Even without a mat, the frame should allow for the expansion of the paper in changing humidities. Frames with a backing board held in place with spring clips are preferable to those with a rigid system of wedges or paper tape.

A variety of techniques can be employed to create a balanced effect when the frame is combined with a mat. Fine lines or bands can be drawn or scored on the mount to lend definition; the mat can be covered in material; both frame and mat can be covered in wallpaper; borders of braid or ribbon can be added; frame and mat can be painted with a design.

Types of moldings
Moldings vary enormously, as this range of corner samples shows. Wooden frames can be plain or stained and varnished; they can be gilded or finished with gesso and painted; lines can be added to give depth and color. Even metal frames (usually aluminum) come in different colors and finishes. Most framemakers carry a range of samples.

BLOCK FRAMES

Simple inexpensive block frames can be bought or made by fitting a piece of glass over the mounted print and securing it by some means to a piece of backing board. Three methods of assembling this type of frame are illustrated here. Spring clamps can be bought from hardware stores and used to hold the glass and board together. Metal cornerpieces secured with screws can also be used, as can special double clamps that are tied together with stout nylon cord. Although these frames do not provide ideal protection and can let in dust, they are suitable for less valuable works and can be easily taken apart and reassembled.

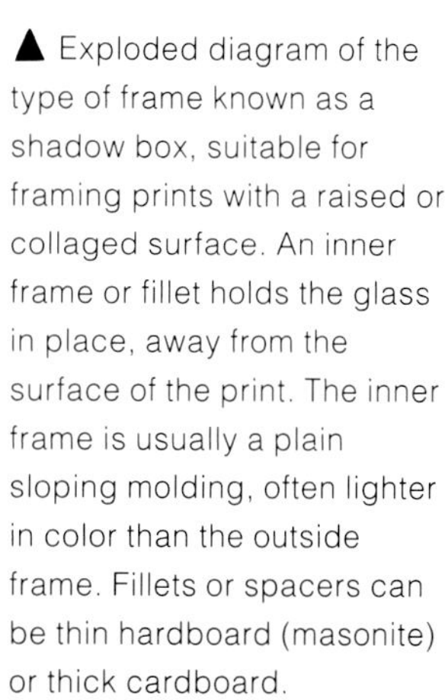

▲ Exploded diagram of the type of frame known as a shadow box, suitable for framing prints with a raised or collaged surface. An inner frame or fillet holds the glass in place, away from the surface of the print. The inner frame is usually a plain sloping molding, often lighter in color than the outside frame. Fillets or spacers can be thin hardboard (masonite) or thick cardboard.

Many simple combinations of mat and frame can give a variety of effects to your print.

MATS

Mats are flat pieces of board or card with a window cut in the center through which the print is visible. Their function is to allow safe handling of the print and to prevent damage which could occur if the glass in the frame came into contact with the surface of the print. They also help to focus attention on the print by isolating it slightly from the frame, and can lend definition to an unobtrusive or plain molding.

Mats should be made from the special board known as conservation or museum board which is made entirely from rag fiber. Never use cardboard; most cardboard is made from wood pulp and is acidic. Over a period of time the print will deteriorate, and become mildewed and stained. The backing board, which supports the print in the frame, should also be conservation board.

The color of the mat should be chosen carefully to complement the print. Lighter colors will tend to make the image appear darker and flatter; dark colors produce the opposite effect.

Mats for prints

A delicate Japanese screenprint of people walking in a garden is shown with a variety of colored mats. It is interesting to note how these mats affect the impact of the print and the balance of color – the blue mat, for example, reinforces the blue so that it dominates the composition. The size of the mat here is not so large that it overpowers the print, but notice how the mat does not frame the print centrally. This takes account of the foreshortening that occurs when the framed print is placed up on a wall.

GLOSSARY

A

Acid The most common acids or acidic solutions for etching plates are nitric acid, sulfuric acid, hydrochloric acid, and ferric chloride solution.

Alum Chemical used with water and nitric acid as a solution, applied to a zinc or aluminum plate in lithography, to remove dirt and oxide from the surface.

Aquatint An intaglio etching process used to create a range of tone. A finely powdered resin is dusted over the plate. The resin is heat-fused to the plate and acid is used to etch through the finely grained resist of resin dust.

Asphalt A type of stop-out varnish used on etched plates which require further work. Asphalt in liquid form is used to protect the ink-receiving image during the preparation of a lithographic stone.

Autographic An image made by hand rather than produced photographically.

B

Bath The liquid used for etching plates, usually acid.

Bevel Any sloping edge but particularly the slope on the edge of an etching plate or lithographic stone. The bevel is at an angle of 45° so that the plate or stone will not cut the paper under the pressure of the press rollers during printing.

Bite The action of the acid in the etching bath on a metal plate.

Bleeding The seepage of ink through or under the stencil can occur when the ink is too thin for the mesh count, when the squeegee blade is blunt, when the printing angle is too low, or when excessive pressure is used during printing.

Blending A technique in which two or more colors are placed on the screen and the squeegee is used to combine them to produce a smooth transition of color before printing.

Block General term for a plate used in relief printing.

Bridge The area of material which holds a character or number together in a cut stencil – for example, the center of 0 or 8.

Burin A cutting tool used for engraving on wood or metal. Also called a GRAVER.

Burnish Apply pressure to a sheet of paper on a plate in order to take a print. Also, the action of using a burnisher, to repair or reduce lines in an etched plate.

Burnisher A rounded steel tool used for removing or reducing the size of etched lines in a plate. Also used for repairing bumps and dents in a plate.

Burr The ridges of metal formed by the cutting action of a drypoint needle or a mezzotint rocker. The burr (on one or both sides of a direct cut) can be left on the plate to produce a soft, furry line in printing, or removed altogether.

C

Chinagraph pencil Grease-based pencil which will accept printing ink.

Collotype Photomechanical process of printing in which the image is transferred from a raised gelatin film surface on a glass support. The printed results are almost continuous tone, with no half-tone screen effect.

Color printing and four-color process Printing by any process in more than one color. The four-color printing process employs the standard colors, cyan (blue), yellow, magenta (red), and black.

Conservation board A high quality board with a low acid content used in framing and mounting. It is usually made from cotton rag fibers and will not damage papers. Also known as MUSEUM BOARD.

Conté pencil A non-greasy black pencil, ideal for any preparatory work on a lithographic plate or stone which is not meant to print.

Copper engraving An engraving produced from a copper printing plate.

Crosshatching Technique of creating tonal variations on a plate by drawing parallel lines in one direction and then more lines at right angles to the first.

D

Direct printing Intaglio and relief printing method when the plate makes direct contact with the paper.

Drawtool A sharp steel tool used for cutting metal printing plates to size.

Drypoint An intaglio technique which does not involve the use of acid. In drypoint, a sharp round point is used to scratch the image into the metal plate.

E

Embossing Impressing type characters, metal plate, or other types of hard flat material on paper or board to produce a raised surface.

Engraving Engraving covers a number of intaglio techniques, all of which involve the cutting of a design or image into metal plates or wood blocks. The metal or wood is removed with an engraving tool called a graver or burin.

Etching An indirect intaglio technique in which the surface of the plate is covered with an acid-resistant material called the ground. The image is cut into this material to expose the metal underneath. The plate is then immersed in an acid bath. Only those exposed parts of the plate are eaten away by the acid. The depth of line (etch) is controlled by the length of immersion in the acid, and also by its strength.

Etching needle A sharp needle-pointed steel tool, used to prepare images on a plate in intaglio printing.

F

Filler A viscous, often water-soluble liquid, used for sealing stencil surrounds, stencil correction and repair, and to make hand-painted stencils directly on the mesh.

Flooding Charging the screen with a thin layer of ink when it is raised above the printing surface. When the screen is lowered, the squeegee is used to press this thin layer of ink through the mesh onto the printing stock.

Frame The rectangular wooden or metal structure over which the mesh is stretched to make a screen.

Frottage A drawing and lithographic technique. A rubbing is made by placing paper over a relief surface or a printed image, taking an impression of the image underneath. Brass and stone rubbings can be classified as frottage. In lithography, a transfer can be taken on paper and put down on a zinc plate or stone.

G

Gesso A finely ground chalk mixed with a pliable glue. Gesso derives its name from the Italian term for chalk or plaster. The material is used extensively in the preparation of ornamental moldings for picture frames.

Gouge The tool used to gouge or scrape out large areas of unwanted surface material in the preparation of a woodcut or linocut.

Gouge chisel Similar to a gouge. A gouge chisel has a strong wooden handle so that it can be struck by a mallet to make deep cuts in the wood.

Grain The grain of wood is the directional growth lines.
End grain is the end of a piece of hardwood, used for wood engraving, not woodcuts.
Side grain is the side of a piece of hardwood, used for woodcuts only.
Paper grain is the direction of the fibers and other materials used in the manufacture of paper. Grain can be determined by flexing a sheet of paper or board – the lightest response indicates the grain direction.
The grain of stone is the surface that is thrown up after graining a lithographic stone so that it is ready to receive a drawing or transfer.
The grain of metal is the surface that is thrown up after graining a zinc lithographic plate so that it is ready for drawing.

Graver A bevel engraving tool (also called a BURIN) used in the preparation of images on metal plates printed by the intaglio and relief methods.

Ground The material used to coat a plate prior to etching. The image is made by scratching away the ground to expose the plate to the acid. Soft ground remains soft after its application to the plate while hard ground becomes firm and hard.

Gum arabic A translucent gum solution used in the preparation of lithographic stones and metal plates and as a resist for greasy ink or lithographic crayon during the drawing stage.

Half tone Like most other printing processes, screenprinting can produce only flat areas of tone or color. By photographing an image through a half-tone screen made up of a grid of lines, the continuous and variable tones of a wash drawing or photographic print can be turned into a matrix of black dots. The number of dots in a given area determines the lightness or darkness of the tones. This effect can readily be seen in the half-tones of newspaper photographs.

Hard ground See GROUND.

Hingebar In screen process printing, the screen frame is attached to the hingebar which in turn is attached to the baseboard. This arrangement enables the screen to be lifted clear of the baseboard so that paper can be slipped in and out easily.

Inks Opaque printing inks, when printed as a solid over other inks, do not allow light to be transmitted from the inks underneath. For example, if blue is printed over yellow the result will be blue and not green.
Water-based inks are formulated so that they can be printed from relief plates and rubber and polyvinyl rollers. The finished print is sensitive to water.
Metallic printing inks are composed of aluminum, bronze, and copper powders which give a lustrous and brilliant finish to the printed surface.
Fluorescent inks are intensely bright, unique in that they reflect and emit light.
Lithographic inks are basically similar to relief printing inks but tend to be more viscous and greasy. Solid blocks of lithographic drawing ink are dissolved in distilled water before use.
Relief inks are designed to print raised surfaces such as type, line, or half tone engravings and electrotypes (reproduction made from an original block or plate). They are usually of moderate tack and viscosity.
Gravure (intaglio) inks must possess sufficient body to be pulled from the engraving on the plate and they must be free of any hard particles that could scratch the plate surface.
Screen process inks print sharply when forced through the screen mesh by the squeegee. They should offer little resistance to the squeegee.
High gloss inks are specially formulated to print on good quality, coated papers, such as art paper, and are manufactured for use in relief, lithographic, and screen process printing. When dry, the colors look varnished and enhance the surface gloss.

Intaglio A process in which the image or design to be printed is cut or etched into a metal plate, usually copper. The technique involves printing from the recesses below the surface of the metal plate.

Key block The printing plate or block (usually black or another dark color) which determines the position (registration) of the succeeding printing plates or blocks in color printing.

Key image In multi-block color printing by the relief process, the key image is the first color (image) to be printed.

Light fast This term refers to the ability of pigments (used in printing ink) to withstand fading due to prolonged exposure to light.

Lithography The process of making a printed impression (lithograph) from images or drawings made on a lithographic stone or metal plates (zinc or aluminum), based on the water-repellent properties of greasy inks. Lithography is a planographic process – that is, prints are taken from a level surface.

Lithographic crayons and pencils Lithographic crayons are greasy black crayons, manufactured in ascending grades of hardness, numbered 1 to 5, for drawing on stone or plate. Lithographic pencils are made of the same drawing material as lithographic crayons, but come in pencil form.

Lithographic oil The oil solvent base used in the manufacture of lithographic printing inks.

Lithographic stone Heavy limestone blocks to allow regrinding and prevent breakage. After the stone is ground, its porous surface is ready to receive drawing lines and tones made with greasy crayons or pencils, or with tusche.

M

Mat The surround to a picture frame through which the image is visible. Mats are usually made from flat sheets of card or board.

Mesh The woven fabric that is stretched across the frame to make the screen, and to which the stencil is anchored.

Mesh count The measure of the fineness or coarseness of the mesh, stated as the number of threads to the inch.

Metal cut Technique of relief printing which involves cutting directly into a metal plate using a graver or a burin, and acid.

Mezzotint A type of intaglio printing in which the surface of the plate is pitted with minute indentations which hold the printing ink. A rocker is used to produce gradations of tone.

Monograph A print (or color wash drawing) made in one color only.

Monoprint A one-off, unique, and therefore unrepeatable print.

Monotype A method of pulling a single reverse facsimile of an image made on a hard surface (perspex, glass, porcelain, metal or stone) by superimposing a sheet of paper and rubbing (burnishing) the reverse side until the whole or a part of the image is transferred.

Multiple tool Cutting tool with two cutters on the head for making parallel lines. Used in preparing plates in relief printing.

Museum board See CONSERVATION BOARD.

N

Nap rollers Lithographic wooden rollers covered with calf skin. Used for rolling black lithographic ink onto the stone or plate.

Negative An image that is the reverse of the positive original in its tonal values. In a photographic negative, the dark areas of the subject appear light and the light areas are dark.

O

Offset, offset printing To offset in color relief printing the key plate or block is inked and the image transferred onto a prepared plate or wood block. This helps to position the next color.
Offset printing is a lithographic printing method, where the image is offset after inking onto a printing.

Oilstone A fine grade carborundum stone or similar stone used for sharpening cutting tools. Oil is usually applied to the stone to reduce friction.

Open area Any part of a stencil that allows ink to pass through the mesh.

P

Paper
Handmade paper is made in a frame, manufactured from pure cotton or linen, usually with deckled edges.
Cartridge paper is a strong white opaque drawing or printing paper. The surface is smooth but not coated or glossy.
Moldmade paper is similar to handmade paper in weight and appearance but is made mechanically. Mold paper is more suitable than handmade for color work because it is more robust.

Perspex Translucent or colored plastic which can be used as a substitute for end grain boxwood in engraving. Similar in density to boxwood, but less expensive.

Photo engraving The image on the printing plate or cylinder is produced photographically or electronically for relief printing.

Photo etching A method of etching a plate using a photographic light-sensitive coating. A film negative is placed in contact with the light sensitive coating on the surface of the plate exposed to a light source. The photo resist hardens where it has been exposed to light; the other areas remain soft and can be washed away. The plate is then ready for etching in the normal way.

Photopositive A photographically reproduced image printed onto transparent film from which a photostencil can be made.

Photostencil A stencil made from light-sensitive material that has been exposed to ultraviolet light through a suitably opaque positive.

Pigment The particles of fine color solids used to give color, body, and opacity to printing inks and paints.

Plankwood Wood used for woodcuts cut so that the grain runs along the surface.

Planographic A form of printing in which the print is taken from a flat surface as in lithography: from a plate, stone, or other matrix.

Plate etch Solution used to condition the printing plate in lithography and help clarify the printing image. Usually, nowadays, a proprietary brand.

Posterization A method of simulating continuous tone. The original is photographed several times with progressively varied exposures, each picking out a part of the tonal range. The greater the number of separate stages, the more effective the illusion.

Print The product of the printing process – in this context, usually an image on paper.

Printing press There are many different types of printing press; some are designed specifically for one process, others can be used to print images originated in a variety of ways. Large commercial presses are often entirely mechanical, but smaller workshop presses are usually hand-operated.

Proof The preliminary print taken to examine the progress of the work at successive stages. Proofs are pulled to check color, weight of ink impression, ink squash, registration, and the effects of different paper surfaces.
An artist's proof is a preliminary pull, inspected and modified by the artist, and retained as a unique work. Artists' proofs are usually numbered to a maximum of six. Proofing is the process of taking a proof pull.

R

Reducing agents Chemical solutions, such as a mixture of potassium ferric cyanide and sodium hyposulfate with water, used to reduce chemically the density of photographic emulsions.

Register The exact positioning of colors, one on top of another, in multicolor printing. When colors are out of register, this is usually seen as a fault and steps are taken to correct the placing of the colors.

Sometimes, however, a degree of misregistration is intended.

Relief printing A process in which the image to be printed is created in relief. Materials such as wood, linoleum, or plaster may be cut away to leave the image in relief, or a relief surface may be built up from the flat by adding objects such as keys, coins, leaves, or card cutouts.

Resin A finely grained substance which forms a porous film deposit that can be used as a ground for aquatints.

Resist Any solution or coating which, after it has hardened in the light or air, resists acid or water.

Rocker A rounded steel tool shaped so that its teeth bite into and pit the surface of the plate. Rocking prepares the surface for a mezzotint.

Roulette A toothed, wheel instrument used to make small perforations in the ground or on the plate surface in etching and drypoint.

Scauper (or **scorper**) Tool used in wood engraving for clearing away large areas of wood around the image.

Screen The frame with the mesh stretched over it on which the stencil is fixed.

Screen process printing Screen process printing is a variety of stencil printing. It differs from other modes of printing in that it does not depend on paper (or other materials) and an image-bearing surface coming into contact through pressure, but on ink being transferred onto a substrate from a stencil bearing an image. It is also known as silkscreen printing and screenprinting.

Screen wash The general term for various brands of solvents which are used to clean printing ink and stencil off screens in screen process printing.

Shim A cardboard, wood or metal insert positioned under the hingebar when printing onto card or board in screen process printing.

Sizing The use of a gelatinous mixture as a sealer or filler in papermaking. Sizing strengthens the surface of the paper and reduces water penetration.

Snakestone A polishing stone used to smooth areas of a plate or lithographic stone.

Snap Sometimes called "off contact" or "lift off," this is the small gap between the print bed and the screen. The pressure of the squeegee brings the two into progressive contact, the mesh snapping away from the printing block in the wake of the squeegee.

Soft ground see GROUND.

Stamp printing Method of making a printed impression upon paper or fabric by stamping the block directly onto the surface, without the use of a press. Examples include potato or carrot cuts, plaster and linocuts.

Stencil A sheet of cut paper, card, metal, wood, or gauze through which ink or paint is brushed to transfer an image.
A **direct stencil** is any stencil which is made or prepared on the mesh of a screen process printing frame. The stencil can be drawn directly using a resist or stop-out solution. The wax resist and tusche method are specialized ways of making direct stencils.
An **indirect stencil** is any stencil which is made or prepared away from the screen mesh. The simplest type of indirect stencil is one which is made of cut-out frame paper or proprietary brands of stencil film (also called a knife-cut stencil).
An **indirect photostencil** is a photographic, light-sensitive, emulsion-coated stencil which, when exposed to light, receives an image through a film positive bearing the image. The mesh on the frame in screen process printing is coated with the light-sensitive emulsion and, after drying, is exposed to the film image.
An **indirect photo stencil** is a photographic, light-sensitive stencil, usually manufactured in the form of a two-layer film. One layer is the emulsion and the other is a transparent backing sheet, which is removed before the stencil is exposed to light through a positive film sheet.

Stretching Attaching the mesh to the frame. This can be done by hand, but for professional work, use of a mechanical stretcher that guarantees correct and consistent tension is advisable.

Sugar lift Sugar lift is a technique used in aquatint where the artist draws a positive image using a special medium containing sugar, thus ensuring that it will never dry completely. When the medium is nearly dry a varnish resist is applied to the plate and the whole plate is immersed in water. Only the sugary drawing underneath the resist is attacked, causing the varnish to "lift" and expose the plate for aquatinting in the usual manner. This technique is also called lift-ground.

Tusche A greasy lithographic ink used to draw or paint directly on the screen to create stencils by the gum and tusche method.

Vacuum forming The process of heating a sheet of plastic and then pulling it over an object on a baseboard by vacuum pressure from a suction pump. The plastic liner in a box of chocolates is an example of a vacuum formed object.

Varnish Any solution which is applied to a plate to resist the action of acid or water; also called stop-out varnish.

Vehicle The liquid component of a printing ink. The vehicle carries the pigment enabling the ink to flow.

V tool Tool used in linocut with a V-shaped cutting edge.

Wax resist A method of tusche application for a screen process printing stencil, which involves the use of wax rather than a greasy ink.

Wood block printing Printing from an engraved wood block.

Woodcut One of the relief processes of printing. Woodcuts are made on side grained or flat grained wood.

Wood engraving A relief process of printing where the image work is usually very fine with minute cut lines. End grain wood is used.

Index

Page numbers in *italics* refer to picture captions.

Picture Credits

Every effort has been made to trace and acknowledge all copyright holders. Quintet would like to apologise if any omissions have been made.

a = above, b = below, l = left, r = right

Pg 5, b Paul Bartlett; Pg 6, Judy Martin; Pg 17, a Paul Bartlett, t Mychael Barratt; Pg 18, a Elisabeth Harden, b Moira Wills; Pg 19, (from top) Judy Martin, Ian Mowforth, Philip Coombs, Judy Martin, Caroline Bilson, Roland Stringer, Moira Wills, Juliet Kac, Elisabeth Harden, Elisabeth Harden; Pg 22, a June Ann Sullivan, b Carole Katchen; Pg 28, John Elliot; Pg 33, a Christie's Contemporary Art Ltd., b Ian Mowforth; Pg 42, Jonathan Heale, Pg 43, The Victoria and Albert Museum, London (Crown Copyright); Pg 51, ar The Victoria and Albert Museum, London (Crown Copyright), al Roland Stringer, b Colin Paynton/Wildlife Art Agency; Pg 58, The Trustees of the British Museum; Pg 60, The Victoria and Albert Museum, London (Crown Copyright); Pg 63, a Carole Katchen, b Philip Coombs; Pg 68, r The Victoria and Albert Museum, London (Crown Copyright); Pg 72, Carole Katchen; Pg 73, l Glynn Thomas; Pg 82, b Trevor Price; Pg 87, Philip Coombs; Pg 90, Editions Alecto; Pg 96, The Victoria and Albert Museum, London (Crown Copyright); Pg 97, a Joy Brand/CCA Galleries, b David Koster/Wildlife Art Agency; Pg 108, a Beryl Cook/London Contemporary Art/Advance Graphics, b Moira Wills; Pg 110, a Yuriko/Colonia Publications/Coriander Studios; Pg 131, Boyd and Evans/Angela Flowers Gallery & Coriander Studios; Pg 137, Terry Wilson/Coriander Studios & Terry Wilson; Pg 138, a Allen Jones/Waddington Graphics/Kelpra, b Wendy Taylor/Ionian Bank/Coriander Studios; Pg 139, Ben Johnson/Norman Foster/Coriander Studios; Pg 140, Gerd Winner/Tate Gallery Print Collection/Kelpra; Pg 143, a Editions Alecto; Pg 144, a Editions Alecto, b London Magazine Editions; Pg 145, London Magazine Editions; Pg 146, Tate Gallery Print Collection; Pg 147, Gemini G.E.L., Los Angeles (1974); Jacket image, Ilana Richardson/Quarto Publishing plc/Coriander Studios & Ilana Richardson.